QUEEN VICTORIA AT HOME

Other titles by the same author
Elgar: the Man
Denton Welch: The Making of a Writer
The Honours System
Acting as Friends: The Story of the Samaritans
Eddy: The Life of Edward Sackville-West
Michael Ramsey: A Portrait
Windsor Castle: Past and Present
Exploring Oxford
The Church of England: A Portrait
The Queen Behind the Throne
The King Who Never Was: The Story of Frederick, Prince of Wales
Mervyn Stockwood: A Lonely Life
Bedford School: A History
The House of Hervey: A History of Tainted Talent

Sutton Pocket Biographies
Scott of the Antarctic
George IV

Edited
The Journals of Denton Welch
The Collected Short Writings of Denton Welch

Queen Victoria
at Home

Michael De-la-Noy

CARROLL & GRAF PUBLISHERS

New York

Carroll & Graf Publishers
An imprint of Avalon Publishing Group, Inc.
161 William Street
NY 10038-2607
www.carrollandgraf.com

First published in the UK by Constable,
an imprint of Constable & Robinson Ltd 2003

First Carroll & Graf edition 2003

ISBN 0-7867-1178-7

Printed and bound in the UK

For Andrew Amerasekera

The author, who died last year, wished this book to be dedicated
to the district nurses at Thrapston, the night carer from the
Marie Curie Cancer Centre, and the nurses at the
Cransley Hospice at Kettering, in gratitude for their skill
and loving kindness during his last year.

I think anyone that has the common sense or honesty must needs bee very wary of everything that one meets in with courts . . . I confess that I was never pleased but when I was a child & after I had been maid of honour some time I wished myself out of the court as much as I desired to come into it before I knew what it was.

Sarah, Duchess of Marlborough

Contents

Illustrations

Author's Note

There can never be a definitive life of Queen Victoria; there are too many angles and facets and there is too much material, and this book purports only to be a deliberately non-chronological distillation of Queen Victoria's more personal life, her relations with her family, household and servants. The most authoritative political biography of Queen Victoria remains Elizabeth Longford's life in two volumes, *Victoria RI* (London, 1964).

Letters from the Royal Archives and those in other collections of which Her Majesty the Queen holds the copyright are quoted by permission of Her Majesty. Material drawn from *Queen Victoria in her Letters and Journals* (John Murray, 1984) is reproduced by the generous permission of Dr Christopher Hibbert, whose *Queen Victoria: A Personal History* (HarperCollins, 2001) would be a pleasure for any historian to have at their elbow.

Letters from Prince Albert to his brother, Prince Ernest, edited by Hector Bolitho in *The Prince Consort and His Brother* (Cobden-Sanderson, 1933), are in the archives at Coburg. Many of Queen Victoria's letters not at Windsor are in the archives of the House of Brandenburg-Prussia at Charlottenburg Palace in Berlin. Letters from Queen Victoria to her eldest daughter, the Crown Princess of Prussia and later Empress of Germany, are at the Friedrichshof near Frankfurt, while letters from the Empress to Queen Victoria are in the Royal Archives at Windsor.

A large selection of correspondence between the years 1837 and 1861 was edited at the instigation of Edward VII by A. C. Benson and Viscount Esher and published by John Murray in three volumes in 1908 as *The Letters of Queen Victoria. Further Letters of Queen Victoria*, edited by Hector Bolitho, was published in 1938 by Thornton Butterworth, and a selection of the letters that passed between Queen Victoria and her eldest daughter between 1861 and 1864, *Dearest Mama* (Evans Brothers, 1968), has been edited by Roger Fulford with immense erudition and scholarship.

Fortunately, and against strict instructions, a number of courtiers who knew Queen Victoria personally kept diaries, or wrote, and had preserved, letters describing court life during the last years of Victoria's reign. Among the most interesting are *Life with Queen Victoria: Marie Mallet's Letters from Court, 1887–1901* edited by her son, Sir Victor Mallet (John Murray, 1968) and *Lady Lytton's Court Diary, 1895–1899*, edited by Mary Lutyens (Rupert Hart-Davis, 1961). The Ponsonby family's knowledge of the domestic and political whirl in which the Queen spent her busy days is probably unrivalled. In 1933, for Duckworth's series Great Lives, Arthur Ponsonby (Lord Ponsonby of Shulbrede) produced a succinct and beautifully written biography, *Queen Victoria*, and in 1942 Macmillan published *Henry Ponsonby: His Life from His Letters* by his son, Arthur. Although he served Queen Victoria for only the last six years of her life, Sir Frederick Ponsonby (Lord Sysonby) was a member also of the households of Edward VII and George V, and his *Recollections of Three Reigns* (Eyre & Spottiswoode, 1951) is one of the most riveting and informative accounts of royal affairs ever written. It was sad that such an important writer as Cecil

Woodham-Smith lived to publish only the first volume of her *Queen Victoria: Her Life and Times* (Hamish Hamilton, 1972), taking the story up to the death of the Prince Consort in 1861.

Many people have tried to summarize the character of Queen Victoria, an immensely complex woman whose life and reign encompassed most of the nineteenth century, but no one has done so as neatly as Arthur Ponsonby in the course of editing his father's letters:

Queen Victoria did not belong to any conceivable category of monarchs or of women. She bore no resemblance to an aristocratic lady, she bore no resemblance to a wealthy middle-class Englishwoman, nor to any typical princess of a German court. She was not in the least like the three queens regnant (omitting Mary Stuart who was just the wife of William III),* her predecessors. Mary Tudor was a fanatic, Queen Elizabeth was an autocrat and Queen Anne in her harassed and ramshackle way was occupied in coping with the intrigues around her. Victoria in religion was an orthodox Protestant with Presbyterian leanings, she had had no Roger Ascham [Queen Elizabeth's tutor] to give her a scholastic education and she did not spend her leisure moments like Queen Anne in playing Bach. Moreover she reigned longer than all the other three queens put together. Never in her life could she be confused with anyone else, nor will she be in history. Such expressions as 'people like Queen Victoria' or 'that sort of woman' could not be used about her. Her simple domesticity appealed to a vast number of her subjects; she was intensely human, but the unique nature of her personality and position claimed special attention and often awe from those who reached her presence.

* This is not strictly true. By Act of Parliament, Mary II and William III reigned jointly.

There might be princesses and duchesses, there might be women distinguished in many spheres, there might be empresses, there might be queen this, that or the other in history, but for over sixty years she was simply without prefix or suffix 'The Queen'.

The Corporal Marries

T here was one sense in which the birth of Alexandrina Victoria, on 24 May 1819, who was to be Queen of the United Kingdom of Great Britain and Ireland and Empress of India, was not all that important: she was only fourth in line to the throne. On the other hand, those with precedence over her were, or looked like remaining, childless. In view of the loveless marriage made by her uncle, George IV, it was remarkable that his wife and first cousin, Caroline of Brunswick, had produced even one child, the ill-fated heiress presumptive, Princess Charlotte, who had died in 1817 giving birth to a dead boy. Although the King's greatest, yet unfulfilled, ambition was to obtain a divorce, his wife, if anything even more disreputable than he was himself, was not to die until 1821, when in theory George IV (from 1811 to 1820 Prince Regent) would have been free to marry again and start another family. But few thought that very likely.

At the time of Victoria's birth, the Prince Regent's heir presumptive was the princess's uncle, Frederick, Duke of York. He was married to the Princess Royal of Prussia but had no children. Next came another uncle, the Duke of Clarence, who was to succeed in 1830 as William IV. It was Clarence who initiated a stampede to the altar, in 1811, the year in which he precipitately abandoned his charming mistress and the mother of his ten illegitimate children, the actress Mrs Dorothy Jordan, although his comical search for a wealthy bride six years before the death of the Prince Regent's daughter was not so much an attempt to secure an heir to the throne as financial security for himself.

Victoria's father was at this time also perfectly content with a mistress, Madame de St-Laurent, with whom in fact he lived for twenty-seven years. Something of a spur to producing legitimate offspring to inherit the throne was provided by the marriage in 1815 of the Prince Regent's fourth brother, Ernest, Duke of Cumberland, whose wife, Princess Frederica of Mecklenburg-Strelitz, produced a son in 1819. But the thought of Cumberland, who in 1830 became King of Hanover, succeeding to the British throne sent shivers down everyone's spine, for he was undeniably mad. Like the Battle of Waterloo, however, it was 'a damned nice thing';[1] for the first nerve-racking three years of Victoria's reign her uncle Cumberland, widely believed to have had an affair with his valet before murdering him, was her heir presumptive, being displaced only by the birth of the Queen's first child in 1840.

Clarence, having deserted his mistress, took a leisurely amble through the ranks of a number of variously eligible brides. He tried for two heiresses – the sister of the Tsar and a princess of Hesse – before he finally gained the hand of the twenty-five-year-old Princess Adelaide of Saxe-Coburg-Meiningen. The diarist Charles Greville thought her 'frightful, very ugly, with a horrid complexion', and unfortunately for the Duke of Clarence's prospects of ensuring direct succession to the throne, his wife had great difficulty in producing healthy children. In 1818 a little girl, Charlotte, was born but lived only a few hours. The Duchess miscarried in 1819, the year of Queen Victoria's birth, and when, the following year, the future Queen Adelaide gave birth six weeks prematurely to another girl, Elizabeth, the infant Victoria found herself only fifth in line of succession. But Elizabeth died at the age of four months, and two years later Adelaide again miscarried, losing twins.

There remained other concerns about the Crown, which seems fairly incredible in the light of George III's numerous progeny: nine sons (two of whom, Octavius and Alfred, died as little boys) and six daughters. But the sixth son, Augustus, Duke of Sussex, was obstinately to remain a bachelor all his life; at least, he was a bachelor in the eyes of his father, in contravention of whose 1772 Royal Marriages Act Sussex had contracted two illegal alliances, first to Lady Augusta Murray, and after her death to Lady Cecilia Buggin. Lady Augusta produced a son and a daughter, but like the Duke of Clarence's bastards they were barred from the succession. Adolphus, Duke of Cambridge, the seventh of George III's sons, thought it proper to propose marriage to Princess Augusta of Hesse-Cassel within days of the death of his niece Princess Charlotte, but his wife, in 1819, did at least produce a legitimate son.

It was while they were trying to economize by living in Brussels that the Duke of Kent and Madame de St-Laurent learned, in November 1817, of the death of the heir to the throne – Princess Charlotte. That was shock enough; but when, the following month, the *Morning Chronicle* arrived on the royal breakfast table it was seen to contain a demand that the Duke should marry for the sake of the succession. Madame de St-Laurent nearly had a fit; the Duke sent word to Thomas Creevey, a popular Whig politician and diarist, who also happened to be cutting down on expenses in Brussels, to say that he would be obliged if Mr Creevey would call on him. The date was 11 December 1817, and fortunately Creevey made an almost verbatim note of the conversation that ensued.

'The Duke,' he recalled, 'began, to my great surprise, a conversation upon the death of the Princess Charlotte, and upon an observation from me upon the derangement to the succession to the throne by this event, if the Crown was to be kept in their family.'

Creevey asked the Duke if he thought the Prince Regent would go for a divorce from his almost certainly adulterous wife, to which the Duke sagaciously replied that if she were found guilty of adultery 'she must be executed for high treason' and he did not think the Regent would ever 'try for a divorce'.[2] The Duke dismissed out of hand any possibility of the Duke of York producing children but told Creevey: 'The Duke of Clarence, I have no doubt, will marry if he can.' But he thought a stumbling block might be his demand that all his debts, 'which are very great', be paid off 'and a handsome provision' be made 'for each of his ten natural children'. Should the Duke of Clarence not marry, the Duke of Kent pointed out, 'the next prince in succession is myself, and although I trust I shall at all times be ready to obey any call my country may make upon me, God only knows the sacrifice it will be to make, whenever I think it my duty to become a married man'. He was sure Mr Greevey could well imagine the pang it would occasion him to part with Madame de St-Laurent.

He went on to say that his brother Clarence had 'certainly the right to marry if he chooses, and I would not interfere with him on any account. If he wishes to be king – to be married and have children, poor man [he meant legitimate children] – God help him! Let him do so. For myself, I am a man of no ambition, and wish only to remain as I am.' So saying, he immediately went on to ask Creevey if he had heard of 'the Princess of Baden and the Princess of Saxe-Coburg mentioned'. The latter connection, he said, 'would perhaps be the better of the two'.[3] 'The latter connection' was Princess Victoria of Saxe-Coburg-

4

Saalfeld, widow of the Prince of Leiningen and sister of the recently bereaved Prince Leopold, who since his marriage to Princess Charlotte had become quite popular in England. He was later to become King of the Belgians and the revered uncle of Queen Victoria, while the Dowager Princess of Leiningen became the mother of Queen Victoria and mother-in-law as well as aunt to Victoria's husband.

The Duke of Kent had no money to speak of but, like most of his family, he had plenty of debts. By 1795 they amounted to £75,000. So he had not really needed a push from the press to get married; the idea had been on his mind for the past two years, for once he was married he felt sure that Parliament would not only take care of his debts but vote him £25,000 a year, the sum obtained on marriage in 1792 by the Duke of York. Although by the age of

The Duke of Kent.

fifty the Duke of Kent, a military martinet who delighted in flog-
gings and executions, whose manic cruelty was such that it was
said the entire British army was planning to have him assassinated,
might not have struck many young ladies as a romantic match,
Princess Victoria of Leiningen, the mother of two children by her
first elderly and bad-tempered husband, was in no position to be
too particular. Although at first her inclination was to reject Kent,
when she pondered the matter further she decided that the prospect
of entering the British royal family, and even the possibility of
producing an heir to the throne, was tempting. Having been assured
that she would be permitted to retain the guardianship of her
twelve-year-old son, Prince Charles, and her daughter, Princess
Feodora, destined to become Queen Victoria's greatly loved half-
sister, on 25 January 1818 the Princess of Leiningen wrote to the
Duke of Kent: 'Monseigneur . . . my hand is yours.'

> The Duke replied: I want you to know, my very dear Princess,
> that I am nothing more than a soldier [he forebore to describe
> himself as universally detested and debarred from military
> employment], fifty years old, and after thirty-two years of service
> not very fitted to captivate the heart of a young and charming
> Princess, who is nineteen years younger.

On 29 May 1818 they were married in Coburg by a pastor of the
Lutheran Church. Perhaps to impress his young bride, who had
set eyes on him only once before, he wore his field marshal's
uniform. He was not always so smartly turned out. In September
1818, at a military review near Valenciennes, on the French–Belgian
border, Creevey noted: 'The Duke of Kent's appearance was atrocious. He was dressed in the jacket and cap of his regiment [the
Royals], and but for his blue ribbon and star [of the Garter] he

The Duchess of Kent.

might have passed for an orderly sergeant.' The Duke of Wellington called Kent 'the corporal'.

The service in Coburg had been held to satisfy the bride's German relations. Four days later the Kents set out for England to share in the Duke of Clarence's Anglican nuptials at Kew. Poor cast-off Madame de St-Laurent, of obscure but almost certainly French origin, was created Comtesse de Montgenet by Louis XVIII.

After their English marriage the Duke and Duchess of Kent continued to retrench on the Continent. Queen Victoria was conceived some time in the summer of 1818, and once it was apparent that the Duchess was pregnant the Duke decided it was imperative that his child should be born on English soil lest some plot be hatched to try to disinherit the infant on the grounds that having been born overseas he or she was not a British citizen. So the Kents planned to rustle up what cash they could, pack their belongings and head for the English Channel. The only regrets the Duke of Kent had about his marriage were financial ones. Parliament had become totally fed up with the royal brothers. They were, the Duke of Wellington told Thomas Creevey, 'the damnedest millstone about the necks of any government that can be imagined' and had personally insulted 'two-thirds of the gentlemen of England'. The result was a miserable £6,000 a year voted for the Duke of Kent. So when it was clear that his wife was pregnant the Duke wrote to Sir Benjamin Bloomfield, Keeper of the Privy Purse as well as private secretary to the Prince Regent, to say that the confinement of the Duchess in May would 'necessarily bear hard upon our limited income', and he was sure 'the goodness' of the Prince Regent and 'his liberality' would ensure 'such indulgences as may be in his power for our comfort'. Unfortunately, the Prince Regent heartily disliked his third brother; the brother he loved was the Duke of York, with whom he had been brought up.

So certain was the Duke of Kent that one day his child would succeed to the throne, if indeed he did not first do so himself, for he believed he was as fit as a fiddle while his brothers ate and drank too much, that he told Sir Benjamin he would require the costs of the journey to England, a yacht (which he spelled 'yatcht') in which to cross the Channel, the loan of apartments, previously occupied in Kensington Palace by the Princess of Wales, for his wife's confinement, his meals to be provided by a department known as the Board of the Green Cloth, and if, after giving birth, the Duchess's doctor prescribed sea bathing (a fashionable fad at the time) then perhaps a house at Brighton or Weymouth might be put at his disposal. He reckoned the journey between Amorbach, an estate in the Leiningen principality, and Kensington would cost at least £1,200, and he sent Sir Benjamin precise details of all the alterations he required to be carried out in his suite of rooms at the palace.

The Prince Regent had taken soundings all round, Sir Benjamin replied, and His Royal Highness deeply regretted that there was nothing he could do. Sir Benjamin was further instructed to inform the Duke of Kent that the Duchess of Clarence was presently preparing for a confinement in Hanover; so was the Duchess of Cambridge. Why did not the Duchess of Kent follow their wise example and save herself the trouble and danger of a journey to England? Since the accession in 1714 to the English throne of Georg Ludwig, Elector of Hanover, the electorate had remained under British protection, and the Prince Regent found it convenient to ignore the fact that the Duchess of Clarence was risking a journey to the Continent, and that as her husband was Regent of Hanover the Duchess of Cambridge was there anyway.

Still up to his eyebrows in debt, and always reluctant to cut down on the expenses of his stable, the Duke of Kent became so frantic that he brought military precision to bear on his costings; he now estimated that the birth of the Duchess's child would come to £1,139 11s. But help was at hand. Friends at home, who had come to realize the significance of the forthcoming birth, were urging the Kents to cross the Channel, and between them they scraped together £15,000. Cock-a-hoop, the Duke of Kent announced that he would be in Calais by 18 April, asked that the Prince Regent should send over the royal yacht and as 'an act of kindness' provide accommodation at Kensington Palace. The Prince Regent, by nature both kind and lazy, capitulated.

Although when speaking to Thomas Creevey the Duke of Kent had airily remarked, 'I shall not require very much, but a certain number of servants and a carriage are essentials', he and the

Duchess set out for the coast in a convoy of ten carriages of one sort or another and with a retinue that included a lady-in-waiting, a valet, a footman, several maids, a female obstetrician, Princess Feodora and her governess, two cooks, a manservant, a clerk and a former naval doctor. The luggage included the Duchess's bed and bedding. The journey was blessed by fine weather and no mishaps, although the size of the entourage made it difficult always to find ample accommodation. After being held up for six days with the wind in the wrong direction, the party crossed the Channel in three hours in weather so rough the Duchess was 'certainly very sick'.

Perhaps by now even the Prince Regent, resentful though he was over the death of his daughter (for whom in fact he never particularly cared), had come to accept the potential importance of the impending birth, for the Kents found spacious apartments on the east side of Kensington Palace furnished for them at considerable expense and, as one would expect of Prinny (as Creevey had nicknamed the Prince Regent), in perfect taste. The fact that ancient window sashes let in the rain could not dampen their enthusiasm for the peace and quiet surrounding the house and 'the advantage . . . of a view over the most magnificent Park, with the most beautiful piece of water that it is possible to see'. They had Queen Caroline, the wife of George II and the Duke of Kent's great-grandmother, to thank for the landscape.

On the evening of 23 May the Duchess went into labour, and as custom decreed, in order to make sure that no foundling impostor was slipped into the mother's bed, various members of the Privy Council, including the Duke of Sussex, the Archbishop of Canterbury, the Duke of Wellington and the Bishop of London, began to arrive. Early in the morning of the following day the Duchess gave birth to 'a pretty little Princess, as plump as a partridge'. The Duke told his mother-in-law, the Dowager Duchess of Coburg, that the child was 'truly a model of strength and beauty combined . . . Thank God the dear mother and the child are doing marvellously well.'

What did not go so marvellously well was the bad-tempered christening of the future Queen Victoria, named of course after her mother, but only so named after a protracted wrangle at the font, set up in the magnificent cupola room at Kensington. Prinny was invited to be a godfather and was not best pleased when he discovered that the other godfather was to be the Tsar, a crowned sovereign, which he was not. The parents had settled on what they thought a suitable string of names for the baby: Victoire (her mother's actual name), Georgina (in honour of the Regent), Alexandrina (as a compliment to the Tsar, Alexander), Charlotte (after her paternal grandmother, and also, perhaps, in memory of Princess Charlotte), Augusta. Prinny would have none of it. He absolutely forbade Georgina, insisted on a private family gathering, and said he would further discuss the child's names at the service.

The Archbishop held the baby while the Prince Regent struggled to make up his mind. 'Alexandrina', he pronounced. There was a long pause. The Duke reminded his brother that they had also chosen Charlotte. The Regent shook his head. The Duke mumbled 'Augusta'. That was blackballed. In desperation the Duke suggested Elizabeth. Another shake of the head. By now the Duchess was in tears. 'Give her the mother's name also then,' Prinny instructed the Archbishop, 'but it cannot precede that of the Emperor.' So the child was christened Alexandrina Victoria, but when she came to the throne she chose to reign as Queen Victoria, the only name by which she was ever known as a child.

And so commenced Victoria's connection with her first home,

Kensington Palace, from the gardens.

Kensington Palace, where, until she was eighteen, she was to spend what – looking back when she was fifty-three – she described as her 'rather melancholy childhood'.

The Kensington System

Kensington Palace, still the home of royalty today, has been a Crown property since 1689, and stood originally in a village within easy walking distance of the capital; Queen Caroline, who enjoyed striding out, once went into town on foot from Kensington to meet her husband, George II, on his return from a visit to Hanover.[1] This was in September 1729, when Caroline set off with her children, walking through Hyde Park and down Piccadilly to St James's Park, where she encountered the King's procession, returning to Kensington in the King's coach. Some idea of the isolated situation of Kensington Palace at the start of the eighteenth century can be gained from the fact that while walking alone in the garden, George II was one day relieved of a pocket watch, and again by an amusing account of an extraordinary escapade in which Queen Caroline was involved. Writing from Marlborough House on 23 September 1732, Sarah Churchill, since 1722 Dowager Duchess of Marlborough, a lively letter-writer and invaluable gossip, told her granddaughter, Lady John Russell:

Two or three days ago, Her sacred Majesty was in great danger of being ravished. She was walking from Kensington to London early in the morning, and having a vast desire to appear more able in everything than other people, she walked so fast as to get before my Lord Chamberlain and the two princesses upon one of the causeways, quite out of sight. Whether this proceeded from their compliments to let her see how much stronger she was than they, or from any other accident, I cannot say. But my Lord Grantham, meeting a country clown, asked him if he had met any person and how far off they were! To which he answered he had met a jolly crummy woman with whom he had been fighting some time to kiss her. I am surprised at the man's fancy! And my Lord Grantham was so frightened that he screamed out and said it was the Queen. Upon which the country fellow was out of his wits, fell upon his knees, cried and earnestly begged of my Lord Grantham to speak for him for he was sure he should be hanged for what he had done. But did not further explain what it was. And Her Majesty does not own more than that he struggled with her, but she got the better of him.

When Kensington Palace was purchased by William III for 18,000 guineas it was called Nottingham House, and it was at Kensington that both William and his wife Mary II died. William's successor and the last Stuart monarch, Queen Anne, embellished the garden with a splendid orangery attributed to Nicholas Hawksmoor, and it was within the mellow red-brick walls of Kensington Palace that Queen Anne had her famous final row, on 6 April 1710, with the high-handed Sarah Marlborough.

Nottingham House had been built in 1605 by Sir George Coppin, Clerk to the Crown at the court of James I. Although it has been described at this time as a small country retreat, the plans included a Great Hall extending the whole length of the building from north to south. In 1620 the Speaker of the House of Commons,

Sir Heneage Finch, purchased the property, and the reason it was known as Nottingham House was because, in 1681, the Speaker's son, Secretary of State to William III, was created Earl of Nottingham.[2] William III saw that the house could easily be adapted to suit royal purposes, but it had another particular appeal for him. His official London residence, until it was almost entirely destroyed by fire in 1698, was Whitehall Palace, built on the banks of the Thames and hence a place that was prone to exacerbate his asthma. Nottingham House, on the other hand, was blessed with clean country air.

William chose as his architect Sir Christopher Wren, who built four pavilions at the corners of the main block with two-storeyed wings attached, created a state entrance surmounted by a clock tower – which naturally enough led into Clock Court – and to the south of Clock Court Wren constructed a long ground-floor corridor known as the Stone Gallery. Wren's alterations were by no means complete when the King and Queen moved in. Nevertheless, the intrepid commentator on other people's homes, John Evelyn, found 'a very sweete Villa . . . very noble, tho not very great'. But 'the Garden about it', he declared, was 'very delicious'. The house may not have been very great but it now had a council chamber, an audience chamber, a library and its own chapel. It was not until 1690 that Wren added the Queen's Gallery, 84 feet long, with a staircase at the northern end leading to the State Apartments. Three floors were set aside for the Queen's maids of honour, eight maids of honour, in addition to her ladies and women of the bedchamber, still being attached to the household when Victoria was Queen.[3]

Once the galleries were finished, John Evelyn noticed they were 'furnished with all the best pictures of all the Houses', for William and Mary had more or less abandoned the State Apartments at

Windsor created by Charles II, removing many of the finest works of art, including paintings by Raphael and van Dyke, to Kensington, where William liked to show off his 'world of Porcelain'. Much of Wren's endeavours went up in flames in November 1691 when fire broke out in the Long Gallery in Clock Court, driving the maids of honour into the garden in their nightgowns. Daniel Defoe, whether or not an actual eyewitness, left an amusing account of the drama:

> The Queen was a little surprised at first, apprehending some Treasons, but King William, a Stranger to Feare, smil'd at the suggestion, chear'd Her Majesty up, and being soon dress'd they both walked out into the Garden, and stood there some Hours till they perceived the Fire by the help that came in, and by the Diligence of the Foot Guards, was gotten under Foot.

The south side of Clock Court was lost, as was the King's Staircase (the King and Queen had separate apartments, as was common practice at the time) and all the renovations being carried out by Wren, who was called back yet again in 1695. By the time Queen Anne inherited the palace in March 1702, Wren had brought to fruition just the kind of house the first two Hanoverian monarchs would appreciate; Kensington very much reminded both George I and his son George II of Herrenhausen, little more than a very large country house, their principal residence two miles outside the medieval walls of Hanover. Unfortunately, however, George I had a mind, albeit a very limited one, of his own, and he saw fit to dismiss Wren, replacing him as Surveyor-General with an architect and builder called William Benson.

In 1718 Wren's remarkable pupil, Nicholas Hawksmoor, best known for his city churches, carried out a survey and discovered the original Nottingham House to be 'very ruinous and out of repair'. So Benson was commissioned to demolish the old building and to provide three new state rooms: the Privy Chamber, the King's Drawing Room and the centrepiece of the palace, the superb Cupola Room, begun in 1722, the room in which Queen Victoria's baptism was to take place. It is so named because the ceiling is formed of four great coves, with a central panel, also octagonal, painted with the Star of the Order of the Garter. But Benson turned out to be a better architect than builder, and some of his work was so shoddy that in 1724 £1,925 had to be spent on repairs.

When he could be spared from his labours at Robert Walpole's Norfolk mansion, Houghton Hall, William Kent was hired by George I to decorate the new rooms. Kent, a protégé of the arbiter of taste to the Whig aristocracy, the third Earl of Burlington, was immensely versatile and the most influential decorator, builder, interior designer and landscape gardener of his time, even designing for Victoria's great-grandfather, Frederick, Prince of Wales, a stupendously ornate state barge, now in the National Maritime Museum at Greenwich. One of Kent's most inspired contributions to Kensington Palace was a *trompe-l'oeil* on the King's Staircase in which are depicted an assortment of court functionaries, including two rather dubious Turkish servants imported by the King, Mohamet and Mustapha, officially employed as valets de chambre; much to the disgust of the English courtiers it was their task cere-moniously to dress and undress the sovereign. But they had other duties besides. Mohamet was appointed Keeper of the Closet, paid the tailors' bills and theatre subscriptions and, like the King's German mistresses, enriched himself by selling sinecures; when he died in 1726 these nefarious duties were taken over by Mustapha. The King's Gallery, designed by Hawksmoor back in 1695, was also painted by Kent.

In 1694 George I, while still Electoral Prince of Hanover, had divorced his foolish young wife, so that when he came to live at Kensington there was no queen consort, and three of his granddaughters, Anne (the Princess Royal), Amelia and Caroline, were given accommodation in rooms intended for the maids of honour. They were not particularly appealing young ladies. Anne, potmarked by smallpox, married a hunchback, Prince William of Orange-Nassau. Amelia, known to the family as Emily, entertained a hopeless attachment to the elderly Duke of Grafton, Lord Chamberlain and a grandson of Charles II, ending her life as a cantankerous old maid. And Princess Caroline was plagued by an equally inexplicable passion for Lord Hervey of Ickworth, the bisexual vice-chamberlain unkindly dubbed Lord Fanny by Pope. She, too, retired from the fray a disgruntled spinster.

Apart from her irrational, manic hatred of her elder son Frederick, the eventual father of George III, it was Queen Caroline, an educated and basically intelligent woman, who kept the family more or less together during the reign of George II, sensibly overlooking her husband's flagrant infidelities. And it was at Kensington that she indulged her passion for landscape gardening. In the early years of the eighteenth century she planted avenues of trees, and in 1731 created the Serpentine by linking together a series of ponds. Declaring that St James's Park 'stank of people', while still Princess of Wales she took to driving to Kensington Palace so that she could walk undisturbed in the gardens, 'gardens so immense that twenty or thirty gardeners work in them', according to a young Swiss visitor to England, César de Saussure. Writing home in 1726 he reported: 'One evening, being surprised at seeing so many of these men going home from work, I enquired how many there were. One of them answered there had been fifty or sixty for the last fortnight.' As soon as it became known that the Princess of

Wales, as Caroline remained until 1727, had deserted St James's Park and could be ogled at in a new location, crowds tramped across the fields between London and Kensington to join her.

George III, who succeeded his grandfather in 1760, loved Windsor Castle and had no desire to live at Kensington, and as his sons were impoverished by debts he found it convenient to grant them apartments at the palace. Hence, Queen Victoria's father had been allowed to live there before his marriage, the King turning a blind eye to the existence of his mistress. And in 1807 Prince Augustus, the morganatically married and bookish Duke of Sussex, was told he might have the south range of Clock Court. His library of 50,000 books occupied the Long Gallery; a further 5,000 copies of the Bible were stacked in a room that came to be known as the Divinity Room. Like his father, Sussex was fascinated by clocks and watches, and their cacophony of ticking and chiming nearly drove his visitors demented.

So it was into their suite on the east side of Kensington Palace that the Duke of Kent and his wife moved on their arrival in England for the birth of their child – their only child, as it transpired, for within eight months of Victoria's birth her father was dead. Victoria's uncle, Prince Leopold (he became King of the Belgians in 1830), said that the Prince Regent hated the Duke of Kent 'most sincerely', partly because he had produced a daughter to replace his own as heiress presumptive, partly because the Duke would keep bragging about it. The Regent did not much care for his new sister-in-law either. The Duchess of Kent was regarded by the British royal family as far too Germanic (an ironic attitude to take as they were half-German themselves), and it is true that she found great difficulty adapting herself to English manners and customs and in learning the language. Most unusually for the time, the Duchess fed her baby herself, dispensing with the services of

The Duchess of Kent and the Princess Victoria at the age
of two years, from a painting by Sir W. Beechey RA.

a wet nurse, a course of action her English relatives by marriage would have regarded as somehow decidedly indelicate. Her action may well account, however, for the close bond that undoubtedly existed between mother and daughter, severely tested though it often was by intrigue and bad advice.

Although she had twice given birth before, the Duchess seems to have been a nervous mother, perhaps because she realized how close to the throne her infant was. Before the Duke's death the royal family would have been glad to see the Kents return to Germany, but the Duchess was to remain – and make sure her precious child remained as well – firmly on English soil. The first-floor rooms in which the Duchess commenced her second widowhood have been described as dark and cramped, but as Victoria grew up, for the most part in robust health, enjoying summer holidays in Ramsgate, and no more children seemed to be forthcoming from Queen Adelaide, it became apparent that a better set of rooms would be more suitable. In middle age Queen Victoria recalled visits to Tunbridge Wells, where she and her mother stayed at a house called Mount Pleasant, later turned into a hotel. 'Many pleasant days were spent here,' she wrote in her journal, 'and the return to Kensington in October or November was generally a day of tears.'

Initially a backward child – she was five before she could read or write – Victoria was also a very lonely little girl. She had no brothers or sisters of her own. With her half-brother Prince Charles, who in any case became a young man while she was growing up, she had little rapport, and although devoted to her half-sister Princess Feodora it was more devotion to an idealized relationship than to a companion; Feodora was fifteen years older than Victoria, and by 1828 she was married. Victoria was unhappy at Kensington because the atmosphere was more like a scene of

Tudor plotting than that of a secure and happy home. The Duchess had brought over with her from Germany John Conroy, a captain in the Royal Artillery, Irish by birth, who had served as her husband's equerry. At Kensington he became comptroller to her household. He would have been better named controller. Conroy was immensely ambitious and saw a brilliant future for himself as private secretary to Victoria when she became queen. By attempting to isolate the princess from her relations both at the English court and in Coburg, and hence making her entirely dependent on her mother, Conroy reckoned that whatever advice he gave the Duchess would be passed on to her daughter.

The 'Kensington system', as Conroy's regimen came to be known, took account of every moment of Victoria's waking life – and even the time she spent asleep, for until she was 'nearly grown up', probably aged about seventeen, she was not even allowed a bedroom to herself; she slept in her mother's room. Meals were spartan. Breakfast was at half-past eight, luncheon at half-past one and dinner at seven, a meal at which Victoria was permitted bread and milk served in a small silver basin. 'Tea,' she remembered, 'was only allowed as a great treat in later years.' No wonder she developed a greedy appetite as an adult. Conroy's insistence that Victoria did not meet politicians or William IV's courtiers, that she remained uncontaminated by opinions other than his, only served to whet Victoria's desire to discover what *was* going on in the outside world, and her innate curiosity about the lives of 'ordinary' people became a marked trait in her character; so, too, did her deep affection and consideration for servants, initiated when, at the age of five, she was supplied with a German governess, Louise Lehzen.

Lehzen took it on herself, for example, to teach Victoria to beg the forgiveness of her maid 'for any naughtiness or rudeness' towards her, 'a feeling I have ever retained', the Queen remarked in later life, 'and think everyone should own their own fault in a kind way to anyone, be he or she the lowest'. Apart from her ladies of the bedchamber, once her craze for dancing had worn off and glittering balls had become a court function of the past (and certainly from the moment she was widowed), Victoria very much kept her distance from the aristocracy, of whose behaviour, and especially the bad influence she thought they had on her eldest son, she strongly disapproved. The sort of people she came to admire and whose company she enjoyed were soldiers, musicians and servants. She would not have been the least surprised when Lord Melbourne told her that Lady Holland, the famous political and social hostess, had excellent old-fashioned servants who would sometimes join in the conversation.

Bishops, on the other hand, remained one of the Queen's *bêtes noires*. She said that in childhood, at Kensington, she had 'a great horror of bishops on account of their wigs and aprons'. During her Diamond Jubilee celebrations, the Queen received a delegation of ecclesiastics at Windsor, and driving in the park afterwards she murmured, more or less to herself, 'A very ugly party.' Warming to her theme, she sharply announced, 'I do not like bishops!' Edith, Lady Lytton, who was in waiting, was somewhat startled and said, 'But Your Majesty likes *some* bishops', mentioning by name the Bishops of Winchester and Ripon. 'Yes,' said the Queen, 'I like the man but not the bishop!'

It has been estimated that Victoria penned some sixty million words in the course of her reign, and recalling her early childhood she admitted on paper to being very passionate, 'but always most contrite afterwards'. It was Fräulein Lehzen's task to be both kind and firm, and the Queen wrote: 'I had a proper respect for her.' But Lehzen, whom the princess loved as well as respected, failed to repress her pupil's passion entirely, and thank goodness for that;

Baroness Lehzen, from a miniature at Windsor Castle.

Queen Victoria's letters and journal entries would have been a good deal duller without their abundance of exclamation marks, under-linings and expressions of the wildest and most partisan prejudices.

In October 1819 Victoria's father travelled south, to Devon, in the hopes of finding an inexpensive home with the chance of some sunshine. He alighted on a 'large cottage *orné*' in Sidmouth called Woolbrook Glen (now the Royal Glen Hotel). Here he, the Duchess of Kent and Victoria spent a somewhat fraught Christmas; a young apprentice shooting birds managed to send a pellet through the nursery window, the house was icy and the weather outside so atrocious that everyone caught colds. The Duke's cold turned to pneumonia, whereas Victoria survived both the bullet and the weather, and a friend in Coburg was informed that the eight-month-old

Vickelchen, as her mother called her, was 'beginning to show symptoms of wanting to get her own little way'. As for the Duke's symptoms, obviously they called for the usual merciless bleeding, but he roused himself sufficiently before he died to sign a will not worth the paper it was written on, for he had nothing to leave. Prince Leopold, who had been summoned to the deathbed of his brother-in-law, along with Christian Stockmar, the Prince's roving factotum, had to provide the funds necessary to get the Duchess and her child back to Kensington Palace.

After Leopold's acceptance of the Belgian throne – having declined the Greek – Stockmar was rewarded for his loyal services with a Belgian barony. Originally a native of Coburg, he had trained as a doctor, and it was as a medical man that he was initially taken into his household by Prince Leopold, accompanying the prince to

Baron Stockmar, from the portrait by John Partridge at Buckingham Palace.

England when he married Princess Charlotte. After the princess's death, for which fortunately Stockmar was not responsible, Leopold, desperately in need of comfort and support from someone he had known at home in Coburg, appointed Stockmar his private secretary, Keeper of the Privy Purse and comptroller – not that such an illustrious list of appointments meant very much; Prince Leopold remained without employment for the next thirteen years. Stockmar's influence, not always as sagacious as it might have been, was to come to fruition when Leopold's nephew, Prince Albert, married Victoria.

At a time when twenty-one was still the normal coming of age, Victoria, as heiress presumptive to the throne, was due to come of age at eighteen, being then permitted to reign without a regency. But in the event of William IV dying childless before Victoria's eighteenth birthday there would have been no certain constitutional precedent for the appointment of a regent. George II, when on his trips to Hanover, always flatly refused to grant the regency to his son and heir, Prince Frederick, passing him over for Queen Caroline; when it was first believed necessary for a regent to be appointed when George III became deranged a battle ensued between those, like Charles James Fox, a political adherent of the Prince of Wales, who purported to believe that the heir to the throne had an inherent right to be appointed regent, and those who, like Pitt, declared that Parliament had the right to choose a regent.

Next in line to the throne after Victoria was the gruesome Duke of Cumberland, whom nobody wanted as regent. The only viable alternative seemed to be Victoria's mother. And it became the ardent desire of John Conroy that if a regency was required, the Duchess of Kent should have it. He even went so far as to spread rumours that Victoria was in permanent ill health, was feeble-minded, and that even if she had come of age by the time of William's death she would be quite incapable of ruling without her mother's help; hence the Duchess should be made regent as a matter of course.

It was when Victoria was sixteen, ill at Ramsgate, some say with typhoid, others with tonsillitis, that Conroy attempted to pull off a dastardly coup, by getting the delirious princess to sign a document promising to appoint him her private secretary.[4] He was egged on by the Duchess, but fortunately Lehzen stood firmly against the plotters and prevented Victoria from signing. The Duke of Wellington told Charles Greville, whose appointment in 1820, when he was twenty-six, to a clerkship-in-ordinary to the Privy Council furnished him with both plenty of money and a grandstand view of society, that Victoria's hatred of Conroy, and the cooling of her relations with her mother, was 'unquestionably owing to her having witnessed some familiarity between them'. Whatever the truth about that (Victoria denied it in later life, when she read Greville's diary on its publication in 1887, for by then she wished to preserve a respectful attitude towards her mother, whose death in 1861 she had mourned extravagantly) there is no doubt that Conroy's conduct in Ramsgate was a watershed in Victoria's development as an independent woman, and as far as Victoria was concerned Conroy became 'that monster and demon incarnate'.

By contrast, we have Victoria's own account of Lehzen's ascendancy. 'Dear good Lehzen takes such care of me,' Victoria wrote in her journal on 5 November 1835, 'and is so unceasing in her attentions to me that I shall never be able to repay her sufficiently for it but by my love and gratitude. I never can sufficiently repay her for all she has borne and done for me. She is the most affectionate, devoted, attached and disinterested friend I have and I love her most dearly.' As well as ingratiating himself with the

Duchess of Kent, Conroy had turned his charm on for the benefit of George III's susceptible daughter, Princess Sophia, who had apartments at Kensington Palace and an illegitimate son by one of her father's equerries, General Thomas Garth. Having relieved the princess of at least £22,000 with which to buy for himself a house in Kensington, an estate in Wales and a country house near Reading, Conroy suggested to the princess that she should ask her brother, since 1820 George IV, to create him a Knight Commander of the Hanoverian Order, an honour in the gift of the sovereign, so that there was no need for the King to consult the Prime Minister. While he was about it, Conroy also thought the Duchess of Kent's household would be enhanced if the King made Louise Lehzen a Hanoverian baroness.

Baroness Lehzen has often been credited with taking responsibility for Princess Victoria's education. What she did was act as schoolmistress, making sure her royal pupil kept her head down and followed a punishing curriculum set out for her by a Fellow of Christ's College, Cambridge (later Bishop of Peterborough), the Reverend George Davys. Much of Victoria's childhood was spent in a world of make-believe, she and the Baroness dressing no fewer than 132 dolls. Victoria must have been amused when, at the age of seventy-three, a lady who was writing a book about dolls enquired, through the Queen's private secretary, whether as a child she had liked dolls. Back came the reply: 'The Queen has no hesitation in saying that she was quite devoted to dolls & played with them till she was 14. Her favourites were small ones which cd be dressed as she liked & had a House. None of her children loved them as she did – but then *she* was an *only* child & except occasional visits of other children lived always alone, without companions.' The Queen was able to recall a good deal of her childhood in considerable detail, and in later life she spent a great deal of energy putting people right about the facts. In 1888 Oscar Wilde put his foot in it – or was he leg-pulling? – by asking for permission 'to copy some of the poetry written by the Queen when young'. 'Really what will people not say & invent,' the Queen minuted. 'Never cd the Queen in her whole life write *one line of poetry* serious or comic or make a Rhyme even. This is therefore all *invention & a myth.*'

The Golden Jubilee of 1887 encouraged a number of authors to write books about the Queen, some of whom were rash enough to offer her presentation copies. 'People shd send their books to the Queen *before* & not *after* they are published with *endless mistakes,*' she told her private secretary. 'Quite wrong', 'stupid story repeatedly contradicted', 'all total myths', 'a complete invention', 'quite untrue', 'never threw her arms round her uncle's neck & sobbed' were some of the angry annotations.

As Victoria's mother spoke both French and German but rather poor English, and Lehzen of course spoke German, Victoria became fluent in both languages. Under the tuition of Richard Westall (and later in life Edward Lear) she became a skilled draughtsman, and the organist at St Margaret's, Westminster, John Sale, undertook with success the training of her very pleasing soprano voice. Her 'naturally beautiful' and 'melodious' speaking voice was frequently commented on. On the academic side, Victoria studied Horace, Virgil and Ovid. Dryden, Pope, Oliver Goldsmith and Cowper, together with Shakespeare of course, were among the English poets and playwrights whose work she read, but she shied clear of novelists, telling the Dowager Lady Lytton in 1897 that she never read a novel before her marriage 'and had been very careful what books her daughters read'. She thought 'even Scott was sometimes coarse'. But she absorbed Voltaire's histories in French, and when she was fifteen Victoria studied a commentary on the laws of England. As she was likely to become Supreme Governor of the Church of England, twenty religious texts were added to her reading list. She learned the Acts of the Apostles by heart. Whether this helped to develop her retentive memory or was a consequence of it is hard to say. As a young girl she was immensely industrious scholastically, and as a constitutional monarch, who might have been expected to sit back and remain content to warn, advise and be kept informed, she drove her ministers to distraction by her own erudite comments and questions on matters of state, in particular foreign affairs, about which she often knew a great deal more than they did. By any standards Queen Victoria was well educated. The fact that she believed Marie Corelli would come to be regarded as one of the greatest writers of her time can only be regarded as a typical Victorian quirk.

Almost as if deliberately to rile William IV, the Duchess of Kent and Conroy stage-managed well-publicised progesses to show the young Victoria off to her future subjects, these excursions serving as an outing for Conroy's daughter, also called Victoria, whom the princess cordially loathed. Much to the fury of the King, in the summer of 1832, when Victoria was thirteen, she and her mother made a journey to Wales, and that autumn they were received at Oxford. For Victoria these jaunts served as a pleasant change from the stifling atmosphere at Kensington, where she was forbidden to receive anyone unless a third party was present. One evening after dinner in July 1833 Victoria played spillikins with her cousin Prince Ernst of Württemberg. That must have been quite an event. The essential sadness of Victoria's incarceration at Kensington can be gauged by the arrival, on 5 June 1834, of her half-sister, whom she had not seen for six years, and Princess Feodora's departure two months later. 'The separation was indeed dreadful,' Victoria wrote in her journal. 'I clasped her in my arms and kissed her and cried as if my heart would break . . . When I came home I was in such a state of grief that I knew not what to do with myself. I sobbed and cried most violently the whole morning . . . My dearest best sister was friend, sister, companion all to me . . . I love no one better than her.'

But as Victoria grew older her horizons did widen a little. On 19 April 1836 she received her first singing lesson, for example, from Luigi Lablache, the Neapolitan bass, and on 3 May she recorded: 'I like Lablache very much, he is such a nice, good-natured, good-humoured man, and a very patient and excellent master; he is so merry too.' And she went on to display an early and vivid example of her ability to note and describe in detail the attributes of almost everyone she met. '*En profile* he has a very fine countenance, I think, an aquiline nose, dark arched eye-brows, and fine long eyelashes, and a very clear expression. He has a profusion of hair, which is very grey and strangely mixed with some few black locks here and there. I liked my lesson extremely; I only wish I had one every day instead of one every week.' Lablache, who made his London debut on the opera stage in 1830, was at this time aged forty-two. He was not conventionally good-looking and became very stout, but all her life Victoria was much smitten by male physique.

It was on 18 May 1836, at Kensington Palace, that Victoria, a stickler for exactitude ('At a ¼ to 2 we went down into the Hall, to receive my Uncle Ernest, Duke of Saxe-Coburg-Gotha'), first met the Duke of Coburg's younger son, her sixteen-year-old cousin and future husband, Prince Albert. 'Albert,' she noted, 'is extremely handsome; his hair is about the same colour as mine; his eyes are large and blue, and he has a beautiful nose and a very sweet mouth with fine teeth; but the charm of his countenance is his expression, which is most delightful; *c'est à la fois* full of goodness and sweetness, and very clever and intelligent.' The fact that already Albert spoke good English is one indication that from birth he had been his uncle Leopold's choice of bridegroom for Victoria.

Sir John Conroy and the Duchess of Kent were not very pleased by visits from potential consorts or to discover the young princess beginning to find her feet. Victoria wrote to King Leopold on 31 May 1836 to tell him about a dance at Kensington Palace (Prince Albert had been her 'dear partner') when 'we all stayed up until ½ past 3'. But she assured the King: 'You are very kind dear Uncle to think of my health and of my not fatiguing myself; I can assure you all this dissipation does me a great deal of good.'

Already Victoria had marriage, and total freedom, on her mind. By 7 June she was writing to King Leopold to say that Albert 'possessed every quality that could be desired to render me perfectly happy . . . He has . . . the most pleasing and delightful exterior and appearance you can possibly see.'

Leopold had become the first of Victoria's father-figures, her 'secondo padre', as she referred to him in September 1836, 'or rather, solo padre! for he is indeed like my real father, as I have none! He is so clever, so mild, and so prudent; he alone can give me good advice on every thing.'

With Baroness Lehzen's encouragement, Victoria was gradually freeing herself of the 'Kensington system'. On 14 March 1837 she wrote to Leopold: 'We had a dinner on Saturday which amused me, as I am very fond of pleasant society, and we have been for these last three weeks immured within our old palace, and I longed sadly for some gaiety.' She had not long to wait. On 24 May she came of age, no regency would be required, and she celebrated with a ball at St James's Palace. By 15 June 'news of the King are [sic] so very bad' that all her lessons, save that due to be given by the Dean of Chester, were cancelled – even Lablache's. 'I regret rather my singing-lesson,' Victoria wrote in her journal, 'though it is only for a short period, but duty and proper feeling go before all pleasures.' At the very moment of writing she heard that the doctors 'think my poor Uncle the King cannot last more than 48 hours! Poor man! he was always kind to me . . . He was odd, very odd and singular, but his intentions were often ill interpreted! At about a ¼p 2 came Lord Liverpool, and I had a highly important conversation with him – alone.' The third Earl of Liverpool, whose father had served as Prime Minister from 1812 to 1827, was a moderate Tory intensely concerned for Victoria's welfare, in whom Victoria had complete confidence; the 'highly important conversation' centred on Conroy's continued insistence on being appointed private secretary when Victoria succeeded, Lord Liverpool urging Victoria on no account to appoint him to her household, but adding that she must seek the advice of Lord Melbourne, soon to become the first of her ten Prime Ministers.

Victoria had, as usual, received advice, too, from King Leopold. 'Your advice is most excellent,' she wrote to her uncle on 19 June, 'and you may depend upon it I shall make use of it, and follow it.' King William 'expired at 12 minutes p 2 this morning,' Victoria recorded on the day of her accession, 20 June, the timing of course denoting the precise moment at which she became Queen. But Victoria was in any case fascinated by death and deathbeds, and having hastened from Windsor Castle to Kensington Palace in the early hours, arriving shortly before 6 a.m., the Archbishop of Canterbury, William Howley, imparted to his new young sovereign the details of her uncle's death, the King having 'directed his mind to religion', dying apparently 'in a perfectly happy, quiet state of mind'. In one of her most famous journal entries the Queen began her account of the arrival of the archbishop, accompanied by the Lord Chamberlain, the Marquess of Conyngham, whose mother, in 1820, had become one of George IV's well-proportioned mistresses: 'I was awoke at 6 o'clock by Mamma . . . I got out of bed and went into my sitting-room (only in my dressing-gown), and alone.' There she received the archbishop and Lord Conyngham, who knelt to kiss her hand, 'at the same time delivering to me the official announcement of the poor King's demise'.

Victoria's several references on the first day of her reign to doing things alone highlights the restrictions on her privacy until so recently insisted upon by Sir John Conroy:

> At 9 came Lord Melbourne, whom I saw in my room, and of course quite alone as I shall always do all my ministers. He kissed my hand and I then acquainted him that it had long been my intention to retain him and the rest of the present Ministry at the head of affairs . . . At about $^{1}/_{2}$p 11 I went downstairs and held a Council in the red saloon.[5] I went in of course quite alone . . . Took my dinner upstairs alone . . . Went down and said good night to Mamma etc. My dear Lehzen will always remain with me as my friend but will take no situation about me, and I think she is right.

The 'Kensington system' had collapsed. Conroy and the Duchess of Kent were isolated. For a few years Baroness Lehzen acted virtually as private secretary, but eventually she fell foul of Prince Albert and left the Queen's employment without even saying goodbye. Queen Victoria was soon to say goodbye to Kensington Palace, her home for the first eighteen years of her life. She returned in 1867 to her old apartments to view for the first time the future Queen Mary but she was the last sovereign ever to live there.

3

'Very Pleasant Large Dinners'

Buckingham Palace has enjoyed a long and complex history, a multitude of alterations, the attention of a good many architects and several changes of name. In addition to his official London residence, St James's Palace, George III acquired what was then known as Buckingham House, presenting the property to his wife, Queen Charlotte, so that it became known as the Queen's House. Queen Victoria was the first sovereign to take up official residence in a building resembling anything like the Buckingham Palace we know today. Indeed, she never even contemplated living at St James's Palace, although ambassadors continued to be accredited to the Court of St James's, as they still are today; and although she came much to prefer the romanticism of Windsor Castle, with the privacy provided by the royal apartments and the Great Park, she retained sufficient ceremonial links with London for Buckingham Palace, after her death, to become the weekday centre of operations for the monarchy, her eldest son, Edward VII, being born and dying there.

Her imprimatur, in the early years of her reign (her uncle William IV had only very reluctantly contemplated moving in, and in the end he never did), was ironic in a way, for Queen Victoria took an aversion to Buckingham Palace; it did not suit her self-imposed conduct as a grieving recluse after Albert's death. At a meal in 1900 her granddaughter Princess Thora remarked that her dog did not like Buckingham Palace. 'I can *quite* understand that!' said Victoria.

The site on which Buckingham Palace stands has been endowed with royal connections since the reign of Henry VIII, who drained the marshy land, laid out gardens now known as St James's Park and hunted from a lodge that became St James's Palace. His daughter Elizabeth's successor, James I, had the brainwave of competing (or trying to compete) with the French silk industry, and in 1608 he paid £935 to have mulberry trees planted on a four-acre plot near the present north wing of the palace. Unfortunately, he planted black mulberry trees, which silkworms detest, instead of white mulberry trees, which they gobble up.

The first house of any substance built where Buckingham Palace now stands was Goring House – the home of Lord Goring, later Earl of Norwich, vice-chamberlain to the wife of Charles I and Master of the Horse. Faced with massive debts due entirely to his extravagance, Goring mortgaged his home to his wife's relatives and then saw it requisitioned by Commonwealth troops. After the Restoration the property was owned by a secretary of state to Charles II, Henry Bennet, ennobled in 1665 as Earl of Arlington. Arlington lavished his wealthy wife's money on Goring House, and when Samuel Pepys called in 1666 he found it 'a very fine house and finely furnished'. In 1672 the fortunes of both Lord Arlington and Goring House were sealed when Charles married off his nine-year-old bastard son, the Duke of Grafton, to Arlington's five-year-old daughter, Isabella.

Goring House became one of the grandest of London homes, John Evelyn finding in 1673 the Countess of Arlington's 'new dressing room with the glasses, silver jars and vases, cabinets and other, so rich furniture as I had seldom seen'. Alas, the Parisian green damask bed curtains, the paintings by Raphael and van Dyke, the drawings by Leonardo da Vinci were all destroyed in a fire that consumed the house and its contents in 1674 while the Arlingtons were taking the waters in Bath. Not in the least down-hearted, Arlington promptly built a replacement, a veritable mansion which he called Arlington House. It had superb views over St James's Park and down the Mall. Deer were imported, nightingales took up their noisy residence, and the gardens and house became a favourite resort for the King, whose son by the Countess of Castlemaine, Henry Grafton, inherited the enticing estate on Lord Arlington's death in 1685.

After a spell when the fourth Earl of Devonshire took a lease on the house a second fire caused considerable damage, and Arlington House became the property of John Sheffield, Marquess of Normanby, created Duke of Buckingham in 1703, an event he celebrated by demolishing the damaged Arlington House and building in its place what became *the* grandest town house in London, Buckingham House, its royal connections, if only on the wrong side of the sheets, being strengthened even further with the marriage in 1705 of Buckingham to Katherine, Countess of Anglesey, an illegitimate daughter of James II. She in turn became the grandest *grande dame* in town. Immensely wealthy and inordinately proud of her Stuart blood, she regarded the Hanoverian dynasty, when they arrived in 1714, with disdain; as far as she was concerned they were mere parvenu, if not actually usurpers. On the anniversary of the execution of her grandfather, Charles I, she would have her drawing room draped in mourning. The Duchess of Buckingham's grandson, Lord Mulgrave, married Lepel Hervey, the eldest daughter of Lord Hervey of Ickworth. Hervey knew the

Duchess well — so well that she bequeathed to him Buckingham House for his lifetime; but perfectly satisfied with the house in St James's Square given him by his father, the Earl of Bristol, Hervey handed over Buckingham House to his daughter.

The Duke of Buckingham had employed two architects, William Talman and William Winde, whose royalist family had sought refuge in Holland, where Winde himself was born. He became one of the most important domestic architects of the seventeenth century. By coincidence, Winde had previously been employed by another Duke of Buckingham, the second duke, son of James I's ill-fated favourite, George Villiers, who in about 1666 had purchased Cliveden, near Taplow, later to become the principal country home of Frederick, Prince of Wales. Winde produced a four-storey brick house and landscaped the garden, but all that remains of Winde's work at Cliveden today (two disastrous fires occurred, in 1795 and 1849) is the south-facing arcaded terrace over-looking the Thames valley.

Winde began work on Buckingham House in 1705, and three years later, for £8,000, he was said to have produced a 'graceful palace, very commodiously situated in the westerly end of St James's Park, having at one view a prospect of the Mall & other walks, and of a delightful and spacious canal; a seat not to be condemned by the greatest monarch'. It certainly made St James's Palace look a bit tawdry. After the death of the Duke in 1721, the Prince of Wales, later George II, opened negotiations to rent or buy Buckingham House, almost certainly in a bid to irritate his father. But he baulked at the sum — £60,000 — the Duchess demanded. The Duchess was nicknamed Princess Buckingham by those in society who thought she cut a ridiculous figure; in 1741 Horace Walpole told Sir Horace Mann she was 'more mad with pride than any mercer's wife in Bedlam, came the other night to the Opera *en princess* literally in robes, red velvet and ermine'.

The Duke of Buckingham had no legitimate heir, but his bastard son Charles Herbert took the name Sheffield, was made a baronet, and in 1763 he sold Buckingham House, with its 30 acres of gardens, for £28,000 to George III. Two years later the King gave the house to his wife, and it was then that it became known as the Queen's House. Queen Charlotte was extremely attached to her own town house, twelve of her fifteen children being born there. This did not necessarily mean the family would outgrow the accommodation, for the two eldest boys, George and Edward, were brought up at the Dutch House in Kew (the only royal residence in Kew that still stands), while an ugly two-storey building, the Queen's Lodge, most unfortunately erected by Queen Anne across the centre of the south range of Windsor Castle, blocking out any view of the park, was utilized to provide accommodation for the six princesses.[1]

George III's most notable addition to the Queen's House was the provision of a library, completed in 1767 by Sir William Chambers – an octagonal room in which the King famously crept up on Dr Johnson while he was reading. In time the King's collection amounted to some 67,000 volumes, the books 'chosen with perfect taste and judgement' in the opinion of the first American minister to the British court, John Adams, who saw the library in 1783. The King was not exactly short of works of art, and he had a number of paintings transported from Hampton Court to the Queen's House, but several astute purchases of foreign collections early in his reign enabled him to embellish the Queen's House with Canalettos and Zuccarellis. Drawings by Poussin jostled with van Dykes and works by Rubens and Titian. Josiah Wedgwood was summoned to the house. In 1781 the King attended an auction near Marlow, bidding for chairs at 14½ guineas each, a couch that

Buckingham House in 1775.

cost 48 guineas and two small cabinets, knocked down for 45 guineas. While money seems to have been no object when it came to furnishing the Queen's House (by the Queen's bed stood a case containing twenty-five watches, all encrusted with jewels) it had a homely atmosphere too; in March 1767 a visitor found the rooms 'full of Roses, carnations, hyacinths etc, dispersed in the prettiest manner imaginable in jars & different flower pots on stands'.

The performing arts came in for due attention. A music room contained an elaborately carved organ and not one but three harp-sichords were purchased for the Queen, who took singing lessons from Johann Christian Bach; the King was a proficient flautist. And it was at the Queen's House that the seven-year-old Mozart was received. He played the organ, the Queen sang, and the child prodigy composed four sonatas in her honour.

It was symptomatic of the King's restless nature, and almost certainly a portent of impending attacks of porphyria that were to wreck his life after 1788, that once he had got the Queen's House arranged to his satisfaction he began to lose interest in it. He had escaped to the relative simplicity of the Queen's House to get away from the formality of court life, yet now he wished to rid himself of London to enjoy the open air at Kew and Windsor. An excuse to leave behind the increasing grime of London was presented in 1779 when a gale 'took off the upper corner of the Queen's House', as Charlotte Papendiek, daughter of the Queen's page, recalled in her memoirs.[2] 'This was the room next to the one in which the Princes Ernest, Augustus & Adolphus slept, which was over the bedroom of their majesties. The King was up, and with his children in a moment. The ceiling was falling fast & had already broken the bedstead of the elder Prince.'

After about 1785 the King and Queen were hardly ever at their Pimlico residence, at least not together. But when the demented

King was finally incarcerated at Windsor, to all intents and purposes clinically mad, Queen Charlotte did sometimes continue to repair to her town house. To cheer up her son the Prince Regent when he was short of money, she threw a party for him at the Queen's House – not, she explained, '*à la manière de* Carlton House, but about 100 or 200 people'. She added: 'If you would like to take a quiet dinner with me *en famille* I will order it at six that we may have a little time to breathe before the company comes.'

With the death in 1820 of George III, the prodigal Prince Regent inherited the Queen's House (Queen Charlotte had died in 1818), and as he now decided to turn it into a palace it became known as the New Palace, and sometimes, perhaps in derision, as the King's House in Pimlico. In view of the prodigious sums of money the King had extracted from the government for Carlton House, the Brighton Pavilion and Windsor Castle it was amazing that he persuaded Parliament to vote £200,000 for 'a repair and improvement of Buckingham House', and true to form he eventually ran up bills for three times as much. But bored with Carlton House, and determined on a real London palace, in 1827 George IV committed probably his only truly wicked act; he demolished Carlton House, his favourite architect John Nash having been called in two years earlier to set to work on Buckingham House. Nash virtually rebuilt it, around a three-sided courtyard, with its principal front of Bath stone overlooking the extensive gardens, newly landscaped by William Alton.

Although it was not until June 1825 that Parliament actually voted their £200,000, in May that year *The Times* was reporting:

Buckingham House is to be converted into a palace, for the residence of the King. The centre building will ostensibly remain, but the interior of it will be entirely renovated. Two magnificent and tasteful wings, which have been projected by His Majesty himself, upon a very large scale, will be added to the centre. The domestic offices, suited to the luxury of these times, and replete with every convenience, will be concealed from the public eye by an ingenious artifice. The workmen have already commenced their labours; the whole will be finished in 18 months.

The following month *The Times* was informing its readers that there were 'nearly 400 artisans of every description at work on the premises, among whom there are no fewer than 120 carpenters'. The old hands were apparently satisfied 'with the usual pay of 5 shillings a day' but Nash found himself with a strike on his hands when the newly hired workmen demanded an increase. When the strikers actually began to use threats, 'one who was armed with a sword flourishing it about in a menacing manner', the Coldstream Guards were called out to evict the 'non-contents'. Increasingly paranoid, hypochondriac and bedridden, George IV spent his declining years at Windsor, and never moved into 'The King's Palace at St James's Park', as *The Times* had announced in January 1826 that Buckingham House was now to be called, adding: 'The entire pile will be of immense magnitude.' It was not until 1837, seven years after the death of George IV and in the year of Queen Victoria's accession, that for the time being, at any rate, work on Buckingham Palace was finished; it had overrun by ten years and six months.

William IV, the former Duke of Clarence, who referred to his brother's art collection as his 'knicknackeries', found a white elephant in Pimlico. He had no intention of taking up residence in Buckingham Palace if he could help it. He was more than content with Clarence House, the residence in the Mall he had occupied before coming to the throne – content, at any rate, after

Nash had brought it up to scratch.³ At the start of his reign William lived at St James's Palace when in London, but he soon returned to Clarence House. He was delighted when in 1834 a fire destroyed the Palace of Westminster; Buckingham Palace, he suggested, could now serve as the new Parliament building. Three years previously the King, who was not very bright ('what can you expect,' Charles Greville enquired, 'from a man with a head like a pineapple?'), wondered if this sumptuous building would not serve rather well as a barracks. In 1831, in a very reluctant manner, the King had agreed that the palace should be completed, by a Derby-born architect called Edward Blore; £100,000 was allocated, the King insisting that money should not be squandered on 'the Decorations which he considers to form part of the Architectural Estimate, especially as he has never calculated upon the use of Buckingham Palace for any purpose of state'.

But although William IV always insisted he had no intention of making formal use of Buckingham Palace, he gave orders that the music room was to be converted into a state dining room. A suite of rooms in the north wing was completed for the use of the King and Queen, and by 1835 they had decided they would, after all, move in. But Blore was a perfectionist, insisting he could not hand over the building until gas lighting had been installed, silk at six shillings a yard had been ordered from Ireland, and furnishings and fittings had been moved in from Windsor. As far as Thomas Creevey was concerned he might as well not have bothered. There 'never was such a specimen of wicked, vulgar profusion', he declared. He thought that instead of being called Buckingham Palace it should be named the Brunswick Hotel. 'The costly ornaments in the state rooms exceed all belief in their bad taste . . . Raspberry coloured pillars without end, that quite turn you sick to look at; but the Queen's paper for her own apartments far exceed everything else in their ugliness and vulgarity.' In May 1837 the palace was declared finished and fit for a king. By 20 June William was dead.

Nash had provided a much-derided dome, which Edward Blore removed, and Blore was back at Buckingham Palace in 1847 to provide additional rooms for Queen Victoria's numerous children by enclosing the courtyard with what has been described as a 'rather dull range in Caen stone facing the Mall'.4 The major, and now irreversible, problem about Buckingham Palace is that it was built back to front; the public face, with its famous balcony, still remains rather dull even following the completion in 1913 by Sir Aston Webb of a façade of Portland stone, while Nash's garden front, only ever viewed by guests invited to garden parties, is infinitely more pleasing. Victoria eventually replaced Blore by a nephew and pupil of Nash, Sir James Pennethorne, who built the south wing containing the state supper room and an enormous ballroom. These palatial additions were finished in 1855, but not much dancing took place after the death of the Prince Consort just six years later.

Victoria had lived for the first eighteen years of her life in one apartment of a provincial palace with much charm but no claims to regality. She could not wait to take over a large, grand palace in the heart of London where she could play at being Queen to her heart's content. She moved in on 13 July. 'I really and truly go into Buckingham Palace the day after to-morrow', she wrote to King Leopold on 11 July, 'but I must say, though I am very glad to do so, I feel sorry to leave for ever my poor old birthplace.' And she was in no hurry to explore the other homes she had inherited: the Palace of Holyroodhouse in Edinburgh, the Royal Pavilion in Brighton or the most venerable of all, Windsor Castle, with which she was already slightly acquainted. 'I shall not go out of town, I think, until the 20th or thereabouts of next month,' she wrote to her uncle Leopold from Buckingham Palace on 25 July. 'Windsor requires thorough cleaning and I must say I could not think of going in sooner after the poor King's death. Windsor always appears very melancholy to me, and there are so many sad associations with it. These will vanish, I daresay, if I see you there after my arrival there.

'I have very pleasant large dinners every day,' she went on to inform the King. 'I invite my premier generally once a week to dinner as I think it right to show publicly that I esteem him and have confidence in him, as he has behaved so well. Stockmar is of this opinion and is his great admirer.'

Her premier, the second Viscount Melbourne, was far more than a political adviser in the early years of Victoria's reign. He was her mentor and second father-figure, a companion as much as a Prime Minister with whom she instinctively relaxed, allowing him some rather extraordinary but endearing liberties; not many Prime Ministers have been granted the indulgence by their sovereign of nodding off after dinner. Charles Greville thought the Queen's feelings for Melbourne were sexual, although she did not know it. He may well have been right; Victoria was a very emotional and passionate women, and at this stage of her life seriously starved of affection. No young man of her own age would have dared approach her on anything like an intimate basis. Melbourne got away with all sorts of eccentric behaviour precisely because Victoria looked up to him. His flippant remarks, often more suited to a male dinner party than to the imagination of a young and inexperienced girl, may not always have been judicious, but although the opportunity to serve such a pliable object as Victoria undoubtedly appealed to Melbourne, and breathed renewed energy into his politically flagging spirits, no one could ever accuse him of making capital out of his relations with the Queen. Even his political enemies acknowledged his essential honesty. One of Victoria's first acts of her reign was to offer Melbourne the Garter, an honour he had no hesitation in declining, believing it had been so debased in his time that he exclaimed there was 'no damn merit in it'.

One reason Victoria had hurried to install herself at Buckingham Palace was because it was from the palace that she planned to make her first state drive as sovereign, only four days after moving in, in order to prorogue Parliament. She records in her journal that she 'did it very well'. She saw Buckingham Palace rather than Kensington Palace as a splendid setting in which to receive 'various foreign Ambassadors', including 'Count Orloff, sent by the Emperor of Russia to compliment me. He presented me with a letter from the Empress of Russia accompanied by the Order of St Catherine all set in diamonds. (I, of course, as I generally do every evening, wore the Garter.)' At a levée that followed she claimed to have had her hand kissed 'nearly 3000 times!' She then held a Council. 'After this I saw Lord Melbourne for a little while, and then Lord Palmerston.'

An old friend of George IV, Princess Lieven, wife of the Russian ambassador, was received by the Queen towards the end of July. She told Charles Greville that the Queen was 'very civil and gracious, but timid and embarrassed, and talked of nothing but commonplaces'. Greville noted that the Queen had probably been warned that Princess Lieven was an intriguer 'and was afraid of committing herself'. Ever in search of gossip, the Princess did indeed shoot off to see the Duchess of Kent the minute her audience with the Queen was over, and she reported to Greville that it was plain to see the Duchess was 'overwhelmed with vexation and disappointment', on account, of course, of the fact that Victoria was sailing along quite happily without her help or advice. If the idea of providing the Duchess with accommodation at Buckingham

Palace was to give the impression that the unmarried young Queen was being suitably chaperoned, matters had not been engineered very astutely. The Duchess had apartments about as far away as they could have been from her daughter's, and unless specifically sent for she never saw Victoria. Baroness Lehzen, on the other hand, had a virtual right of entrée; as one door closed on the exit of a minister the door opposite quietly opened to admit the Baroness. Friction in the household was inevitable, especially as the Duchess felt humiliated by the dismissal of Sir John Conroy from the Queen's employ, and instead of waiting until the Queen married it would have been far more sensible for the Duchess to have been given Clarence House as a London residence from the very beginning of the reign.

The truth was that Victoria had come into her inheritance while still a girl. She was headstrong by nature, and the full and dazzling round of activities, all the obsequious bowing and curtsying, and the overwhelming sense of freedom and independence turned her head, and she scarcely gave a thought to her mother's predicament. As far as her aunt Queen Adelaide was concerned, however, Victoria behaved with perfect dignity and consideration, going to Windsor to see her and assuring her she should stay on at the castle as long as she pleased. By the beginning of August Victoria felt it was permissible to resume her singing lessons with Lablache 'twice a week', as she told King Leopold. 'He is such a good old soul, and greatly pleased that I go on with him.' In preparation for taking the salute at a parade of Guardsmen and Lancers in Windsor Great Park in September, on 15 August Victoria got around to inspecting the Buckingham Palace stables. 'Put on my habit and went to the Mews, which are in the garden,' she recorded in her journal. 'I first rode a bay horse, a delightful one called Ottoman, and cantered about a good while. I then tried for a minute another horse which I did not like so well. I then remounted Ottoman. After him I mounted a beautiful and very powerful but delightful grey horse, a Hanoverian, called Fearon.'

'I am very pleased with my rooms,' Victoria told Princess Feodora in October. 'They are high, pleasant and cheerful.' Aunt Louise, King Leopold's second wife, was informed: 'There are no less than five fine large rooms, *besides* the [Picture] Gallery and dining room, and they are so high, the doors so large and they lie so well near one another that it makes an ensemble rarely seen in this country.' She was determined to have fun, and so what if, the day after her arrival, Sir John Hobhouse, President of the Board of Control, found the place 'in great disorder' with the apartments 'full of housemaids on their knees scrubbing the floors, and attendants putting down the carpets'. With a gracious wave of her hand the Queen invited Sir John to sit down. Unfortunately, after the death of Prince Albert the seemingly imperious side to Victoria's nature took over, and for most of her reign not even the Prime Minister was offered a chair when received in audience – which was no great deprivation for Disraeli, who spent much of his time grov-elling on his knees. It was perfectly understandable that no one sat until the Queen had done so, but she did not endear herself to her ladies by remaining standing after dinner until the gentlemen had arrived from the dining room to play whist, by which time the women were dropping; but at least the Duchess of Kent was able to slip away to her own apartments to put her feet up. At the theatre the Queen's ladies took it in turns to stand behind her.

A tradition inaugurated by Queen Victoria on the death of Prince Albert in 1861, that meetings of the Privy Council should be conducted with everyone, even the monarch, standing, persists to this day. Whereas there had previously been no limit on the numbers of Privy Councillors attending, after 1861 a quorum of three was decided on (it remains three even now), and the quaint idea that everyone should stand, and very few need attend, was 'designed to ensure that the Queen was required to spend no more time than was necessary and consistent with her duty on affairs of State'.⁵ At Victoria's accession Council at Kensington Palace no fewer than ninety-six Privy Councillors had turned up, 'notwithstanding', as Greville recorded, 'the short notice which was given'.

Victoria almost invariably received her royal guests at Windsor in preference to Buckingham Palace, and at the castle, which had presumably been thoroughly swept and dusted, on 29 August 'I and Mamma as well as my whole court were all at the door' to receive 'my dearest most beloved Uncle Leopold and my dearest most beloved Aunt Louise'. It was, the Queen recalled in her journal on

HM Leopold I, King of the Belgians, from a portrait by Diez 1841.

receiving her first crowned guest, 'an inexpressible happiness and joy to me, to have these dearest beloved relations with me and in my own house. I took them to their rooms, and then hastened to dress for dinner. At 8 we dined . . . I sat between dear Uncle and my good Lord Melbourne; two delightful neighbours. Dear Aunt Louise sat opposite. After dinner I sat on the sofa with dearest Aunt Louise, who is really an angel, and Lord Melbourne sat near me. Uncle talked with Lord Palmerston. It was a most delightful evening.'

The Belgian King and Queen remained at Windsor for three weeks, on what to all intents and purposes was a state visit, the castle being constantly host to senior government ministers. Victoria stayed on at Windsor until the end of September, reviewing her troops in the park and enjoying 'delicious rides', during which 'Lord Melbourne rode near me the whole time. I have seen a great deal of him, every day, these last 5 weeks . . . I have seen him in my Closet for Political Affairs, I have ridden out with him (every day), I have sat near him constantly at and after dinner, and talked about all sorts of things . . . I am very fond of him.'

Presumably on information supplied through the gossip of servants, Charles Greville tells us that the Queen rose 'soon after eight o'clock' and 'breakfasts in her own room'. She would spend the morning attending to business, and 'At eleven or twelve Melbourne comes to her and stays an hour, more or less, according to the business he may have to transact'. Presumably Melbourne remained to lunch, for at two o'clock the Queen would ride out 'with a large suite (and she likes to have it numerous)', Melbourne on her left hand, 'and the equerry-in-waiting generally on her right'. Greville maintained she rode for two hours 'along the road, and the greater part of the time at full gallop', but no one in their right mind would gallop a horse on a made-up road. In any case, as Victoria rode side-saddle and did not hunt it seems unlikely that she galloped at all.

Rather surprisingly, for Victoria disliked very young children and had no great rapport with her own even when they were older, Greville also tells us she might spend time in the afternoon 'romping with children, if there are any in the Castle (and she is so fond of them that she generally contrives to have some there)'. In the evening, guests having assembled by half-past seven, 'the lord-in-waiting comes into the drawing-room and instructs each gentleman which lady he is to take into dinner'. On entering the drawing room, the Queen apparently spoke to each lady, bowed to the men and went immediately into the dining room. 'Melbourne,' Greville observed, 'invariably sits on her left, no matter who may be there.'

It was household management that interested and amused the young Queen as much as politics. 'She organizes and regulates every detail herself . . . settles about the riding or driving, and enters into every particular with minute attention.' Yet Greville reckoned she spent at least six hours with Melbourne every day – 'an hour in the morning, two on horseback, one at dinner, and two in the evening'. He thought the Prime Minister's manner towards the Queen was perfect, 'always respectful, and never presuming upon the extraordinary distinction he enjoys'. But Greville marvelled at the way in which Melbourne had adapted his way of life and personal tastes, swapping 'the good talk of Holland House [Lady Holland's entertaining home] for the trivial, laboured and wearisome inanities of the Royal circle'.

Not only was the Queen, as she said herself, fond of her Prime Minister (perhaps even a little in love with him), but she was becoming dangerously dependent on him, believing him to be a

Viscount Melbourne, from a portrait by Sir Edwin Landseer RA.

political prop no one could ever take away. In a leisurely age he was always on hand, to proffer advice and to make the sort of amusing remarks that a polished courtier and man of the world is expected to come out with to keep the conversation at dinner, and in the drawing room afterwards, sparkling. At her first Lord Mayor's dinner it would have been Melbourne, who had coached her in her conduct at her first Council, who told the Queen before-hand to knight the sheriffs and to confer a baronetcy on her host. 'There is no end to the amusing anecdotes and stories Lord Melbourne tells,' the Queen noted on 8 December, 'and he tells them all in such an amusing funny way.' On 22 December she wrote: 'I was delighted to see Lord Melbourne in excellent spirits . . . He was very clever and funny about education at dinner.' On

19 January 1838: 'Lord Melbourne was amazingly funny and amusing . . . ' The Queen was shocked by the treatment of slaves, and when the government introduced a bill to ameliorate their conditions Lord Melbourne read to her 'the principal Heads of it explaining to me each part in the most clear and agreeable manner possible'.

'I asked Lord Melbourne how he liked my dress. He said he thought it "very pretty" and that "it did very well". He is so natural and funny and nice about *toilette* and has a very good taste I think.'

Melbourne discoursed with his attentive young apprentice on railways, Lord Byron, George III, the peerage, Dr Johnson, Garrick, George IV's mimicry, Queen Caroline, Schiller, the novels of Dickens, the correct use of English grammar. The Queen told him she 'often stood before a person not knowing what to say, and Lord Melbourne said that the longer one stood thinking the worse it was; and he really thought the best thing to do was to say anything commonplace and foolish, better than to say nothing'.

Lord Ribblesdale, who dined frequently with the Queen much later in her reign, wrote in his memoirs that 'I personally never heard her say anything at dinner which I remembered next morning'. Charles Greville was invited to dine at Buckingham Palace on 10 March 1838. He has left us not only an account of a rather stilted conversation with Queen Victoria, which he swore was true, but a lively picture of court etiquette, much of it improvised; George III never gave dinner parties, George IV depended on his current mistress to act as hostess, and usually ended up under the table drunk, and William IV's dinners were liable to be interrupted by tirades against the French. Hence Victoria's decorous evenings were very much her own invention.

'There was a very numerous party,' Greville recalled. 'We assembled in the round room next the gallery, and just before the dinner was ready the Queen entered with the Duchess of Kent, preceded by the Chamberlain, and followed by her six ladies. She shook hands with the women, and made a sweeping bow to the men, and directly went into dinner.' The Queen sat between the Lord Chamberlain, Lord Conyngham, and the Hanoverian Minister, Baron von Münchhausen. Greville thought it in very bad taste for her health to have been proposed 'by her own officer', the equerry-in-waiting, Henry Cavendish, 'at her own table'. Apparently the Queen 'sat for some time at the table, talking away very merrily to her neighbours, and the men remained about a quarter of an hour after the ladies. When we went into the drawing-room, and huddled about the door in the sort of half-shy, half-awkward way people do, the Queen advanced to meet us, and spoke to everybody in succession.' Her conversation with Greville went as follows:

The Queen: 'Have you been riding today, Mr Greville?'
Greville: 'No, Madam, I have not.'
The Queen: 'It was a fine day.'
Greville: 'Yes, Ma'am, a very fine day.'
The Queen: 'It was rather cold though.'
Greville: 'It *was* rather cold, Madam.'
The Queen: 'Your sister, Lady Francis Egerton, rides, I think, does not she?'[6]
Greville: 'She does ride sometimes, Madam.'
In order to cover an embarrassing pause, Greville asked: 'Has Your Majesty been riding today?'
The Queen: 'Oh, yes, a very long ride.'
Greville: 'Has Your Majesty got a nice horse?'
The Queen: 'Oh, a very nice horse.'

Victoria celebrated her nineteenth birthday with a ball at

Buckingham Palace, 'dancing till past four o'clock this morning', she told King Leopold the next day. 'I have spent the happiest birthday that I have had for many years; oh, how different to last year! Everybody was so kind and so friendly to me.' She had felt 'a little shy' on entering the ballroom, but her cousin Prince George, who succeeded as second Duke of Cambridge in 1850, thought 'she danced really very nicely and seemed to be very much amused'. Some of the older guests were not so amused, however, when the Queen ate her supper standing up in the ballroom, accustomed as they had been to the royal family retiring for a private supper.

The first coronation procession ever to drive from Buckingham Palace did so on 28 June 1838, Victoria having been woken at four in the morning by the firing of guns. Who should have stood 'very close' to her 'throughout the whole ceremony' in Westminster Abbey but her 'excellent Lord Melbourne'. When the eighty-two-year-old Lord Rolle attempted to ascend the steps of the throne to pay homage and managed to roll all the way down again, the Queen instinctively advanced to help the old man up and was universally lauded for doing so. Needless to say, when her 'good Lord Melbourne knelt down and kissed my hand, he pressed my hand and I grasped his with all my heart, at which he looked up with his eyes filled with tears and seemed much touched, as he was, I observed, throughout the whole ceremony'.

There was, Victoria noted, 'another most dear Being present at this ceremony, in the box immediately above the royal box, and who witnessed all; it was my dearly beloved angelic Lehzen, whose eyes I caught when on the Throne, and we exchanged smiles . . . 'At eight we dined . . . Lord Melbourne came up to me and said, "I must congratulate you on this most brilliant day".' Melbourne told the Queen there had been a large breakfast in the Jerusalem Chamber, 'where they met before all began; he said, laughing, that whenever the Clergy, or a Dean and Chapter, had anything to do with anything, there's sure to be plenty to eat'.

4

Lady Flora and Others

Queen Victoria's brief honeymoon, with her subjects and her new home, was about to come to a very abrupt end, for Buckingham Palace was to witness, in quick succession, two dramas Victoria was to regret and brood over for the rest of her life, one strictly domestic in which nevertheless her Prime Minister was involved, the other strictly political but directly affecting the Queen's personal happiness and domestic harmony.

In January 1839 Lady Flora Hastings, a sister of the second Marquess of Hastings, a lady-in-waiting to the Duchess of Kent and a friend of the troublesome Sir John Conroy, was observed to be in a condition that everyone, including the Queen, presumed to be that of pregnancy. The Queen was in no doubt by whom Lady Flora was pregnant: her *bête noire* Sir John. Her judgement was no less clouded on account of her dislike of Lady Flora – an 'odious' person, an 'amazing spy who would repeat everything she heard'. Both Lord Melbourne and the Duke of Wellington became involved in discussions about Lady Flora's alleged indiscretion, and both counselled hushing the whole matter up.

But that was easier said than done. On 2 March Charles Greville was writing in his journal: 'The whole town has been engrossed for some days with a scandalous story at Court.' Lord Hastings was on the rampage; the Queen's ladies-in-waiting believed the honour of the court – how times had changed – demanded the matter be resolved. Victoria was thrilled to think that Sir John was in trouble, but by 25 March Greville was reporting: 'Nobody cares for the Queen, her popularity has sunk to zero.' Lady Flora reluctantly agreed to be examined jointly by the Queen's doctor, Sir James Clark, and by her own family doctor, the similarly named Sir Charles Clarke, both of whom came to the conclusion that Lady Flora was not, nor ever had been, pregnant; indeed, that she was a virgin. Two of Victoria's enemies had been vindicated at a stroke, and it must have been a gratifying outcome for Sir John, whose contempt for the Queen had been fuelled long ago because he entertained a fantasy that his wife, Elisabeth Foster, was the daughter of the Duke of Kent; this would have made her Victoria's illegitimate half-sister. In an attempt to get rid of Conroy Victoria had offered him a pension of £3,000 a year as soon as she came to the throne, and in the coronation honours he had been given a baronetcy, but he still hankered after an Irish peerage. He could not have been in a more unforgiving mood when the Lady Flora Hastings scandal broke. Far from being pregnant, she had cancer.

The Queen begged Lady Flora's forgiveness. Lord Melbourne kept his head down, so another scapegoat was required; Lord Hastings alighted on Baroness Lehzen. Sensational letters from Lady Flora, her mother and Lord Melbourne all found their way into the *Morning Post*. The Queen needed a scapegoat, too, and chose her mother. She felt 'a growing dislike for Mamma', she told the Prime Minister; it was 'like having an enemy in the house'. Victoria even managed to convince herself that Lady Flora was suffering from nothing more serious than a bilious attack. Melbourne's cynical advice to the Queen was to send to enquire after Lady Flora, 'First of all because she is under your roof, and then because it shows feeling'.

A week before Lady Flora died the Queen did go to see her, finding her 'literally a skeleton'. The Queen refused to feel or show remorse, however, and was hissed at Ascot by 'two foolish, vulgar women' the Queen thought ought to be flogged. One was a duchess. Never having been cultivated by the Queen, the aristocracy felt perfectly at liberty to put her in her place. Victoria sent Lady Flora's maid £50; the Dowager Marchioness of Hastings returned it. As for the incident at Ascot, many years later the Queen's private secretary, Sir Henry Ponsonby, was bold enough to ask her whether it was true, as alleged in a magazine article, that she had been hissed by the Duchess of Montrose and Lady Sarah Ingestre. The Queen's immediate reaction was to say, 'Quite true', but then she corrected herself for the record, saying: 'They sent to let me know privately they didn't hiss me. They hissed Lord Melbourne. He was an excellent man but too much a party man and made me a party Queen. He admitted this himself afterwards.'

While Lady Flora Hastings had been slowly dying so, too, had Melbourne's government. It survived, however, until the first week of May, when the Queen wrote in her journal: 'The state of agony, grief and despair into which this placed me may be easier imagined than described! All, all my happiness gone! That happy peaceful life destroyed, that dearest kind Lord Melbourne no more my minister . . . I sobbed and cried much.' When she received the Prime Minister she begged him not to forsake her, for she still imagined she had only to wave her magic wand and anyone she fancied could carry on in government for her benefit even if he had lost the support of Parliament, a fact of constitutional life even her great-great-grandfather George II had come to realize was no longer the case when he lost Sir Robert Walpole in 1742 after

Walpole had lost the support of the House of Commons.

Not only was Victoria on the point of losing Melbourne but with a change of government her household also, and hot on the heels of her loss of popularity over her treatment of Lady Flora came the first political upset of her reign. Still only twenty and almost totally inexperienced, she decided to put her foot down and have a fight. To follow the course of the battle it would be a mistake to imagine that if a new Tory administration insisted on placing Tory ladies at court the Queen would have been separated from her closest female friends. She had no friends, or at least, until she came to the throne and got to know and rely on the companion-ship of her household she had no friends; her life at Kensington Palace had been so restricted that she scarcely knew anyone in society or among the aristocracy. Her first ladies and women of the bedchamber – her ladies-in-waiting – were recommended to her by Melbourne, who had made an error in selecting only the wives of Whig ministers. To all intents and purposes Victoria was a Whig because her adored Melbourne was a Whig; Whigs were nice people because Melbourne was a Whig; Tories were nasty people because their most influential leader, Sir Robert Peel, was a stiff and starchy man who wanted to replace her household with Tory women.

Melbourne's advice was to ask only that those members of the Queen's household engaged in politics be changed; in other words, her ladies would remain in her service. Having tendered his resig-nation, Melbourne very properly declined to see the Queen, but Victoria was so desperate she tried to coerce him into a suppos-edly surprise meeting while out riding in the park. She had an aversion to the obvious choice of Tory leader, Robert Peel, and invited the deaf and aged Duke of Wellington to form an admin-istration. He declined and advised her to send for Peel. This she did, and when Peel raised the question of her household the Queen penned one of her most telling journal entries – a spirited defence of her right, as she saw it, to appoint ladies of her own choice. Although the Queen was encouraging a constitutional crisis, it should be remembered that any Queen, regnant or consort, depends for everyday companionship and often close friendship on her ladies.

Soon after this Sir Robert said, 'Now, about the Ladies,' upon which I said I could not give up any of my ladies, and never had imagined such a thing. He asked if I meant to retain all. 'All,' I said. 'The Mistress of the Robes and the Ladies of the Bedchamber?' I replied, 'All.' . . . He said they were the wives of the opponents of the Government . . . I said that [they] would not interfere; that I never talked politics with them, and that they were related, many of them, to Tories, and I enumerated those of my Bedchamber women and maids of honour; upon which he said he did not mean all the Bedchamber women and all the maids of honour, he meant the Mistress of the Robes and the Ladies of the Bedchamber; to which I replied that they were of more consequence than the others, and that I could not consent, and that it had never been done before. He said I was a Queen Regnant, and that made the difference. 'Not here,' I said – and I maintained my right.

She stuck to her guns, telling Melbourne: 'We shall see what will be done. The Queen would not have stood so firmly on the Grooms [she meant grooms of the stole, not those who tended the horses] and Equerries, but her Ladies are entirely her own affair, and not the Ministers'.' The list of the Queen's ladies – and it was a formidable one – had been settled by 30 August 1837. In addition to the

Mistress of the Robes, the thirty-one-year-old Duchess of Sutherland (she was to serve four times in that capacity), Victoria had eight ladies of the bedchamber, including two marchionesses and three countesses, eight maids of honour, who went into waiting in pairs for a month at a time, so that each maid of honour spent three months at court every year, and a further eight women of the bedchamber. The ladies of the bedchamber received £500 a year, the maids of honour £300, and the annual cost of the Queen's household at the start of her reign came to £131,250, paid for out of a total Parliamentary annuity of £385,000.

A new rash of applicants for royal warrants had followed a change of sovereign, too. In August 1838 the following appointments were made: 'Mr Charles Page to be Maker of Waterproof Dress Clogs and shoemaker in ordinary to Her Majesty'; 'Mrs Lydia Amelia Curling to be Lace Cleaner in ordinary'; 'Messrs Daniel Foot Tayler and Henry Foot Shuttleworth, trading under the firm of D. F. Tayler and Company, to be Patent Solid Headed Pin Manufacturers in ordinary to Her Majesty.'

Melbourne found it quite as difficult to disengage from the Queen as she did from him, and on 10 May, on Melbourne's advice, she wrote to Peel to say: 'The Queen having considered the proposal made to her yesterday by Sir Robert Peel, to remove the Ladies of her Bedchamber, cannot consent to adopt a course which she conceives to be contrary to usage, and which is repugnant to her feelings.' Peel backed off, Melbourne was back as Prime Minister, and he and the Queen celebrated by sitting up until midnight together, when Melbourne fell asleep and began to snore.

It was small wonder Charles Greville came to believe that Melbourne seemed to hold office 'for no other purpose but that of dining at Buckingham House', nor that he believed there was something 'which shocks one's sense of fitness and propriety in

the spectacle of this mere baby of a Queen setting herself in oppo-
sition to this great man', by whom he meant Wellington. Victoria
remained, not surprisingly, very immature, and it was not until she
took the plunge and married that a steady hand – that of Prince
Albert – came to rest on her shoulders. Rather like Elizabeth I,
Victoria both wanted domesticity and a loving husband yet dreaded
her loss of independence. She declared herself – in the privacy of
her journal – 'quite in love' with Grand Duke Alexander of Russia
when he paid a three-week visit to Windsor in the early summer
of 1839. 'I danced with the Grand-Duke,' she recalled, 'and we had
such fun and laughter . . . I never enjoyed myself more. We were
all so merry; I got to bed by $^1/_4$ to 3, but could not sleep till 5.'[1]

For some reason she had 'so disliked the idea of the Grand-
Duke's coming', and now 'I was so very very sorry at his going'.
She told Lord Melbourne that it was so seldom that she had 'young
people of my own rank with me'. She had two English cousins
who were princes, both the same age as she and both called George,
the heirs to the Dukes of Cumberland and Cambridge; Victoria
saw something of them but never contemplated an English alliance,
and marriage to an English commoner – or any commoner – was
out of the question. On her mother's side there were, of course,
cousins Ernest and Albert of Saxe-Coburg and Gotha, whom
Victoria had met but kept at a distance, Ernest because he was
destined to inherit his father's somewhat meagre domains, Albert
because she was perfectly well aware that for a long time it had
been Uncle Leopold's desire that she should one day marry him,
and Victoria did not much care for the idea of having a husband
foisted on her. She went out of her way to remind the King of the
Belgians that no promise of marriage, on her part, had ever been
made. None the less she kept an open mind, even though she tells
us she was 'terrified (foolishly)' when 'Lord M' said, 'Now, Ma'am,

The Prince Consort, from a painting by F.X. Winterhalter.

for this other matter', the matter of her marriage. Although genuinely concerned for the Queen's happiness, Melbourne saw it as his duty to urge the Queen gently towards matrimony for the sake of the succession. He must have been rather alarmed when, having discussed the 'various princes, of whom not one, I said, would do', the Queen announced that her feeling 'was quite against ever marrying'.

Exhibiting a refreshing candour and self-awareness, Victoria told Melbourne that she dreaded the thought of marrying because she was so accustomed to having her own way. She thought it was '10 to 1 that I shouldn't agree with any body'. Melbourne's inept response was to assure the Queen that even though married she would still be able to have her own way, the worst possible idea to put into the mind of a headstrong young girl full of her own importance who was about to become engaged to one of the most intelligent and well-intentioned young men in Europe. The miracle of Victoria's marriage was the swiftness with which it subjugated her egocentricity, if only until she was widowed, and transformed, almost overnight, a flighty princess into a conscientious monarch, a reasonably devoted mother and a besotted wife.

On 12 July 1839 Victoria recalled in her journal talking with Lord Melbourne 'of my Cousins Ernest and Albert coming over – my having no great wish to see Albert'. She was in quite an interior muddle. 'There was no engagement between us, I said, but that the young man was aware that there was the possibility of such a union.' In September Victoria told Melbourne she did not like people because they were handsome, but that she was not insensible to beauty. Melbourne's response to this comment, a very obvious one where Victoria was concerned, was to 'take port wine to keep himself awake'. Melbourne by this time was virtually *en famille*, not hesitating to sit down even if the Queen was standing.

On the last day of September Victoria received a letter from Albert, whose visit she was dreading, to say that he and Ernest could not set out before 6 October. 'I think they don't exhibit much *empressement* to come here,' she told King Leopold, 'which rather shocks me.'

The young Princes arrived at Windsor Castle on 10 October ahead of their luggage, and having no clothes to change into 'they couldn't appear at dinner'. At '1/2p 7' Victoria had gone to the top of the staircase rather than the front door, which was one way of keeping them in their place, to receive 'my two dear cousins'. She found them 'grown and changed'. And 'embellished'. 'It was,' she wrote, 'with some emotion that I beheld Albert – who is beautiful.' By the following day Albert had become 'quite charming' and 'excessively handsome', with 'such beautiful blue eyes, an exquisite nose and such a pretty mouth'. He had a beautiful figure, broad shoulders and a fine waist. 'My heart is quite going,' the Queen confessed.

The entertainment laid on by Victoria for her German cousins was not very sophisticated. 'I played 2 games at Tactics with dear Albert, and 2 at Fox and Geese. Stayed up till 20m p 11. A delightful evening.'

By 14 October Victoria told Lord Melbourne that she had made up her mind – to marry Albert. But how was she to tell him? 'In general,' she remarked, 'such things were done the other way – which made Lord M laugh.' The following day Victoria, noting it had been 'about 1/2p 12', sent for Albert when he came in from hunting, who found the Queen alone and could have had few doubts what was expected of him: to renounce his homeland, take British nationality and marry the Queen. Physically, Albert was a great catch, and there is no doubt that Victoria was head over heels in love with him. As many German princesses went, and the Queen had a good deal of German blood (on her paternal side alone George I, George II, Frederick, Prince of Wales, George III and her father had all married Germans), Victoria was certainly not ugly, but she was no beauty. Pauper princes cannot afford to be choosy, however, and what Victoria had to offer (if Albert played his cards adroitly) was a dazzling future, even if it did get off to a rather unpromising start; two weeks after they had become engaged Victoria was signing 'some warrants and papers etc' when Albert 'was so kind as to dry them with blotting paper for me'.

At twenty Albert was as young in every way as the Queen, and in affairs of the heart as ignorant. He expressed surprise at the smallness of Victoria's hands, and told the Queen 'he could hardly believe they were hands, as he had hitherto only been accustomed to handle hands like Ernest's'. In what way Albert had 'handled' his brother's hands we may never know. The couple exchanged many passionate kisses, Albert was given a ring and obliged with a lock of his hair. On 14 November Albert departed for Coburg. Victoria wrote up her journal, then went for a walk and had a good cry. She arranged to have the Order of the Garter sent to Albert and broke the news that the Cabinet were against his being given a peerage.

One of the bugbears of having the Duchess of Kent living in Buckingham Palace was that as Sir John Conroy was still hanging on as the Duchess's comptroller (a situation which was bound to irk the Queen anyway) it meant that Conroy continued to haunt the palace too. Now that Victoria was about to exchange her spinsterhood for the state of matrimony she saw a God-given opportunity to get rid of both mother and Conroy, and braced herself to give the Duchess her marching orders. It was, in fact, the wily old Duke of Wellington who finally persuaded Conroy to retire and go abroad. Conroy's successor as comptroller to the Duchess discovered that for nine years Conroy had kept no household accounts. A gift of £50,000 to his sister by King Leopold had vanished; so had £10,000 rather surprisingly given by her brother-in-law, King William. George III's daughter, Princess Sophia, into whose coffers Conroy had also dipped, was left with a bank balance of £1,608.

Shortly after Albert's lamented departure Victoria returned to Buckingham Palace to deliver to the Privy Council the declaration of her engagement: her intention 'to ally myself in marriage with the Prince Albert of Saxe-Coburg and Gotha'. This she did on 23 November, with some eighty Privy Councillors present. According to Charles Greville, the Queen 'read the declaration in a clear, sonorous, sweet-toned voice, but her hands trembled so excessively that I wonder she was able to read the paper which she held'.

It was not long before 'the Prince Albert of Saxe-Coburg and Gotha' was made to realize that on his marriage as consort to the Queen he need not imagine he would be master in his own house, yet alone master in his wife's house. He had assumed, not unreasonably, that he would be free to appoint his own household, and in particular his private secretary, and that no objection could possibly be raised if his closest advisers were fellow countrymen. In a letter dated 8 December the Queen had no qualms about disillusioning him; she and Lord Melbourne had decided that George Anson, Melbourne's private secretary, should be seconded to the Prince. 'As to your wish about your gentlemen, my dear Albert, I must tell you quite honestly that it will not do.' These were the tones of a schoolmistress. In desperation, Albert pleaded to be allowed to place about himself, in a country 'in which everything is new and strange to me', two or three people in whom he already had confidence. He was told, for his pains, that the Queen knew what was good for him. 'Once more I tell you that you can perfectly rely on me in these matters.'

Had Victoria forgotten, or chosen not even to acknowledge, her two very recent and very serious misjudgements, over Lady Flora Hastings and her refusal to surrender any of her Whig ladies? Albert could not possibly have broken off the engagement, but he may have felt tempted to wish that he could, and certainly he must have felt apprehensive about the future, an apprehension that would only have been confirmed when he discovered that Victoria, who had made all her wedding arrangements without consulting anyone, not even her fiancé, had refused to invite more than a handful of Tories. Charles Greville thought her conduct in this respect 'as wilful, obstinate and wrong-headed as usual'. But Victoria was a great hater and a great seeker after revenge. On 24 January 1839 Lord John Russell had proposed an allowance of £50,000 a year for Prince Albert, which would have been a reasonable sum. The Tories got it reduced to £30,000. 'As long as I live, I'll never forgive these infernal scoundrels, with Peel at their head . . . for this personal act of spite!!' the Queen thundered in her journal. She got her own way over the length of her honeymoon, however, which she intended should be spent at Windsor: just three days.

You have written to me in one of your letters about our stay at Windsor [the Queen wrote to Prince Albert on 31 January 1840], but, dear Albert, you have not at all understood the matter. You forget, my dearest Love, that I am the Sovereign, and that business can stop and wait for nothing. Parliament is sitting, and something occurs almost every day, for which I may be required, and it is quite impossible for me to be absent from London; therefore two or three days is already a long time to be absent. I am never easy a moment if I am not on the spot, and see and

The Marriage of the Queen, from a painting by Sir George Hayter.

hear what is going on, and everybody, including all my Aunts (who are not knowing in all these things), says I must come out after the second day, for, as I must be surrounded by my Court, I cannot keep alone. This is my own wish in every way.

The Queen of England had spoken. Eight days later Albert arrived, accompanied by his father and brother, and on 10 February Victoria drove in state from Buckingham Palace to St James's Palace, there to be married in the Chapel Royal. She was attended by a dozen bridesmaids and ten members of the royal family. Charles Greville says there was no cheering on the way, attributable to 'torrents of rain and violent gusts of wind'. According to the Queen's account, there were crowds of people in the park, who 'cheered most enthusiastically'. She and Albert returned to Buckingham Palace for the wedding breakfast, leaving for Windsor at four o'clock 'in a very poor and shabby style' – the caustic Greville again. 'Instead of the new chariot in which most married people are accustomed to dash along, they were in one of the old travelling coaches, the postillions in undress liveries, and with a small escort, three other coaches with post-horses following. The crowds on the road were so great that they did not reach the Castle till eight o'clock.'

Very few people, royal or otherwise, leave such vivid accounts of their honeymoon as did Queen Victoria. Before dinner, Albert took her on his knee. Despite a sick headache that put her off her dinner, the Queen considered the evening 'bliss beyond belief!' Her journal entry for the following day is charmingly uninhibited. 'When day dawned (for we did not sleep much) and I beheld that beautiful angelic face by my side, it was more than I can express! He does look so beautiful in his shirt only, and with his beautiful throat seen. We got up at $1/4$p 8. When I had laced I went to dearest Albert's room and we breakfasted together.' With her 'precious

Angel' and his dog Eos she went for a walk on the terrace at noon, 'arm in arm!' and 'talked a great deal together'. After lunch it was Albert's turn to feel sick and have to rest in Victoria's room. 'He looked so dear, lying there and dozing.'

On 12 February she wrote: 'Already the second day since our marriage; his love and gentleness is beyond anything, and to kiss that dear soft cheek, to press my lips to his, is heavenly bliss.'

On 13 February: 'My dearest Albert put on my stockings for me. I went in and saw him shave; a great delight to me.'

Back at Buckingham Palace there were domestic problems to deal with, one concerning security. A boy called Edward Jones, who had been fourteen when he broke in in December 1838 (although it would be more true to say that he just wandered in; a jury acquitted him), was back in December 1840. He managed to penetrate the kitchens, where no doubt the staff thought he was one of them, and claimed, although he may have made this up, to have sat on the throne and seen the Queen. But he was almost certainly telling the truth when he said he heard a baby squall, for he was finally discovered under a sofa in the room where the Princess Royal, born on 21 November that year, slept. For reasons best known to the Victorian judicial system, he was sent to prison for three months, condemned to a treadmill. Nothing deterred, within a fortnight of his release 'the urchin Edward Jones', as *The Times* saw fit to refer to him, seventeen years of age by this time and very undernourished, managed once more to make his way undetected into the palace kitchens. Now labelled 'a rogue and a vagabond' the lad was again sentenced to three months in prison and was honoured by a visit from the inquisitive Charles Dickens. 'Supposing he had come into the bedroom, how frightened I should have been,' the Queen is said to have remarked, yet she certainly did not lack physical courage. She had already supposedly been shot at without turning a hair. It was left to the Countess of Sandwich to immortalize the enterprising Edward by suggesting his name must really have been In-I-Go Jones.

It had been in June 1840 that the first of six real or pretended assassination attempts were made, as the Queen, four months pregnant, was driving up Constitution Hill in an open phaeton with Prince Albert. Two shots appeared to be fired at point-blank range. The culprit was another Edward – Edward Oxford, a young waiter, who was found guilty but insane. Whether he actually fired live bullets remained uncertain; also uncorroborated was a rumour that he had been hired by the Queen's uncle, Cumberland, now King of Hanover, who was certainly as insane as Edward Oxford and, until the Queen gave birth, heir to the British throne.

Another domestic problem with which Prince Albert felt obliged to come to grips was the overbearing influence exercised by Baroness Lehzen. After three months of marriage Albert was telling a friend on the Continent, Prince William of Löwenstein, that although in his home life he was very happy and contented he remained only the husband 'and not the master in the house'. While the Queen had remained unmarried, Lehzen dominated domestic affairs, even acting as Privy Purse, and by allowing outmoded practices to flourish she had conducted the day-to-day running of Buckingham Palace with spectacular inefficiency. She showed no inclination to renounce her privileged position now that the Queen was married; she had, after all, known her since she was a little girl. Melbourne believed that the Queen was influenced more than she realized by Lehzen and that, while it had been all very well for the Baroness to stand between the Queen and her mother when protecting Victoria from the machinations of Sir John Conroy, it would be the former governess's downfall if she attempted to make trouble between husband and wife. But as far as the short-sighted Lehzen was concerned, Albert was an interloper.

There was another thorn in Lehzen's side, Baron Stockmar, who on Victoria's marriage had in a sense been loaned to Albert and the Queen in the guise of a sage *éminence grise*. He and Albert became devoted to one another. Stockmar was quite happy to leave his wife and daughter in Coburg from autumn through to the spring each year while he tried to untangle the waste and over-manning now endemic in the royal establishments, and although his political advice was not always sound (he implanted in the Queen's eager ear the notion that she was a kind of permanent Prime Minister), historians have generally found his influence on the early years of Victoria's reign both beneficial and disinterested.

Stockmar could see very well there was no longer any role for Baroness Lehzen to play if disaster was to be avoided; she had been acting virtually as private secretary to the Queen, and her contempt for Prince Albert was patently obvious. Albert himself told Stockmar that the Baroness was 'a crazy common stupid intriguer, obsessed with lust of power, who regards herself as a demi-god and anyone who refuses to recognize her as such was a criminal'. These may have been the heated words of a young man in a hurry, but clearly one of them had to go, and it would not be Albert. But he did not rush his fences. He had plenty of other problems to deal with, in the nursery and in the management of Buckingham Palace. But the autumn of 1842 saw the sad, silly Baroness, who could have remained in honourable retirement at the palace until the end of her life had she been more circumspect, sailing for Germany, comfortably provided for by the Queen to the tune of £800 a year.

On 22 August 1840 Albert was able to boast to his brother about what he called his 'masterstroke'; he had driven the Lord

Chamberlain and another courtier 'out of their rooms, back to St James's Palace'. With the aid of Baron Stockmar, so at home in the royal household that he was permitted to slop around in his dressing gown and slippers, to dine in trousers instead of breeches and to retire immediately dinner was over, he set about a total reorganization. He had discovered that one man might lay a fire but it was the duty of someone else to light it. The Lord Steward, the Lord Chamberlain and the Master of the Horse were all vying for control; the staff, when they bothered to turn up to look after guests, were untrained, and whereas pages and housemaids answered to the Lord Chamberlain, the footmen, for some inexplicable reason, came under the Master of the Horse. The reason Stockmar retired early was because he was at work on a comprehensive memorandum, which was even to include advice on reorganizing the archives. By his reckoning, two-thirds of the servants were completely unsupervised, and when an inquest was held on how young Edward Jones had managed to gain access to Buckingham Palace so easily and to wander around undetected it was considered unfair and indeed impossible to pin the blame on anyone, so poor was the chain of command. One of Stockmar's revelations was the existence of dormitories where as many as a dozen footmen slept, and if smoking, drinking or 'any other irregularities' took place they went unchecked.

Sinecures, many of them remnants of the reign of George III, were rife. Albert found an under-butler receiving £1 15s. a week for wine no longer consumed. Candles were purloined and replaced even if they had not been burned. Differentials in salaries had gone unregulated for years. The Mistress of the Robes, a largely honorific title usually accorded a duchess, who was nominally in charge of the rota of ladies-in-waiting and would accompany the Queen on state occasions, like the opening of Parliament (the Mistress of the

Robes had ridden to Victoria's wedding in the Queen's carriage), received £500 a year, the housekeeper, with a huge staff under her, £112. The steps were scrubbed by housemaids earning 15 guineas a year while the First Page of the Back Stairs took home £320. A ratkiller employed at Windsor Castle got £80 a year and the chimneysweep £111, which was just £11 less than the dentist.

Albert found the system for making purchases and repairs bizarre, requisitions being signed and countersigned by an army of minor officials. In one year alone, it transpired, no fewer than 700 brushes had been bought. At Windsor the housekeeper estimated that there were some 400 dusters 'in constant use, scattered all over the castle'. The staff had good cause to be grateful to Prince Albert; by 1867 a maidservant at Windsor Castle was being paid £45 10s. a year, the equivalent of about £2,000 a year today, and she would also, of course, have received free food and accommodation.

Whenever he could, Albert went hunting, and fell off his horse near Slough. He was also keen on skating, and in the garden at Buckingham Palace, on 9 February 1841, he nearly came to grief. The ice on the pond broke and Albert fell in, but while Victoria's lady-in-waiting screamed for help Victoria kept her head and somehow fished him out. A rather less hazardous pleasure the young couple shared was music-making, and with various members of the household they organized some ambitious concerts in the music room at Buckingham Palace, featuring pieces by Rossini, Haydn and Mendelssohn. In 1842, when Felix Mendelssohn was thirty-three and had only another five years to live, Prince Albert invited him to play the organ at Buckingham Palace, when the composer found the Queen 'so friendly and courteous'. She asked him to play seven of his *Songs without Words*. On his second visit that year the Queen came into the room to find sheets of music scattered all over the floor, and without thinking to call a footman she knelt down to gather them up herself. After she had had a parrot removed from the room she sang Mendelssohn's *Schöner und Schöner*, a brave thing to do in the composer's presence, who reported to his mother that the Queen 'sang beautifully in tune, in strict time and with very nice expression'.

The other more than merely modest gift the Queen possessed – quite apart from her genius as a diarist – was for portraiture. She never attempted anything on a large scale, and some of her sketches do not quite come off, but others display a very real talent. A sketch she made of Lord Melbourne was extremely skilful. So

Pen and ink sketch made by the Queen for the dresses of the bridesmaids at her own wedding. The design was faithfully copied.

was a profile of the future Edward VII, executed just before his ninth birthday. And drawings of her singing teacher Luigi Lablache and Baroness Lehzen show a very shrewd yet sympathetic understanding of human character.

5

'Windsor is Beautiful and Comfortable'

Queen Victoria had some slight acquaintance with Windsor
Castle before she came to the throne, having first been
invited, together with her mother, her half-sister and her governess,
to visit George IV when she was about seven; recalling some of
her earliest childhood memories when she was fifty-three, the
Queen thought the year had been 1826. Her memory, especially
for dates, was good, so it probably was. But at Balmoral, only a
few months before her death, she was asked by one of her granddaughters, Princess Marie Louise, to recall her very earliest remembrance. After a moment's thought the Queen replied: 'Going to
Carlton House Terrace to watch Sir Thomas Lawrence painting
the Duchess of Gloucester.' Windsor Castle was undergoing extensive renovation in 1826, and George IV was still living at the Royal
Lodge in the Great Park, transformed for him by Nash into a
charming cottage *orné*. So it was to another house on the estate,
Cumberland Lodge, that Princess Victoria was first of all escorted.
At the Royal Lodge her uncle said, 'Give me your little paw',
presented her with his portrait set in diamonds, and sent her off
in a pony carriage for a drive round the park. The following day
the King caught up with his niece while driving his phaeton

(something he did with great skill) and this time he said: 'Pop her in.' She was much impressed by the scarlet and blue livery worn by the King's servants, and was taken to a cottage where one of George IV's pages lived. Here she was given some fruit and then 'amused' herself 'by cramming' the page's little girl with peaches.

Two of Victoria's cousins, Prince Ferdinand of Saxe-Coburg and his brother Prince Augustus, were staying at Windsor Castle in March 1836, when Victoria and her mother were invited to join a dinner party in St George's Hall 'with an immense number of people'; Victoria sat between the King – William IV – and another cousin, Prince George of Cambridge. Afterwards there was a ball in the Waterloo Chamber (Queen Victoria often referred to this room as the Waterloo Gallery, for it is liberally festooned with portraits of people connected with the Battle of Waterloo), at which Victoria danced three quadrilles, all of them partnered by her cousins. It had been an enjoyable occasion, in no way a curtain-raiser to the disastrous birthday dinner for William IV on 21 August that year. William's dislike of Victoria's mother was almost pathological, and the Duchess of Kent had in any case a few days previously infuriated the King by appropriating to herself additional rooms at Kensington Palace. She and Victoria had been invited to stay at the castle the night before the King's birthday, and when they sat down to dinner – the Duchess beside the King, Princess Victoria opposite him – they had no inkling of the storm about to break.

Simmering with rage, the King rose. 'I trust in God,' he told the startled assembly, 'that my life may be spared nine months longer, after which period, in the event of my death, no Regency would take place.' Pointing to his niece, he continued: 'I should then have the satisfaction of leaving the royal authority to the personal exercise of that young lady, the heiress presumptive to the

Crown, and not in the hands of a person, now near me, who is surrounded by evil advisers and who is herself incompetent to act with propriety in the situation in which she would be placed. I have no hesitation in saying that I have been insulted – grossly and continually insulted – by that person, but I am determined to endure no longer a course of behaviour so disrespectful to me.'

By now the atmosphere was electric. The King went on to complain that Princess Victoria had been kept away from court, and he demanded that in future she attend his drawing rooms. By the time he sat down Queen Adelaide was seen to be 'in deep distress', Princess Victoria was in tears and the Duchess herself behaved in the only way possible under the circumstances; she sent for her carriage. In point of fact the King, like so many of his family, was virtually off his head, and, as we know, he had the satisfaction of staying alive long enough to know that Victoria had indeed come of age, and that his arch-enemy the Duchess of Kent would never be called on to act as Regent. He died, as had his brother George IV, in the Blue Room at Windsor, less than four weeks after Princess Victoria's eighteenth birthday.

It was small wonder that Victoria had something of an aversion to her oldest and far and away historically most interesting home, the longest continually occupied royal residence in the world. George III may have been the first monarch to die there, but in Victoria's time only one sovereign, Richard I, had failed to live at the castle since the Norman Conquest.[1] It was William the Conqueror who spotted the useful defensive position at Windsor with superb views of the River Thames and a practically unscaleable escarpment to the north. Here he threw up a mound of earth, which, a century later, once it had settled, became the foundations of the great Round Tower. Some time between 1066 and the Domesday Survey of 1086 a keep was erected, and the original primitive edifice covered what was then known as a half-hide of land. Long before Victoria's reign the castle, divided into three wards, the upper ward eventually containing the royal apartments, the lower ward the Chapel of St George, had occupied thirteen acres.

To enumerate every event of importance that has occurred at Windsor, to trace in full its architectural development and to record the names and deeds of the myriads of inhabitants who have stamped their personalities on the place would require a book to itself.[2] It was at Windsor, as early as 1072, that the supremacy of the Archbishop of Canterbury over the primate of York was settled. Henry II began work on the Round Tower in 1180, and it was he who provided Windsor with a stone-built castle, using heath stone quarried near Bagshot – a silicate and crystalline material which instead of retaining the dirt of centuries is washed clean by every shower. Hence visitors often cannot credit the true age of the outer walls. It was from Windsor Castle that King John's frustrated barons rode out to Runnymede in 1215 to sign the Magna Carta; they felt safer in the open air. And John's grandson, Edward I, was brought up at Windsor, the first indication of the castle serving as a home. Edward's father, Henry III, had so enhanced the place that a contemporary chronicler, Matthew of Westminster, declared that Windsor was the most magnificent palace in Europe.

An even greater benefactor was Henry's great-grandson, Edward III, who was actually born at Windsor, on 23 November 1312. By 1330 Windsor had become Edward's principal residence, and his fifty-year reign coincided with the Age of Chivalry; hence a hectic series of jousting tournaments took place at Windsor, followed by meals 'abounding in the most alluring drinks'. And after dinner, according to one of the guests, 'dances were not lacking, embraces and kissings alternately commingling'. Edward was well aware of the myths concerning 'King Arthur' and his Round Table, and in 1344 he had a table built 200 feet in diameter for tournament dinners served in the Round Tower.

Returning to England in 1347 flushed from his victory at Crécy Edward decided to celebrate by instituting a new order of knighthood, the Order of the Garter, which, with its often misquoted motto, 'Honi soit qui mal y pense' ('Shame on him who thinks evil of it'), today ranks as the senior order of chivalry in the British honours system. The twenty-fourth of June 1348 is now regarded as the probable day on which the fraternity of the Knights of the Garter first met, and the order has been indelibly linked with the chapel at Windsor ever since. Ransom paid by the French helped considerably to finance Edward III's building costs at Windsor; both the King of France and his son were captured at the Battle of Poitiers and taken to Windsor, where they found waiting to welcome them Edward's own brother-in-law, King David II of Scotland – taken prisoner at the Battle of Meville's Cross in 1346; he was still waiting for his ransom to be paid.

There have been some surprising as well as appropriate appointments as Surveyor or Clerk of the Works at Windsor; they have included Geoffrey Chaucer and Sir Christopher Wren. In 1356 William Wykeham, founder of Winchester College and New College, Oxford, Lord Chancellor and Bishop of Winchester, was appointed Surveyor of the King's Works. He was paid a shilling a day, whereas expenditure on the King's new chapel, dedicated to St George, was running at £3,000 a year. This building, demolished by Edward IV a century later, would have been in the English Gothic style. Edward IV had no very serious claim to the throne; he was third cousin to Henry VI, who was deposed in 1461, Edward being proclaimed King at the age of nineteen. A dashing and romantic character, six feet four inches tall and extremely handsome, Edward IV would invite the Mayor and Aldermen of London to Windsor 'for none other errand but to have them hunt and be merry with him'.

It was in 1474 that Edward demolished his great-grandfather's chapel and began work on the present glorious building. Edward's second child, Mary, was born at Windsor in 1466, and when she died at the age of fifteen she was buried in the chapel. Within a year, in 1483, not yet forty-one and probably a victim of typhoid, Edward was laid to rest there too, under a large stone on the north side of the altar. Over his tomb was hung his coat of mail 'covered over with crimson velvet, and thereon the arms of France and England quarterly, richly embroidered with pearl and gold, interwoven with divers rubies'. And there it remained until, on 23 October 1642, the chapel was plundered by Parliamentary forces.

By dint of careful management and the cutting out of waste at Windsor, in 1509 Henry VII left his second son, Henry VIII, a colossal fortune by the standards of those days – £1 million. In the first year of his bloodthirsty reign (not many men have condemned to death two Chancellors and a couple of wives), Henry VIII built the gateway to the lower ward that bears his name, through which visitors to the castle pass today. It was at Windsor, on 1 September 1531, that Henry created Anne Boleyn, mother of Elizabeth I and the first of Henry's wives to lose her head, Marchioness of Pembroke. Her uncle was a canon of St George's, and one of the many sinecures held by Henry's Archbishop of York, Cardinal Wolsey, was also a canonry of Windsor. Yet Henry was a learned and gifted man, and when the fastidious Dutch humanist Erasmus came to visit Windsor during Henry's reign he declared that he found the place 'more like a house of the Muses than a court'.

Queen Victoria was not the first sovereign to experience an aversion to Windsor Castle. 'Methinks I am in prison,' the poor little twelve-year-old Edward VI groaned. 'Here be no galleries, nor no gardens to walk in.' His elder sister Mary, as bloody-minded as her father, married the equally murderous Philip of Spain at Winchester and escorted him to Windsor, where she invested him with the Garter and heard in the chapel a Te Deum and a De Profundis sung. With alarming swings of religious allegiance from one Tudor monarch to another, the dean and canons hardly knew what they were doing. Elizabeth restored the Anglican rite but, denied a husband herself, she saw no reason why other people should be happy, and although she had to put up with a married Archbishop of Canterbury, Matthew Parker, 'a commandment came from the Queen unto the College of Windsor' ordering 'that the priests belonging thereunto that had wives should put them out of the College; and for time to come lie no more within that place'.

Elizabeth was an astonishingly well-educated woman. With plague raging in London, the Queen took refuge at Windsor for the winter of 1563–4, even though she found the castle deadly cold. She spent much of this enforced incarceration in study, and her teacher, the redoubtable scholar Roger Ascham, reported 'that beside her perfect readiness in Latin, Italian, French and Spanish, she readeth here now at Windsore more Greek every day than some Prebendarie of this church doth read Latin in a whole weeke'. At Christmas 1593, while at Windsor, the Queen spent much of her time in the dean's and canons' library on a translation of Boethius.

Elizabeth's successor, James I, particularly enjoyed women being immodest, and when a masque and banquet were staged at Windsor in 1606 in honour of his brother-in-law, King Christian IV of Denmark, the ladies present were observed to abandon 'all sobriety' and to 'roll about in intoxication'. As constable of the castle he

Windsor Castle in the reign of Queen Elizabeth, showing St George's Chapel.

installed what school history books would euphemistically refer to as one of his favourites, George Villiers, later created Duke of Buckingham. As Dean of Windsor, James chose one Marcus Antonius de Dominis, a former Archbishop of Spalato. When the renegade priest returned to Rome, both literally and liturgically, he was promptly imprisoned by the Inquisition for his former heresy, and died in 1625 'of grief and hard treatment'.

Windsor Castle was about to enter one of its saddest periods, for under Charles I it became an embattled fortress, and for a time it was even lost to the Crown. Having so foolishly, on 4 January 1642, put at risk what was left of his authority by trying, in person, to arrest five Members of Parliament, Charles I retreated to Windsor, leaving a few weeks later, never to return again a free man. During the winter of 1642–3 Windsor became the head-quarters of the Parliamentary army. The organ and windows of the chapel were smashed, and plate was melted down to make coins, but the Dean, Christopher Wren, father of his namesake the great Restoration architect, managed to smuggle out invaluable records relating to the Order of the Garter. (Christopher Wren junior was bought up in the deanery.) In July 1647 the King returned to Windsor, as a prisoner, was moved to Hampton Court, from whence he escaped, only to be recaptured and returned to Windsor on 22 December 1648. He was permitted to walk on the North Terrace, and £20 a day was allowed for his upkeep. He even continued to dine in state. But the patience of his captors was gradually worn away; he refused to negotiate, was denied a chaplain, and when not engrossed in prayer he spent his time rereading the plays of Shakespeare.

Charles's final connections with Windsor were truly surreal. On 18 January 1649 he was led away to St James's to await his trial, and after his execution Parliament gave orders that he should 'be buried at Windsor in a decent manner, provided that the whole expense should not exceed five hundred pounds'. On 7 February his decapitated body was taken to the castle in a hearse driven by his former coachman. The corpse was laid in the royal bedroom, and next day it was taken to the dean's hall. Two lighted tapers were placed on the coffin. At about three o'clock in the afternoon William Juxon, Bishop of London, who had attended King Charles on the scaffold in Whitehall, asked permission to bury the King according to the Book of Common Prayer, but this was refused. When the Duke of Richmond and three other peers entered the chapel to select a spot for interment they found the place so ransacked, with windows smashed and ornaments stolen, that it was almost unrecognizable.

Having disposed of the King, Parliament set about trying to get rid of Windsor Castle, and the House of Commons resolved 'that the Castle of Windsore, with all its Houses, Parks and Lands there, belonging to the State, be sold for ready money'. A bill for this purpose was introduced and debated, but when members were advised they might not obtain more than £2,700 they abandoned plans to sell the entire estate, and merely got rid of the 'Little Parke and meadowes there'.

Life at the castle was a good deal more merry with the restoration of Charles II. He arrived at Windsor on 15 April 1661 and promptly installed a dozen new Knights of the Garter. Feasts of St George were now destined to last three days. In 1670 the gravy for one meal alone required 249 pounds of beef, 74 pounds of bacon, four cases of veal, two of mutton and one of pork, ten dozen pullets, nine dozen sheep's tongues, eighteen dozen sweetbreads and seven dozen marrowbones, not to mention the 'small guts of an Ox'. The bill for a meal consisting of prawns, crawfish, lobsters, crabs and scallops, capons, pullets and chickens, ducklings, pigeons, geese, turkeys, eggs and asparagus came to £2,394 17s. 8½d.

Yet despite the vulgarity, and largely on account of the beauty of the services in the chapel, Samuel Pepys came to regard Windsor as 'the most romantique castle in the world'. But large numbers of people had taken up squatters' rights in the lower ward during the Commonwealth, leaving much of the fabric 'ragged and ruinous', and these unwelcome intruders had to be evicted. Then Charles took the opportunity of turning the castle into a palace by transforming the royal apartments on the north side of the upper ward, sweeping away a large section of Edward III's buildings and engaging the architect Hugh May to create a series of rooms now known as the State Apartments. Grinling Gibbons was commissioned to carve much of the wooden decoration, and several magnificent ceilings, three of which survive, were painted between 1676 and 1681 by the Neapolitan artist Antonio Verrio. This grand suite of rooms included separate bedrooms, dressing rooms and drawing rooms for the King and Queen, a ballroom, and a dining room for the King.

In 1685, the year of his death, Charles made his last and one of his most effective contributions to Windsor Castle by planning the Long Walk, in imitation of André Le Nôtre's grand vista at Versailles. The intention was to integrate castle and park, giving the impression that the King's lands rolled away from his front door for ever. It was to be left to George IV to clear the south front of the castle of extraneous buildings, to commence the Long Walk at the walls of the castle themselves and to bring the three-mile vista to a focal conclusion by the placing of a statue. But the original concept was Charles II's, and together with Henry II, Edward III, Edward IV and George IV, Charles II must be reckoned one of the main architectural benefactors of Windsor Castle.

The death at Windsor, on 30 July 1700, of the twelve-year-old Duke of Gloucester, the only surviving child of Queen Anne, effectively spelled the end of the Stuart dynasty, and with the arrival in 1714 of the Hanoverians Windsor Castle found no favour with George I or George II, and it was seriously neglected until the accession, in 1760, of George III. George turned the castle into a family home, if rather an uncomfortable one, and the estate into a prosperous farm. But once again squatters had to be evicted; so did the fishmongers and grocers who had been plying their trade in the lower ward and the prostitutes theirs on the North Terrace. On hand to record the King's tragic derangement at Windsor was the novelist Fanny Burney, assistant keeper of the wardrobe to Queen Charlotte.

In 1785 Fanny Burney left a description in her diary of the King's easy-going nature where visitors to Windsor Castle were concerned:

The king and queen and the Prince of Mecklenburg, and Her Majesty's mother, walked together. Next to them the princesses and their ladies, and the young princes, making a very gay and pleasing procession, of one of the finest families in the world. Every way they moved, the crowd retired to stand up against the wall as they passed, and then closed in to follow.

Other frequent visitors to the North Terrace were the painters Paul and Thomas Sandby, and George III had the sagacity to purchase many of Paul Sandby's delicious watercolours.

During the last decade of George III's life, with the King shuffling about in two rooms on the North Terrace, his wife living at Frogmore and the Prince Regent also living in the Great Park, at the Royal Lodge, Windsor Castle once again became neglected.

George IV inherited a castle constructed in many areas of small, dissimilar rooms often without proper connecting corridors. Leading architects were consulted – John Nash, John Soane, Robert Smirke – and an estimate of £150,000 was accepted based on suggestions sent in by Jeffry Wyatt, the nephew of James Wyatt, who changed his name to Wyatville. Such a sum was soon found to be inadequate, which was hardly surprising; once Wyatville got down to work he found it necessary to remove fifty wagon loads of rotten timbers for a start. By 1828, the year in which Wyatville was knighted, the bill had mounted to £644,500.

On the south side a dozen houses were pulled down. The Brunswick Tower, at the furthest extremity of the North Terrace, was found to be split from top to bottom and had to be entirely rebuilt. New windows were positioned; the Round Tower was raised by thirty-three feet; a sunken garden in front of the East Terrace was constructed. His masterstroke was the sequence of sumptuous green, crimson and white drawing rooms and the Grand Corridor linking the private apartments. A workforce of 700 men was employed, and between them George IV and Sir Jeffry Wyatville more or less prevented Windsor Castle from falling down. George VI's librarian, Sir Owen Morshead, has written: 'Beset as he was by many difficulties, Wyatville achieved a great work, despite his natural limitations and the taste of the generation which his style reflects . . . He found a workhouse and he left a palace.'[3]

When William IV became King in 1830 all ten of his illegitimate children moved in with him. They brought with them their husbands and their wives, and set about demanding money and quarrelling with their father. But money seems to have been no object. William entertained on average 2,000 people a week- but not always with civility. 'What's that you're drinking, sir?' he bellowed one evening at Prince Leopold. 'Water, sir? God damn

Win

le.

it! Why don't you drink wine? I never allow anybody to drink water at my table.'

Once Queen Victoria had taken charge at Windsor Castle, she moved the hour of dinner from the Georgian custom of late afternoon to the newly fashionable hour of eight o'clock (later in her reign she did not dine before nine). By contrast with the gloomy years of her widowhood, in 1841 an astonishing 113,000 people were entertained at the castle. But it was not long before Victoria was bemoaning her fate. 'Windsor is beautiful and comfortable,' she admitted to King Leopold on 16 January 1844, 'but it is a palace, and God knows how willingly I would always live with my beloved Albert and our children in the quiet and retirement of private life, and not be the constant object of observation, and of newspaper articles.'

One way in which the Queen came to terms with what she saw as an inequality in her married life, having come firmly to believe that the husband should after all be the master in his own house (had she had it in her power, she would have shared her throne with Albert), was to raise him to an equal in matters of state. Windsor was the setting in which this totally unconstitutional change took place. At a time of Cabinet crisis, Victoria sent for Lord John Russell and a former Foreign Secretary, the Marquess of Lansdowne. Charles Greville noted on 16 December 1845:

Formerly the Queen received her Ministers alone; with her alone they communicated, though of course Prince Albert knew everything; but now the Queen and Prince were together, received Lord Lansdowne and John Russell together, and both of them always said *We* – '*We* think, or wish, to do so and so; what had *we* better do, etc.' The Prince is becoming so identified with the Queen that they are one person, and as he likes business, it is

Royal Group, Windsor 1843, by Sir Edwin Landseer.

obvious that while she has the title he is really discharging the functions of the Sovereign. He is King to all intents and purposes. I am not surprised at this, but certainly was not aware that it had taken such a definite shape.

William III and Mary II had reigned jointly by Act of Parliament. Queen Victoria had decided to take the law into her own hands.

6

A Strange Chinese-Looking Thing

In addition to Buckingham Palace and Windsor Castle there was a third home in England Queen Victoria inherited, the Royal Pavilion at Brighton, the seaside extravaganza created by George IV over a period of some forty years with the aid of two outstanding architects, Henry Holland and John Nash. The Royal Pavilion had its origins in a visit – his first – paid by George IV in 1783, when he was Prince of Wales, to a small Sussex town, formerly a fishing hamlet called Brighthelmstone. His precise destination was Grove House on the Steine, there to stay with his aunt and uncle, the Duke and Duchess of Cumberland. This Duke of Cumberland was one of George III's dissolute brothers; his adultery at the age of twenty-five with the Countess of Grosvenor had cost £10,000 in compensation to the Earl, and his marriage in 1771 to a widow, Mrs Anne Horton, said to be 'vulgar, noisy and indelicate', was one of the spurs to George III instigating the Royal Marriages Act the following year.[1]

Cumberland had spent several summers at Brighton since discovering the alleged benefits of bathing in the sea and drinking the spring waters at nearby Hove. When the young Prince of Wales, still endowed with somewhat florid good looks, arrived in 1783, bells were rung, guns were fired and the Prince lost no time in taking advantage of the informal atmosphere at Grove House; it came as a breath of fresh air after the stifling atmosphere of his father's court at Windsor. He returned the next year, again to enjoy visits to the theatre in North Street, balls in the Assembly Rooms and racing on the Downs, and he determined he must have a home of his own at Brighton. Money was a slight problem. He had already been forced to economize by shutting down Carlton House, disbanding his racing stables and dismissing most of his staff, and in an ostentatious show of poverty he now took the public coach to Brighton, travelling on the outside like any gentleman too hard up to possess transport of his own.

But the Prince was seldom deterred by debts. The potential home he alighted on was a modest farmhouse on the Steine, the property of Thomas Kemp, MP for Lewes, the speculator later responsible for the elegant Regency Kemp Town estate on the coast to the east of the town. Once Parliament had obligingly agreed to pay off £161,000 of Prince George's debts he wasted no time in summoning Henry Holland to Brighton, with orders (in 1787) to transform the farmhouse into a Marine Pavilion. Up went a small neoclassical house with a central domed rotunda surrounded by Ionic columns, and with bow-fronted wings enhanced by a style of ironwork balcony so typical of the Regency houses in Brighton inspired by the Prince Regent's patronage.[2] On the ground floor was a dining room, breakfast room and library. Even after a new dining room and conservatory had been added the house was dwarfed by stables for sixty horses designed, between 1803 and 1808, in the Indian fashion.

So in 1815, by which time the Prince of Wales was Prince Regent, John Nash was called in. Over a period of seven years were built the saloon, music room and banqueting room, in which a chandelier

The banqueting room at the Brighton Pavilion.

weighing nearly a ton was hung. By 1823 the interior décor, with its magnificent chinoiserie, was completed. Meanwhile, oriental domes and minarets went spiralling into the air. A modern commentator on architecture, Simon Jenkins, has neatly described the overall effect as 'witty and light-hearted'. The Pavilion, in what one might call its second stage, was certainly intended for entertainment, and often on the grandest imaginable scale; in 1817 Grand Duke Nicholas of Russia sat down to a banquet comprising over a hundred dishes.

George IV was an indolent man who atoned for his youthful advocacy of the Whig cause by abdicating almost all political responsibility in middle age. The less business he had to attend to the better, and what place could be more delightful from which to escape importunate ministers, not to mention the fickle London mob who dared to stone his carriage, than the Royal Pavilion. George IV's arrival in Brighton had brought the town enormous prosperity, building and trade now catering for a population of 7,000. In Brighton George was seen as a splendid adornment to the place, an acknowledged patron of the arts, a jovial benefactor, a popular local squire. 'God bless you all!' he would say to his guests, with a gracious wave of his hand, as he retired to bed. And always late to bed – he was a notoriously late riser. But once dressed and coiffed he could rely, in Brighton, on a seemly promenade alone the Steine.

Fun and amusement were the order of the day, and the King would invite guests to Brighton who could be relied on to help entertain the company. The brilliant and delightful playwright Richard Sheridan played endless pranks and kept everyone laughing. Until his sad disgrace, Beau Brummell, the arbiter of fashion who taught the Prince Regent the correct way to take snuff, was another favourite guest. On 31 October 1811 Thomas Creevey arrived at the Pavilion to find the newly appointed Prince Regent 'in the best humour', looking 'uncommonly well, though very fat'. At the Pavilion, Creevey recorded, the Prince was 'always merry and full of his jokes'. At first the Prince's morganatic wife, Mrs Fitzherbert, acted as hostess; later the task was allotted to the current matronly mistress. Dinner was served at six o'clock, and afterwards the Prince would sometimes wend his somewhat unsteady way to the Assembly Rooms. Or he might sit on a sofa tapping his foot in time to the band. Precisely at midnight the band would pack up and in were wheeled sandwiches and more wine.

With the death of George IV in 1830 the Pavilion passed to his brother, William IV, and on his death to Queen Victoria. She lost very little time travelling down to Brighton to investigate her legacy, deciding she needed an autumnal holiday in early October 1837, the first year of her reign. She had always had a penchant for the seaside, and was disappointed to discover at the Pavilion that she could 'only see a little morsel of the sea' from one of her sitting room windows. The Pavilion itself she thought 'a strange, odd Chinese-looking thing, both inside and outside', and she considered most of the rooms too low. Compared with the State Apartments at Buckingham Palace they *were* low, but she seems to have missed the whole point of the Pavilion, that in royal terms at any rate it was intended to be on an intimate scale. And when one considers the taste she was to favour as an adult woman – Scottish baronial at Balmoral, Italianate at Osborne – it is little wonder that her limited imagination failed to appreciate the sheer exuberance, the deliberate absurdity, even, of the architecture and décor at Brighton which so successfully complemented the quixotic character of its creator. Fortunately, Victoria was never there long enough, or late enough in life, to start cluttering the place up with the hordes of framed photographs and figurines that came to dominate her private rooms at Windsor. The wallpaper in her bedroom at Brighton, for example, was a hand-painted Chinese paper, whose ravishing effect would have been ruined by having paintings of dogs and deer strung all over it. As befitted the intimate size of the rooms upstairs, furnishings were relatively sparse, although the Queen did have a mahogany four-poster bed, in contrast to the three-foot six-inch tent bedstead supplied for her maid in the room next door. Yet she was not insensible to the theatrical effect intended on the ground floor. She returned to the Pavilion in 1838, perhaps to put her feelings to the test again, and in 1842 she had the stupendous banqueting room chandelier rehung; it had been put into store by William IV in 1833 because Queen Adelaide was terrified it might crash down on the diners.

The west front of the Pavilion, from a drawing by Pugin, 1838.

This was the occasion of Albert's first sight of the Royal Pavilion, two years after his marriage, and already accommodation had to be found for two very young children, the Princess Royal and Bertie, born on 9 November 1841. The marriage had struck its first rocks, Albert accusing the Queen of starving their little daughter while, unrecognized by both of them, the Queen was suffering from post-natal depression. 'We think of going to Brighton early in February,' she wrote to King Leopold on 14 January 1842, 'as the physicians think it will do the children great good, and perhaps it may me; for I am very strong as to fatigue and exertion, but not quite right otherwise; I am growing thinner, and there is a want of tone which the sea may correct.' It was actually the dismissal at this time of Baroness Lehzen, who had been trying to control the nursery, that did more good than anything.

It had never been intended that the Pavilion should be large enough to sleep other than essential domestic staff; the Queen's four dressers were lodged in four attic rooms, while most members of the household were accommodated in neighbouring houses that had sprung up in the wake of George IV's descent on the town. The royal couple were back at the Pavilion briefly the following year, accompanied by Prince de Joinville, a son of King Louis-Philippe of France. The Prince 'was very much struck with the strangeness of the building', the Queen wrote. Ideally, the Royal Pavilion should have provided a ready-made holiday home for the Queen and her family, but already the view of the sea from the Pavilion had been obscured by residential development, and a visit by the Queen quite naturally excited the interest of the local people. She had never been keen on overattentive subjects, and if she needed an excuse to rid herself of the Pavilion she had one handed to her on a plate in 1845. She and Albert took a stroll to the famous Chain Pier, when 'the crowd behaved worse than I have ever seen them do', she complained in her journal, 'and we were mobbed by all the shopboys in the town, who ran and looked under my bonnet, treating us just as they do the Band, when it goes to the Parade! We walked home as fast as we could.'

By about this time Victoria had already been toying with the idea of acquiring a new seaside retreat with plenty of private land between her inquisitive vassals and herself, somewhere on an island, perhaps. Another factor had entered the equation; the need for more money to be spent on Buckingham Palace. Sir Robert Peel, Prime Minister since 1841 and now much liked and appreciated by the Queen, was initially horrified at the idea of money being spent so soon on a building so recently finished. But from the Pavilion itself, on 10 February 1845, the Queen decided to put pressure on him, writing to say that there was a 'total want of accommodation for our little family, which is fast growing up'. In addition, 'most parts of the palace' were 'in a sad state, and will ere long require a further outlay to render them *decent* for the occupation of the Royal Family or any visitors the Queen may have to receive. A room, capable of containing a larger number of those persons whom the Queen has to invite in the course of the season to balls, concerts etc than any of the present apartments can at once hold, is much wanted.' Equally necessary, she added, were 'improved offices and servants' rooms, the want of which puts the departments of the household to great expense yearly'. She thought the exterior of the palace 'a *disgrace* to the country'.

The Queen had a plan up her sleeve to help offset the expense of alterations at Buckingham Palace, a plan that she felt sure would compel Peel to fall in with her wishes; she would dispose of the Pavilion and put the money it fetched – £53,000 in the event – towards whatever sum Peel might feel obliged to come up with. In fact, a new Whig administration under Lord John Russell voted a generous £150,000 in 1846, the estimate including the cost of providing much-needed improvements in ventilation. Meanwhile, 143 van loads of furniture, china, carpets and clocks were on their way from Brighton to Buckingham Palace and Windsor Castle, and at Buckingham Palace on 10 June Victoria exclaimed with delight: 'We breakfasted as we already dined last night in the new room . . . very handsomely fitted up with furniture etc from the Pavilion at Brighton, including the Chinese pictures that were on the wall there, and the doors with the serpents etc . . . A dragon has been painted on the ceiling and harmonizes with the rest. The small sitting room is also furnished with things from the Pavilion – all arranged according to my dearest Albert's taste.'

Yet a great deal was still left to be desired, caused to a large extent by the Queen's very intermittent use of Buckingham Palace. She organized a series of costume balls, and in 1853 there was a grand banquet in the picture gallery to celebrate the birth, on 7 April that year, of her fourth son and eighth child, Prince Leopold, brought into the world with the aid of chloroform, which the Queen found 'soothing, quieting and delightful beyond measure'. But between these set occasions long periods of time elapsed when the place stood empty, unaired and unheated. In 1855 Victoria's German dresser, Frieda Arnold, was complaining: 'I have never been so cold in my whole life as I was for two days at the palace. We arrived in bitter weather at this huge building that had stood empty for a long time; in spite of all the heating, the tomb-like atmosphere only disappeared after several days' occupation.'[3]

The year 1847 had seen the sale of some of the surplus Brighton furniture. On 6 June the following year a further sale took place on the Pavilion lawns, and the following day George IV's seaside Pavilion, depleted of all its beautiful Regency furnishings, was locked up. But interest in this unique building was so great that,

The music room at the Brighton Pavilion.

although quite empty, in the summer of 1849 27,563 curious people flocked through its deserted rooms. It was suddenly realized what a potentially valuable asset the Royal Pavilion could become to the town, and on 19 June 1850 the Royal Pavilion Estate was purchased from the Queen by Brighton Town Council.[4]

7

'A Perfect Little Paradise'

Queen Victoria's first visit to the Isle of Wight was made when she was twelve, when she carried out what was almost certainly her first public engagement by laying the foundation stone of a new church at East Cowes. She was back again two years later, accompanied, as always, by her mother. And her thoughts turned again to the Isle of Wight once she realized that the Royal Pavilion in Brighton would never supply the privacy for which she craved. As the original Osborne House, a charming eighteenth-century property built by Robert Blachford and now owned by Lady Isabella Blachford, sister of the Duke of Grafton, was only a mile from East Cowes, Victoria would definitely have recalled it from her childhood, and she would have known the Duke. By 1843 the Queen was negotiating with Lady Isabella to take a lease on the property with an option to buy, and Prince Albert was sent across the Solent in March the following year to cast an eye over the prospect. His report was favourable, and in August Victoria was at Osborne House herself. She declared that she was delighted with it; she thought it 'complete and snug' and considered that with some 'alterations for the children' it might be made 'an excellent house'.

Osborne House, Isle of Wight.

By taking sound financial advice from his private secretary, George Anson, Prince Albert had already begun to make money for the Queen, investing her savings in land and on the stock market, thus establishing the basis of the royal family's private fortune. Victoria was the first sovereign not to go cap in hand to Parliament every time she ran into debt; she was never in debt. Early in 1845 Lady Isabella agreed to sell Osborne House and about 1,000 acres of grounds for £26,000 (it was 'a perfect little Paradise', the Queen told Sir Robert Peel on 22 June), and by March 1847 Anson, who had long since earned the respect and affection of Prince Albert, was reporting to Charles Greville that 'the Queen's affairs are in such good order and so well managed that she will be able to provide for the whole expense of Osborne out of her income without difficulty, and that by the time it is furnished it will have cost £200,000'.[1]

Although on 23 April 1845 Victoria was writing to Lord Melbourne to say that she and Albert were delighted with their new home, with its private beach and its woods that 'grow into the sea' (the calm and blue of the sea reminded Prince Albert of Naples, one of the towns on the itinerary of a tour he made of Italy in 1838, when he was nineteen, and it is certainly true that there is a Continental atmosphere to the area, the present gardens almost resembling a landscape by Poussin), it was only a matter of time – weeks, in fact – before the foundation stone of a new marine mansion was laid, on 23 June. The architect George Barry had already been influenced by the Italianate style, made popular by increasing numbers of wealthy Belgravian clients able to holiday on the Continent in relative comfort now that roads had been properly made up, hotels dusted and steam-driven cross-Channel boats had taken the place of sail, and the successful West End builder Thomas Cubitt had in turn been influenced by Barry.

Albert, so much more cosmopolitan than the Queen (she had yet to go abroad), invited Cubitt, in one of whose houses, in Eaton Place, George Anson lived, to put into effect his own Italianate designs.

Even before the new house was anything like under way the Queen had summoned a meeting of the Privy Council to East Cowes. A room specifically set aside for meetings of the Council was to be incorporated into the new house. Meanwhile, there was nowhere for the Council members to congregate other than in the entrance hall of the doomed old house, so, as Greville recorded, they 'walked about looking at the new house the Queen is building; it is very ugly and the whole concern wretched enough'. But at least, as he hastened to add, 'it is her own money and not the nation's'.

The first part of the demolition and building operation concentrated on a pavilion for the royal family. Cubitt did not mess about, and Victoria and Albert were able to spend their first night there on 15 September 1846. On hand to record the event was Lady Lyttelton, a lady-in-waiting to the Queen who had been appointed superintendent of the royal nursery when trouble was brewing over Baroness Lehzen's high-handed conduct. It was a surprising appointment in some ways. She was a kindly widow with five children of her own, and was grateful for the salary, but the Queen was distinctly Low Church and Lady Lyttelton High. Worse still, her brother was a Roman Catholic priest and monk. He was, nevertheless, permitted occasional visits to Windsor to visit his sister. When Lady Lyttelton first took up her duties she had only the welfare of Vicky, the Princess Royal, and Bertie, the future Edward VII, to concern herself with. But the nursery had been rapidly filling up: Alice, now three, had been born in 1843, Alfred the following year, and

Helena, by the time Victoria took possession of the pavilion at Osborne, was sixteen weeks old.

'Nobody caught cold or smelt paint,' Lady Lyttelton wrote, 'and it was a most amusing event coming here. Everything in the house is quite new, and the dining room looked very handsome. The windows, lighted by the brilliant lamps in the room, must have been seen far out to sea.' Punctilious in her own Anglican observances, Lady Lyttelton was pleased when, after dinner, everyone rose 'to drink the Queen's and Prince's health as a *house-warming*' and the Prince responded by quoting two lines from Luther in German, a prayer, he explained, to 'bless our going out and coming in'. It was 'dry and quaint', Lady Lyttelton thought, 'but we all perceived that he was feeling it. And truly entering a new house, a new palace, is a solemn thing to do.'

Ultimately Osborne House was built around an open courtyard facing a drive, with the pavilion block in the middle and the main block, containing the kitchens, a visitors' entrance, a grand corridor and rooms for the household, to the right of the courtyard. Not really much given to slumming, there is no doubt that although the Queen was anxious to acquire a private home, she intended the State Apartments on the ground floor to reflect her regal status. Some concession to informality was achieved by placing the billiard room at right angles to the drawing room, so that although technically in attendance courtiers could relax and even sit down out of sight of the monarch while remaining within easy call should they be summoned to the next room. The chances are that such niceties would have been thought up by the Prince, whose imagination in most areas of life ran well ahead of the Queen's.

In the centre of the main block, on the garden side and reached via the Grand Corridor, Osborne was fitted up with an audience room, in which ministers were to be received, and next to it a

Council room with French windows leading on to the upper terrace. The original carpet in the Council room, like much else at Osborne, was purchased by the Queen when the Great Exhibition of 1851 closed. Although a good many Council meetings were held (it was at Osborne that by letters patent Queen Victoria created Albert Prince Consort in 1857), the room was used more frequently for dances, charades and theatrical performances staged on an egalitarian footing (it is difficult for an equerry to keep calling a princess ma'am during rehearsals), the royal family, household and servants all taking part. But the inclusion of a Council room at the very start is a clear indication that the house was never intended as a weekend retreat. In point of fact, the pantomime of transporting servants, household, family and luggage from Windsor to Osborne, by train and then by ship, presented such a logistical headache for those responsible for the arrangements that a summer visit of less than six weeks would have been absurd.

It has often been assumed that in Victorian and Edwardian England billiards was a game played exclusively by men, usually after dinner, when they could smoke as well, but Victoria learned to play billiards at Osborne, and she roped in some of her ladies to play with her after lunch. The Queen thought the adjoining drawing room, in which the Swedish soprano Jenny Lind was invited to sing in 1847, 'extremely handsome, with its yellow damask satin curtains and furniture to match'. Not everyone agreed. One of Victoria's Prime Ministers, the fifth Earl of Rosebery, remarked that having seen the drawing room at Osborne he thought he had seen the ugliest drawing room in the world until he saw the one at Balmoral. A large pair of doors led from the drawing room to the dining room, and it was in the dining room at Osborne that in the wake of the Prince Consort's death a subdued marriage took place, in July 1862, of Princess Alice, the Queen's second daughter, to the Grand Duke of Hesse-Darmstadt. The Queen, whose dreary plan it was anyway, thought this marriage 'more like a funeral', and she could not have imagined that fifty-nine years later her own body would lie in state in the dining room before being taken to Windsor.

There could be no greater contrast in any royal establishment between the opulence of the State Apartments at Osborne and the relative simplicity of the Queen's chintzy little private rooms on the first floor, where she retired (admittedly to work on the ministerial boxes) in her role as a German hausfrau. In the centre of the first floor of the pavilion is her sitting room, with a pair of writing tables so that Albert could sit beside her and peruse confidential state papers, offer the Queen advice, reply to her queries and, when not at work in his own dressing and writing room, pen innumerable memoranda. The room served a more homely purpose as well. 'When I am not particularly occupied,' the Queen wrote during her first autumn at Osborne, 'Vicky [aged six] and Bertie [aged five] alternately always take their supper in our room. [Why alternately, one wonders?] Then little Helena is brought down for a quarter of an hour, followed by Affie [Alfred, aged two], and then Alice [aged three].' No upper-class parents of the time, all of whom employed nannies, would have thought it the least odd to spare just fifteen minutes for their new baby, Helena having been born on 15 May that year.

By royal, and even aristocratic, standards, Victoria and Albert's marriage was an extraordinarily domestic one, neither partner ever contemplating for an instant taking a lover or a mistress. The difference between their conduct, and the way in which they thought other people should behave, separated their generation from that of Victoria's notorious uncles as if by some great mountain gorge; it was a transformation that laid down the code of middle-class

The nursery, Osborne House.

morality for a century. The children had not far to walk or be carried to visit their mother's sitting room at Osborne; the nursery was on the second floor so as to allow the parents easy access to the children, who eventually numbered nine in all. The children usually remained in the nursery suite, where there was a comfortable sitting room, until they were six, when they were promoted to the schoolroom on the first floor. But even when all the Queen's children had become fledglings, the spacious nursery bedroom, with its cots and beds and clutter of ingenious German toys, remained in use for her grandchildren.

While they were lavishing money on furniture, paintings and statues, Victoria and Albert provided themselves with luxurious bathrooms, way ahead in their design of the standard fixtures commonly manufactured in the middle of the nineteenth century. It is very apparent at Osborne, the first property she could call her own, how Queen Victoria, once she was financially independent as well as free of maternal restraints, made up for an emotionally deprived childhood by supplying security in the form of personal possessions. Visitors to Osborne today may care to wander round armed with a 'summary catalogue' that 'refers only to the main items among the thousands of nineteenth-century paintings and objects that belonged to Queen Victoria'. She seems to have needed also an overabundance of attendants, all of whom had to be housed and fed; in 1866, for a ten-day stay at Cliveden, in order to get away from 'the noise and turmoil of Ascot', she took with her an entourage of ninety. At Osborne, as at Windsor, there was a permanent housekeeper (a 'dear, sweet old lady', according to one of the Queen's dressers), accommodation for forty staff and, once the Queen had added Barton Manor and another 1,000 acres to the estate, there was no shortage of accommodation for equerries.

'Nearly all the men-servants sleep in another house that cannot be seen from here,' a dresser, Frieda Arnold, reported home from Osborne in 1855, 'so that it is quite quiet in the house: they are taken there in a wagon each night at eleven o'clock.' Frieda, who together with the other dressers slept in rooms on the third floor, directly above the Queen's apartments, and could be rung for from the sitting room by means of an elementary electric bell, had arrived from Karlsruhe shortly before Christmas the previous year on three months' trial and remained with the Queen until the summer of 1859. She loved Osborne, although, she wrote, 'the Queen's staff, without exception, dislike staying there'. The Queen revelled in the 'purest air' and the chance of getting away 'from all the bitterness which people create for themselves in London', whereas the bracing weather disagreed with many of the staff, most of whom were married, missed their wives, and had nothing to do and nowhere to go on their time off.

Although the crossing to Portsmouth took an hour and a half, by dint of the use of a private railway station at Gosport and a royal train that never stopped, when returning to Windsor the Queen and Prince Albert were only a matter of three and a half hours from door to door; they saw the journey to the Isle of Wight as merely a pleasant jaunt, but while at Osborne they put down firm domestic roots. In 1855 they built a substantial Swiss Cottage for the children, who were encouraged to cultivate their own plots of garden and to try their hand at cooking – so substantial that even a resident housekeeper and her husband were installed. Albert himself directed landscaping operations by semaphore from the flag tower. He was not to live to see the final appendix to what so far had been entirely his own creation, the Durbar Block, consisting of a corridor and an ornate state banqueting hall, built by Queen Victoria in 1890 to the left of the courtyard. Although not declared Empress of India until 1876, a title engineered for her by Disraeli, she had always had a soft spot for Indians, she and Albert entertaining the fifteen-year-old Maharajah Duleep Singh at Osborne in 1854. The Queen discovered on her return to Windsor on 17 June 1887 that the Duke and Duchess of Connaught (Connaught was Prince Arthur, her third son) had imported 'an Indian boy of 10 years old, an orphan & a Christian, who waited at lunch. He is very quick and attentive & a pretty boy.' Eleven days later she recorded having breakfast at Frogmore 'under the trees. The Indians always wait now, & do so so well & quietly.' The Queen's most famous Indian servant was the bogus Abdul Karim, who taught her a little Hindustani and was at Osborne in 1887, during his first year in service. Two portraits of him hang in the corridor.

It would appear that when on holiday as a child Victoria was not permitted by her overprotective mother to venture into the sea, for in 1847 she recorded her first experience of the brine. She had a bathing machine constructed that ran on stone rails. It contained not only a changing room but a plumbed-in lavatory. 'Drove down to the beach with my maids and went into the bathing machine, where I undressed and bathed in the sea (for the first time in my life), a very nice bathing woman attending me. I thought it delightful till I put my head under the water, when I thought I should be stifled.' After Victoria's death, the bathing machine had the ignominy of being used as a chicken shed. Like so many people since the mid-1760s, Prince Albert believed in the curative effects of sea-bathing, had the children taught to swim and took a daily dip with the boys.

Her purchase of Osborne House inspired the Queen to try her hand as a watercolourist. She took lessons from W. L. Leitch, who left some moderately accomplished paintings of the garden and one of the house under construction, and it is tempting to describe his pupil's work as more advanced; a painting of the six eldest children in the garden is charming, and the Queen's handling of foliage in what was called the valley footpath, with the pavilion in the background, is very accomplished. There was a good deal of genuine talent in the family; a pen drawing by Prince Albert of Vicky and Bertie playing at Windsor in 1843 would have served very well as a book illustration. Alfred painted with a sure touch at thirteen, only outshone by his sister Louise, whose talent for drawing and painting was established by the age of three. She became an honorary fellow of the Royal Society of Painters and Etchers. Not too much credence should be given to the royal family's acting abilities on the evidence alone of their passion for putting on *tableaux vivants*; what appealed to them mainly was the opportunity to dress outrageously and pretend to be someone else. When it actually came to acting – and a performance of *She Stoops to*

Conquer was put on at Osborne in 1893 – it was said of Princess Louise that she could act but could not learn her lines (she took the part of Miss Hardcastle), whereas Princess Beatrice (Constantina Neville) could learn her lines but could not act. In case anything too unprofessional occurred, it was arranged that a row of obliging footmen should start applauding to cover the hiatus caused by a premature entrance or a case of drying up. The Queen thought one performance 'not quite so successful as it might have been owing to the ladies getting the giggles and shaking'. But Princess Helena 'played the piano exquisitely', and it was generally acknowledged that Princess Alice could have earned her living in the decorative arts 'by making designs for wallpapers, chintzes etc'. She drew 'unerringly, never rubbing out or correcting a single line'.

Billiard room, Osborne House.

It was only with the greatest difficulty that Victoria tore herself away from Osborne in 1848, spending 123 days watching over building and planting. Eventually, a fairly regular pattern of visits was established: early spring, early summer, part of July and August and late autumn, leaving for Windsor in time for Christmas. Wherever she was living the Queen liked, whenever possible, to breakfast out of doors, and as Osborne had no breakfast room even moderately fine weather would find her out of doors from first thing in the morning. Until the death of the Prince Consort she invariably celebrated her birthday, on 24 May, at Osborne. At 7 a.m. a band would strike up on the terrace. The Queen would give Albert one or two presents, as she had always distributed gifts on her birthday as a girl, and the children all greeted her carrying nosegays. Her own presents would be displayed on a table in a room elaborately decorated with flowers. The Prince also celebrated his birthday without fail at Osborne, on 26 August, when the estate workers would be treated to an outdoor fête and dinner in a marquee. After dinner on the Queen's birthday there was often a dance in the Council room but oddly enough Princess Helena's third birthday, in 1849, in which she could surely have taken very little conscious part, ended with the entire family prancing about in the drawing room with the Duchess of Kent strumming on the piano.

8

'No Pudding and no Fun'

Queen Victoria's discovery of Balmoral Castle, on the upper Dee in Aberdeenshire, and her purchase of the estate and rebuilding of the house shadow her purchase and rebuilding of Osborne. She paid her first visit to her Scottish kingdom in 1842, when she and Prince Albert sailed from Woolwich to Edinburgh, the 'extreme beauty' of which, she told Lord Melbourne on 10 September, writing from Drummond Castle, the home of Lord Willoughby de Eresby, they greatly admired. Indeed, she thought the situation of Edinburgh 'as well as the town' most striking, 'and the Prince, who has seen so much, says it is the finest town he ever saw'. Lord Willoughby's barony dated from 1313, but his castle she dismissed as 'quite a cottage'. During this visit they stayed also at Taymouth Castle in Perthshire as the guests of the Marquess of Breadalbane, both the Queen and the Prince falling in love with the countryside and the country people, 'marked by that honesty and sympathy which always distinguish the inhabitants of mountainous countries', Albert wrote to his grandmother. This first visit concluded at Dalkeith Palace in Midlothian, to stay a night with a major Scottish landowner, the Duke of Buccleuch and Queensberry. Victoria was following in the footsteps of George IV, who had been entertained by the Duke in August 1822 when his young host was only sixteen, the King installing his own staff in the palace kitchens.

It may seem odd that the Queen did not further follow in her uncle's footsteps by staying in Edinburgh, at the Palace of Holyroodhouse, where in 1822 2,000 enthusiastic Scottish subjects had been presented to him at a levée. But it had been little used since then and may not have been in a fit state to receive the Queen and Prince Albert. There were also rumours of scarlet fever at Holyrood. The Queen made intermittent use of the palace later in her reign, realizing its historical importance. 'On the 28th [of August 1857] we slept in sombre Holyrood and on the 29th in dear Balmoral,' Albert wrote to his brother. King David I had established an Augustinian abbey on the site in 1128, dedicated to the Holy Rood – the Holy Cross – because he had presented the community with a reliquary allegedly containing a fragment of the cross on which Christ was crucified. It was at Holyrood Palace, as the house begun beside the abbey by James IV was at that time known, that in 1566 the secretary of Mary, Queen of Scots, David Rizzio, was dragged from supper with the Queen and murdered by her second husband, the Earl of Darnley. When he was twelve years old, Queen Mary's son, James VI of Scotland and from 1603 James I of England, took up residence at the palace and spent more time at Holyrood than any other monarch before or since. A somewhat dubious claimant to the kingdom, the Young Pretender, had the nerve to hold court at Holyrood in 1745, giving a state ball, touching for the king's evil and living in rooms normally occupied by the Hereditary Keeper of Holyroodhouse, the Duke of Hamilton and Brandon. When Victoria occupied the palace as a staging post to Balmoral she made use of the West Drawing Room, in which Prince Albert was painted studiously studying some document or other. In the 1850s she opened the royal apartments to the public.

In the early autumn of 1844 the Queen and Prince Albert were back in Perthshire, staying at Blair Castle with Lord Glenlyon, shortly to succeed his uncle as Duke of Atholl, when somewhat controversially they attended the local kirk instead of the Episcopal church. But by this time they had been carried away by everything of native Scottish origin, bagpipes and all. 'I can only say that the scenery is lovely,' the Queen wrote in her journal, 'grand, romantic, and a great peace and wilderness pervades all, which is sublime.' They were taken hill-climbing by one of Lord Glenlyon's servants in Highland dress. 'Here we were,' Victoria wrote, 'with only this Highlander behind us holding the ponies, not a house, not a creature near us, but the pretty Highland sheep with their horns and black faces.' Back at Windsor in October she was instantly pining for 'the hills, the pure air, the quiet, the retirement, the liberty', she told King Leopold.

Impatient to continue her search for *Gemütlichkeit* (cosiness) in Scotland as well as on the Isle of Wight, the Queen had to wait an agonizing three years before another obliging host, the Marquess of Aberdeen (in 1852 he became Prime Minister), placed a fishing lodge at Ardverikie on the shore of Loch Laggan in Invernesshire at her disposal. It poured with rain but nothing could now dampen the Queen's determination to find a northern hideaway of her own, an ambition in which she was encouraged by her physician-in-ordinary, Sir James Clark, himself a Scot and the author of works recommending pure fresh air as a cure for 'chronic diseases', especially 'pulmonary consumption'. Sir James knew the eminent diplomatist Sir Robert Gordon, who had a lease on a 'pretty little castle in the old Scotch style', as the Queen described Balmoral Castle, not far from Ardverikie, when she first clapped eyes on it. At breakfast on 8 October 1847 Sir Robert obligingly dropped dead. Sight unseen, the Queen purchased the remainder of his lease, paying her first visit to her new property the following year.

The 'pretty little castle' contained 'a nice little hall', a billiard room and a dining room. 'A good broad staircase' led to a sitting room above the dining room, 'a fine large room opening into our bedroom etc'. Perhaps on reflection it was a little too cosy; after all, members of the Privy Council – as at Osborne – would be expected to attend, staff would need accommodation, by 1848 there were half a dozen children, and ladies-in-waiting would need sitting rooms. It was not long before the builders were called in. Meanwhile, a summons was sent out for a Council to be held at Balmoral at 2.30 p.m. on 5 September. Its purpose: to 'order a Prayer for relief against the colora'. But for once Charles Greville seems to have enjoyed a trek of considerable proportions to achieve perhaps five minutes' work.

He left London by train at 5 p.m., dined at Birmingham, and went on by mail train to Crewe, where he spent the night. After breakfasting at Crewe Hall, he continued by express train to Perth, arriving at half-past twelve in the morning. Leaving Perth six hours later, he arrived at Balmoral at exactly half-past two. He thought the road from Perth to Balmoral beautiful, and much though he disliked 'Courts and all that appertains to them' he had to admit he was glad to have made this expedition, 'and to have seen the Queen and Prince in their Highland retreat, where they certainly appear to great advantage'. The place was very pretty, the house very small, and 'They live there without any state whatever; they live not merely like private gentlefolks, but like very small gentle-folks, small house, small rooms, small establishment'. There were no guards, he noted, just a single policeman 'who walks about the grounds to keep off impertinent intruders or improper characters'.

Greville had been invited to stay for a couple of nights, and reported the routine: every morning the Prince went shooting (he was not a good shot), and after lunch he and the Queen walked or rode. 'The Queen,' he noticed, 'is running in and out of the house all day long, and often goes about alone, walks into the cottages, and sits down and chats with the old women.' After breakfast on the Thursday morning Prince Albert joined Greville and the Prime Minister, John Russell, for a chat, and Greville was very much struck by his intelligence and cultivated mind, his 'gay, pleasant' demeanour and total lack of 'stiffness or air of dignity'. After luncheon the house party repaired to the Highland gathering at Braemar, Bertie and Affie in Highland dress, which they now wore all the time. There were only nine people at dinner 'and it was all very easy and really agreeable, the Queen in very good humour and talkative'. The Queen had travelled a long way, in more ways than one, since her stilted conversation about ponies with Charles Greville at Buckingham Palace. After dinner the Queen and Prince Albert were given a private lesson in the Highland reel in the dining room while Greville and Lord John made shift in the billiard room, which was serving as library and drawing room as well.

Such intimacy was not to last, much though the Queen enjoyed the idea of being able to talk to people on a pony trek who had no idea who she was; one old lady offered her some bread and milk. There were salmon to be speared or netted (on one fishing expedition there was 'a horrid moment' when a man who could not swim very nearly drowned) and a bothy – originally an outbuilding on a farm or a hut to provide shelter for mountaineers – called Shiel of Allt-Na-Giuthasach in which to stop off 'after a long hill expedition to the Lake of Loch Nagar. It was,' the Queen wrote to King Leopold on 30 September 1851, 'one of the wildest spots imaginable . . . We are not snowed, but rained up.' But she said: 'Our little Shiel [an alternative name for a bothy] is very snug and comfortable and we have got a little piano in it.'

'I love my peaceful, wild Highlands,' the Queen told her uncle a week later, 'the glorious scenery, the dear good people who are much attached to us . . . One of our Gillies, a young Highlander who generally went out with me, said, in answer to my observation that they must be very dull here when we left: "It's just like death comes all at once."'

On 24 August 1848 Albert wrote to his brother to say:

We are impatiently awaiting the end of the tedious Parliamentary session to go to Balmoral for a fortnight. Balmoral is a castle which I have bought in Scotland. It has 10,000 acres of forest. I bought the lease from Lord Aberdeen for twenty-seven years, for £2,000. It belonged to his brother, Lord Robert Gordon, who had just built the castle and entered it shortly before he died. It is said to be situated in the healthiest place in the Highlands.

In 1852, for £31,500, the Queen purchased the Balmoral freehold together with 17,400 acres, and then she acquired the adjacent Birkhall estate of 6,000 acres.[1] Although he was still only eleven, the Queen purchased Birkhall for Bertie, but as the Prince of Wales did not much care for Scotland, one of many black marks against him, he returned it to his mother in 1885. All this expenditure was made possible because 1852 was the year that saw the death of an eccentric old miser (he was probably about seventy), who lived in squalor in Chelsea. His name was John Nield, and he left some £250,000, for some unknown reason bequeathing most of his fortune to the Queen. She did all the proper things, donating a sum to his parish church and increasing the legacies to his executors, and then gave Albert carte blanche to rebuild Balmoral, which was in fact hopelessly cramped.

The result – as with Osborne House – was not to everyone's taste. It was on 28 September 1853 that the Queen had laid the foundation stone of the new house. Just two years later, on 7 September 1855, she arrived at 'dear Balmoral' to find Albert's handiwork looking 'beautiful', although many of the rooms were only half finished 'and the offices are still unbuilt'. As the Queen entered the hall, 'an old shoe was thrown after us into the house, for good luck'. She thought the part of the house that was habitable 'charming: the rooms delightful; the furniture, papers everything perfection'. By 30 August 1856, 'On arriving at Balmoral at seven o'clock this evening we found the tower finished as well as the offices, and the poor old house gone! The effect of the whole is very fine!' Everything had been her 'dearest Albert's own creation, own work, own building, own laying out, as at Osborne; and his great taste, and the impress of his dear hand, have been stamped everywhere'.

Lady Augusta Bruce, lady-in-waiting to the Duchess of Kent, thought Balmoral had 'a certain absence of harmony of the whole'. Which was not surprising: Albert had been influenced not only by Scottish baronial but by what one might call Germanic fairy tale. Built of grey Invergelder granite, the house ended up 'multi-turreted with castellated gables, a *porte-cochère* and a 100-ft tower'.[2] Albert and his Aberdeen architect William Smith had constructed sixty-seven fireplaces and installed central heating, four bathrooms and fourteen water closets. The Queen had what she called a 'little room' in a turret from which she could gaze across to Loch-na-Gar. But she did not neglect to have created as well a Grand Corridor, for once again Balmoral was to display two sides of Victoria's nature, her desire for both domesticity and regal splendour. A suite for ministers in attendance had its own entrance hall.

Balm

tle.

The largest room, sixty-eight by twenty-five feet, was the ball-room. As for the décor, the place was draped in tartan, so much so that one of the Queen's granddaughters thought the place 'more patriotic than artistic', Albert having designed his own Balmoral tartan of black, red and lavender on a grey background.

The princes were segregated, with their tutors, on the north side of the house, the princesses on the south side. And there was now a state drawing room, a proper library and a separate billiard room. Despite the provision of central heating and so many fireplaces, guests and household froze, for the Queen went round flinging the windows open. Possibly with some slight exaggeration, the Earl of Clarendon, who said the Queen was quite a different person in Scotland (perhaps he caught her putting on a Scottish accent, which she did from time to time), claimed that at dinner his toes became frostbitten. The Tsar of Russia, Nicholas II, thought Balmoral colder even than Siberia, and any number of guests said they only ever felt warm when in bed. The Marchioness of Dalhousie thought she 'never saw anything more uncomfortable' than Balmoral, a complaint frequently echoed by government ministers. Disraeli objected to trying to carry on the government of the country 'six hundred miles from the Metropolis', while another of Victoria's Prime Ministers, the Marquess of Salisbury, declared he was always 'heartily glad' to leave the place. Both Salisbury and Disraeli were obliged to produce medical evidence of their need for a reasonable level of warmth before orders were given for their rooms to be properly heated. One of the Queen's private secretaries, Sir Henry Ponsonby, never again found fault with any private house 'after the severe dreariness' of the accommodation provided at Balmoral. One of the Queen's ladies, the Countess of Lytton, discovered, to her amazement, four laundry maids sharing one bed. Perhaps they were just trying to keep warm.

It was at Balmoral that the Queen mingled most freely with her outdoor staff. On 28 September 1855 she recorded: 'I and the girls were all in Stuart satin dresses, with Royal Stuart scarves . . . after dinner we went to the Iron Ballroom where there was a Gillies Dance. All our children there. Three officers with the detachment of the 93rd Highlanders stationed at Ballater, and 18 of the men who had been in the Crimea, came. It was very gay and our children each danced two or three times.' And it was at Balmoral that the Queen really did make contact with 'ordinary' people in a way she had never done before or, apart from contact with her servants, was she ever to do elsewhere. (Mary Ponsonby thought both the Queen and Prince Albert more at ease with their servants than their guests.) The Queen's journal entry for 26 September 1857 would be easy to dismiss as an account of Lady Bountiful in action were it not for her evident sincerity:

Albert went out with Alfred for the day, and I walked out with the two girls [Vicky and Alice] and Lady Churchill, stopped at the shop and made some purchases for poor people and others; drove a little way, got out and walked up the hill to Balnacroft, Mrs P. Farquharson's, and she walked round with us to some of the cottages to show me where the poor people lived, and to tell them who I was. Before we went into any we met an old woman who, Mrs Farquharson said, was very poor, eighty-eight years old, and mother to the former distiller. I gave her a warm petticoat, and the tears rolled down her old cheeks, and she shook my hands, and prayed God to bless me: it was very touching.

It had been a matter of courtesy on the Queen's part, not a way of attracting obeisance, to forewarn country folk that the Queen

Royal Sports – the Queen and Prince Consort with the Prince of Wales in the Highlands, 1853, by Sir Edwin Landseer RA.

was about to descend on them, but the countryside still remained so insulated that in September 1860 Prince Albert was able to arrange a jaunt in which he and the Queen were to travel incognito, as 'Lord and Lady Churchill and party'. Jane Churchill, who died only the year before the Queen and was one of her favourite ladies-in-waiting (she was in the Queen's carriage in 1872 during an assassination attempt), pretended to be Miss Spencer, and Lieutenant General Charles Grey, who had succeeded George Anson as private secretary to the Prince, became Dr Grey (General Grey wrote *The Early Years of the Prince Consort*). They took only two servants, the head keeper John Grant and the Prince's most trusted gillie, John Brown. Having breakfasted at 7.30 a.m. they left Balmoral shortly after 8 a.m., looking as inconspicuous as they could by travelling in a vehicle called a sociable. The Balmoral police inspector had been sent ahead 'to order everything in a quiet way, without letting people suspect who we were; in this he entirely succeeded'. They crossed Loch Inch by ferry, 'a very rude affair' in which they were obliged to stand, Grant and Brown assisting with the oars. They were met by 'two shabby vehicles, one a kind of barouche, into which Albert and I got, Lady Churchill and General Grey into the other – a break'. Each vehicle had 'a pair of small and rather miserable horses, driven by a man from the box'. Grant accompanied 'Lord and Lady Churchill' while Brown got up behind the real Lady Churchill and the General. There were two uncomfortable moments when Brown forgot the subterfuge and out of habit addressed the Queen as 'Your Majesty', Grant in turn addressing the Prince as 'Your Royal Highness', 'which set us all laughing, but no one observed it'.

They were certainly determined – up to a point – to see how the other half lived, making for an inn in 'a long and straggling toun'- Grantown, in fact – the Queen slipping into her newly acquired Gaelic brogue. They were shown to a bedroom, which was 'very small – but clean – with a large four-post bed which nearly filled the whole room'. It transpired, however, that they had taken the precaution of booking a private sitting room-cum-dining room (as would any nineteenth-century peer and his wife, if they could), a dressing room for Albert, and of having two maids driven over from Balmoral by another route in a waggonette. Grant and Brown were supposed to wait at dinner, but by the time the meal was ready to be served they were drunk and incapable, so 'a ringletted woman did everything; and, when dinner was over, removed the cloth and placed the bottle of wine (our own which we had brought [a wise precaution; the inn probably served only spirits, but one bottle between four does not sound very festive]) on the table with the glasses, which was the old English fashion'. The Queen reckoned that the dinner was 'very fair, and all very clean'. They began with a mutton broth which 'I did not much relish'. There followed 'fowl with white sauce, good roast lamb, very good potatoes, besides one or two other dishes, which I did not taste, ending with a good tarte of cranberries'. After dinner, while the Prince played patience, the Queen tried to write up her account of the day while it was fresh in her mind, 'but the talking round me confused me'. It was 11.30 p.m. before they fell into bed.

'What a delightful, successful expedition!' the Queen enthused next day. She wrote in her journal that 'Dear Lady Churchill was, as usual, thoroughly amiable, cheerful, and ready to do everything. Both she and the General seemed entirely to enjoy it, and enter into it, and so I am sure did our people' – by whom she meant her tipsy gillies. But 'the secret came out through a man recognizing Albert in the street'. No doubt some other alert passer-by had spotted without too much difficulty the royal crown they had omitted to camouflage on the dogcart. A woman observed, '"The lady must be terrible rich" as I had so many gold rings on my fingers! – I told Lady Churchill she had on many more than I had.' Rather a case of lese-majesty surely? Apparently, when it was revealed who the 'terrible rich' lady really was, 'they were ready to drop with astonishment and fright'. One does wonder why 'Lord Churchill's' German accent did not cause raised eyebrows from the start.

A year later they were at it again, this time accompanied by Princess Alice and her future husband, Prince Louis, in addition to Lady Churchill and General Grey. Travelling in two sociables their destination was the Ramsay Arms in 'the small quiet town, or rather village, of Fettercairn'. Here they were provided with another small bedroom but separate dining and drawing rooms. Although the bedroom was 'excessively small', the Queen thought it was much better furnished than the one at Grantown. Prince Louis and General Grey were lodged in a temperance hotel opposite. At eight o'clock they dined on 'a very nice, clean, good dinner', this time Grant and Brown remaining sober enough to wait. 'They were rather nervous, but General Grey and Lady Churchill carved, and they only had to change the plates, which Brown soon got into the way of doing. A little girl of the house came in to help – but Grant turned her round to prevent her looking at us! The landlord and landlady knew who we were, but no one else except the coachman, and they kept the secret admirably.'

A supposedly incognito visit to an inn at Dalwhinnie could not be counted a success. The Queen was recognized by one of the maids, who had seen her in Aberdeen and Edinburgh. The inn was larger than the others had been, Lady Churchill having her own maid with her and the Queen one of her wardrobe maids, Mary Andrews, whose father, Charles Andrews, had been in the service of King Leopold. 'But unfortunately there was hardly anything to eat, and there was only tea, and two miserable starved

Highland chickens, without any potatoes! No pudding,' the Queen snorted, 'and no fun . . . It was not a nice supper.'

This 'mountain expedition' lasted seven days, and things could only get better. 'We have had a most beautiful week,' the Queen wrote to King Leopold, 'which we have thoroughly enjoyed – I going out every day about twelve or half-past, taking luncheon with us, carried in a basket on the back of a Highlander, and served by an invaluable Highland servant I have.' She was referring to John Brown. He was, she explained to her uncle, 'my factotum here, and takes the most wonderful care of me, combining the offices of groom, footman, page, and maid, I might almost say, as he is so handy about cloaks and shawls, etc. He always leads my pony, and always attends me out of doors, and such a good, handy, faithful, attached servant I have nowhere; it is quite a sorrow for me to leave him behind.'

John Brown.

138

9

Poor Bertie

Although Queen Victoria gave birth to nine live children, all of whom survived into adulthood, she had little patience with children unless they both looked and behaved well, and entertained very ambivalent feelings about her own considerable brood. And the older they grew the more ambivalent her feelings became. She positively detested babies, most probably never having seen one before she gave birth to her own first child, Princess Victoria, on 21 November 1840, to whom she wrote eighteen years later to confess that she felt like a cow or a dog when pregnant. Indeed, the whole concept of pregnancy revolted the Queen. 'I positively think those ladies who are always *enceinte* quite disgusting; it is more like a rabbit or guinea-pig than anything else and really it is not very nice,' she informed Vicky, by that time Princess Frederick William of Prussia, on 15 June 1859. As an only child, the Queen would never have shared a bath night with brothers or sisters, and although she had two cousins exactly the same age as herself, Prince George of Cumberland and Prince George of Cambridge, Victoria's was not exactly the sort of family who stayed the weekend with relatives and whose babies romped together.

'Abstractedly,' the Queen told her daughter, she had no *tendre* for babies 'till they have become a little human; an ugly baby is a very nasty object – and the prettiest is frightful when undressed – till about four months; in short as long as they have their big body and little limbs and that terrible frog-like action.' The Queen had an aversion to frogs at the best of times, one rainy morning encountering 'an immense number of little frogs' at Frogmore, of all places, 'hardly bigger than a bluebottle fly, hopping and crawling all over the grass and paths . . . quite disgusting'.

Even for mid-nineteenth-century royalty the hazards of childbirth and childhood were considerable, and Victoria, living to such a great age as she did, was fortunate not to lose any of her children until fairly late in life. She was fifty-nine when her second daughter, Princess Alice, born on 25 April 1843, succumbed to diphtheria at the age of thirty-five. The death of Prince Leopold in 1884 at the age of thirty-one, when the Queen was sixty-five, could not have been unexpected; he had haemophilia, a hereditary bleeding disease from which, more famously, the only son of Tsar Nicholas II of Russia suffered. Women are merely carriers and do not themselves endure the consequences. Why Queen Victoria was a carrier is a mystery, and at least she passed the disease to only one of her sons, but two of her daughters, Princess Alice and Princess Beatrice, became carriers. And the Queen was an old lady of eighty-one when her second son, Prince Alfred, who had inherited the dukedom of Coburg, died at the age of fifty-six.

Judging by a letter Victoria wrote to King Leopold of the Belgians on 5 January 1841, Victoria initially never intended having so many children:

I think, dearest Uncle, you cannot really wish me to be the 'Mamma d'une *nombreuse* famille', for I think you will see with me the great inconvenience a large family would be to us all, and particularly to the country, independent of the hardship and inconvenience to myself; men never think, at least seldom think, what a hard task it is for us women to go through this very often. God's will be done, and if He decrees that we are to have a great number of children, why we must try to bring them up as useful and exemplary members of society.

So far the Queen had experienced only one birth, but it is true it was a difficult one; Vicky was born three weeks premature, and the Queen's labour, which was very painful, lasted twelve hours. Albert was present, surely an unusual occurrence at the time. Just as unusual, it seems that Privy Councillors were dispensed with; apart from Albert, only a doctor, Charles Locock, and a midwife were present. Told by the doctor that she had given birth to a princess, the Queen replied: 'Never mind, the next will be a prince.'

So it seems equally clear that the Queen had no plans to draw the line at just one child, whatever the 'great inconvenience' the birth of others might entail. It would in any case have been natural for her to hope for a male heir; she never felt comfortable in her role as queen regnant, and finding a suitable bride for an heir apparent would be far easier than searching Europe for an eligible prince to marry the Princess Royal were Vicky to remain the heiress presumptive.[1] The great drawback all her daughters would have, she told Vicky in 1858, was being exiled from their native land (she had not foreseen the possibility of Louise breaking with protocol by marrying a Scottish peer), but 'one great advantage however you all have over me, and that is that you are not in the anomalous position in which I am – as Queen Regnant. Though dear Papa, God knows, does everything – it is a reversal of the right order of things which distresses me much.' As far as the country was concerned, Victoria did not need reminding what a drain on public funds her 'singular' uncles had been, and how unpopular their constant sponging off Parliament had made the whole institution of monarchy. In the event, Victoria gave birth to four sons; the state would expect to provide for the Prince of Wales, Leopold was too ill to fend for himself other than by assisting with his mother's secretarial work, and the other two proved perfectly capable of taking up successful careers in the navy and the army, Arthur, Duke of Connaught, becoming a field marshal.

As for the Queen's reference in her letter to King Leopold to God's will, this was either the language of a Roman Catholic (which most decidedly the Queen was not, a Roman Catholic being forbidden to practise any form of birth control) or of a woman who knew nothing about contraception, which few Victorian women did, and truly believed that God alone was responsible for human fertilization. Of all the possible reasons for Victoria's large family, a good deal larger than the average middle-class Victorian family, the only one that stands up to scrutiny is her ignorance, and Albert's too, of contraception, including abstinence at a time of ovulation. Had she not wished to sleep with her husband the whole of her married life, she would not have done so; and Albert would never have forced himself on her. On the contrary, knowing quite well what the consequences of sleeping with Albert were likely to be, she blithely went on from the birth of an heir apparent in 1841 to provide the throne with another seven potential sovereigns, producing children at an average rate of approximately one every twenty-one months. She gave birth to her last child, Princess Beatrice, in 1857, when she was thirty-eight. This was quite an achievement for a woman whose first seven confinements were extremely painful, who could not bear the sight of a baby, 'particularly not in their baths till they are past 3 or 4 months', and who found fault with most of her own children to an obsessive degree.

But as four and a half years were to elapse between the birth of Beatrice and the death of Prince Albert, and the Queen, although she looked much older than her years, was still a young woman and almost certainly still capable of bearing children, it is a reasonable assumption that she and Albert decided to call it a day in 1857; or that they at last devised some reliable method of birth control. Sir James Clark is reputed to have advised the Queen not to have any more children following the birth of Beatrice, and if he did (and it would have taken some courage even for a medical practitioner to advise Queen Victoria on such a personal matter), his grounds, kept to himself, were more likely to have been emotional rather than physical, for the Queen did fear that the strains of childbirth might bring on an attack of the family malady, porphyria. But her alleged rejoinder – 'Oh, Sir James, can I have no more fun in bed?' – can be dismissed as nonsense. It was not her style to speak so indelicately.[2] However, it may have been because of the absence of any more announcements of royal births after that of Princess Beatrice that stories began to circulate about the mental health of the Queen. In the year of his death, 1861, Prince Albert was writing to his brother in Coburg to say: 'Victoria is very well and I cannot understand how these horrid, vile rumours about her mental state could arise. People here and on the Continent are much occupied with these rumours. They have annoyed me tremendously as I know what the consequences may be. She herself is perfectly unaware of all this scandal.'

The Queen's first Christmas as a mother was spent at Windsor Castle, decorated with Christmas trees, a German custom first imported by George III's wife, Queen Charlotte. 'I go skating every day on the pond at Frogmore,' Prince Albert told his brother, and a very comical print was published depicting Albert wearing the Garter star while propelling the Queen across the ice in a luxuriously padded sleigh; she wears a bonnet, and a fur coat and muffler to match, with a rug over her knees made out of the skin of some unfortunate animal, possibly meant to be a tiger but looking more like a large, contented pussycat, its head and legs stretched out in front of the Queen. Albert is in the pose of a very camp ballet dancer, and beneath a storm-stricken tree stand a pair of footmen.

Victoria's recovery from Vicky's birth had been remarkably swift, considering its difficulty. 'Victoria is well and happy,' Prince Albert scribbled to his brother. 'It is hardly to be believed that only a few hours ago she lay in dreadful pain.' By 24 November, writing from Buckingham Palace, Albert told Prince Ernest: 'V has not suffered the least since her confinement and feels as well as if nothing had happened. The little daughter is considered beautiful by all the ladies and she really is pretty . . . You can imagine that I have my hands very full, as I also look after all V's political affairs. I should have preferred a boy, yet as it is, I thank Heaven.' Already, on 16 July 1840, the Prince's authority had been immeasurably strengthened by the passing of a Regency Bill, opposed only by the Queen's uncle, the Duke of Sussex, who was to die three years later. 'In case of Victoria's death and her successor being under eighteen years of age, I am to be Regent – *alone* – Regent, without a Council', Albert trumpeted to his brother in Coburg. 'You will understand the significance of this matter and that it gives my position here in the country a fresh importance.'

The Queen had managed to do one or two other things for Prince Albert off her own bat. He had received the Garter on 16 December 1839. By royal warrant dated 8 February 1840 he was granted the style Royal Highness, and again by royal warrant, dated 4 March the same year, he was granted precedence immediately after the Queen. On 11 September 1840 he was made a Privy

Councillor. That year he was gazetted a field marshal, and in case he felt a bit exposed on the parade ground, in addition to the Garter the Queen invested him, on 6 March 1840, as a Knight Grand Cross of the Order of the Bath. On 15 January 1842 he became a Knight Grand Cross of the Order of St Michael and St George, and two days later Victoria invested him as a Royal Knight of the Most Ancient and Most Noble Order of the Thistle.

The Queen had a fixation about dates, and expected everyone else to observe and acknowledge those significant dates by which each succeeding year seemed to follow its sacred course. When the thirteen-year-old Prince Alfred, who happened to be at sea, forgot his parents' eighteenth wedding anniversary he received a rap over the knuckles by telegram. So it is no surprise that Vicky was baptized, at Buckingham Palace, on 10 February 1841, 'our dear marriage-day'.

The birth of an heir apparent had been announced by Albert from Buckingham Palace on 9 November 1841. 'You have become an Uncle again,' he wrote to his brother, 'and this time it is a nephew. Victoria was confined at 10.45 o'clock. Mother and son are well. I am over-tired and have no end of letters to write, therefore I must close.' Bertie's birth came as a godsend to the people of Windsor; everyone got 4 pounds of beef, 2 pounds of bread, a pound of plum pudding, a peck of potatoes, 2 pints of ale and a sack of coal. The boys of Derby Grammar School, together with those of Harrow, Winchester and Rugby, got an extended holiday. But there had been a great brouhaha over the choice of godparents for the first prince born heir to the throne since 1762. 'Papa [the Duke of Saxe-Coburg and Gotha] is annoyed about the arrangement for the Christening,' Albert reported to his brother from Windsor Castle on 16 December, 'and has reproached me very seriously, because the child is not to be called Ernst and because neither he nor you are to be godfathers. The godfathers are the King of Prussia, The Duke of Cambridge and Uncle Ferdinand [Prince Ferdinand of Saxe-Coburg, later King of Portugal]. The godmothers are Princess Sophie [Victoria's aunt], Grandmamma and Mamma. The little one is to be called Albert Edward. Papa is very angry on account of the choice of the King of Prussia.' To help cool tempers, the Prince sent his brother as a Christmas present 'Two silver vessels . . . to be used as Champagne coolers. You must put ice in them,' he explained, 'and lay the Champagne bottles on the ice. Here in England it is the custom to place them at the corners of the table, as you will remember.'

The choice of the King of Prussia as a godfather to Bertie served to introduce into the family circle a fellow sovereign with whom Victoria could communicate on equal terms, and the ultimate outcome was marriage between the King's nephew and the Princess Royal. 'Sire, my most honoured Brother' was the flourish with which Victoria opened her correspondence with the King, from Windsor Castle on 12 December 1841.

These few words which I am venturing to write to you in German are only intended to repeat and to confirm what Albert has already conveyed to you, and to assure you how delighted I should be at this opportunity of making the personal acquaintance of Your Majesty and of the Queen.

In true friendship, Your Majesty's sincerely devoted Sister, Victoria R

The King and Queen duly arrived, and a guest at dinner, Baroness Bunsen, observed Victoria 'laughing heartily (no *company* laugh) at things which [the King of Prussia] said to entertain her'. At a cost of £530 18s. the Queen gave him the Garter.

As it transpired, Albert's father had not long to live, and when, on 3 February 1844, letters arrived at Windsor Castle from the French royal family breaking the news that he had died, both Albert and Victoria went into contortions of exaggerated grief. 'How I should like to be with you and weep with you and see the beloved face once again, though it is cold!' Albert wrote to his brother. 'We are deeply bowed in grief,' he announced the following day. 'Our poor little children do not know why we cry and they ask us why we are in black.' His German servants could not 'stop their tears'. The Duke, a great womanizer, had died on 29 January after a lifetime of dissipation, and his elder son was behaving no better. But on 6 February Victoria was telling her uncle Leopold: 'You must now be the father of us two poor bereaved heart-broken children. To describe to you all that we have suffered, all that we do suffer, would be difficult. God has heavily afflicted us. We feel crushed, overwhelmed, bowed down by the loss of one who was so deservedly loved, I may say adored, by his children and family. I loved him and looked on him as my own father.' Victoria scarcely knew her disreputable father-in-law, and hers was not a very tactful comment to make to King Leopold, who was himself supposed to be the Queen's surrogate father. That makes a collection of three father-figures if one includes Lord Melbourne. It also marked the commencement of a life devoted to an almost psychotic identification with death.

The seeds of a hopelessly unsuitable education for Bertie can be seen already germinating in a letter Victoria wrote to King Leopold shortly after her first son's birth: 'You will understand how fervent my prayers and I am [sure] everybody's must be, to see him resemble his angelic dearest Father in every, every respect.' Unfortunately, by 20 September 1842 King Leopold was told 'The Baby' (Bertie) was 'sadly backward', whereas by the age of two, if her mother can be believed, Vicky spoke French. On 6 June 1843 the Queen was writing very amusingly to King Leopold about the christening of Princess Alice. Rather surprisingly she had invited the former Duke of Cumberland to be a godfather. 'The King of Hanover arrived just in time to be too late. He is grown very old and excessively thin, and bends a good deal. He is very gracious, for him. Pussy [Princess Victoria] and Bertie (as we call the boy) were not at all afraid of him, fortunately; they appeared after the *déjeuner* on Friday, and I wish you could have seen them; they behaved so beautifully before that great number of people, and I must say looked very dear, all in white, and very *distingués*: they were much admired.'

On 25 April Albert had reported to his brother that at the birth of Alice, Victoria 'suffered much, but for only a short time'. Somewhat dismissively, he added: 'The little girl is said to be very pretty, so experts say. I am over-tired after a night without any rest or sleep and I have endless letters to write to all parts of the world.' In *his* account of the christening, Albert said that the King of Hanover actually arrived an hour after the banquet was over – in a hackney coach. And he informed his brother: 'The present expected for little Princess Alice should be some article of silver with a value of about £50.' The dotty old King of Hanover caused considerable chaos on 28 June that year when he attended the wedding of Princess Augusta, a granddaughter of George III and a cousin of the Queen, to the Duke of Mecklenburg-Strelitz, which took place at Buckingham Palace. 'It almost came to a fight with the King,' Albert told Prince Ernest:

He insisted on having the place at the altar, where we stood. He wanted to drive me away and, against all custom, he wanted to accompany Victoria and lead her. I was to go behind him. I was forced to give him a strong push and drive him down a few steps. We had a second scene, when he would not allow me to sign the register with Victoria. He laid his fist on the book. We manoeuvred round the table and Victoria had the book handed to her across the table. Now the table was between us and he could see what was being done. After a third trial to force Victoria to do what he commanded, but in vain, he left the party in great wrath. Since then, we let him go, and happily he fell over some stones in Kew and damaged some ribs.

When it came to the birth of Princess Louise, on 18 March 1848, the Queen again endured a painful labour, and things got a bit hectic at her christening too. The Queen's aunt, the Duchess of Gloucester, a daughter of George III, who was seventy-two and lived to be eighty-one, may have been showing mild symptoms of Alzheimer's disease, or perhaps of what was then called senile dementia. 'The poor Duchess of Gloster,' the Queen wrote to King Leopold on 16 May 1848 (the idiosyncratic spelling was her own), 'is again in one of her nervous states, and gave us a dreadful fright at the Christening by quite forgetting where she was, and coming and kneeling at my feet in the midst of the service. Imagine our horror!' When Victoria's eighth child and fourth son was born (on 7 April 1853) he was given the name Leopold in honour of his great-uncle. It was a name, the Queen told King Leopold, 'which is dearest to me after Albert, and one which recalls the almost only happy days of my sad childhood'.

At Buckingham Palace in the early spring of 1841 the Prince was reading to Victoria what he believed to be a masterpiece, Goethe's *Leiden des jungen Werthers*, although he admitted 'the beginning is dry'. Some of the Queen's reading sounds more dutiful than pleasurable. 'I have not read *Barchester Towers* all through,' she once wrote to Vicky after her marriage, 'but I am told it is not meant to be so ill-natured. But I don't like reading it aloud to Papa as there is not enough romance in it. The people I could not interest myself in.' But *The Mill on the Floss* 'I must say . . . made a deep impression upon me. The writing and description of feeling is wonderful and painful!' It would be interesting to know if George Eliot's *The Mill on the Floss* has been read by any member of the royal family since. *Middlemarch* the Queen thought fine but a disappointing book, for all the people were failures; *Jane Eyre* she considered 'a wonderful book though very peculiar in parts'. Her poet laureate Alfred Tennyson she admired extravagantly, approving a peerage for him in 1883.

The Queen's fourth child and second son, Alfred, nicknamed Affie, was born at Windsor Castle on 6 August 1844, again 'after much pain'. Victoria 'let us wait a long time and consequently the child is unusually large and strong', Albert told his brother. 'Both are very well. How sad poor Papa did not live to have this pleasure. I cannot write much as I have to trumpet this news to all parts of the world.' The reason for Albert's busy letter-writing on this occasion was because Alfred was regarded as heir presumptive to the dukedom of Saxe-Coburg and Gotha, Prince Ernest being childless, Prince Albert being tied to England and Bertie being presumed content with one day inheriting the English throne.

Writing from Buckingham Palace to his brother on 26 May 1846, Prince Albert announced: 'To-day I can send you the happy news of Victoria's confinement yesterday afternoon. Heaven gave us a third little daughter. She came into this world rather blue; but she is quite well now. Victoria suffered longer and more than the other times and she will have to remain very quiet to recover from all.' The heaven-sent third little daughter was Princess Helena, always called by her family Lenchen. She was joined in the nursery less than two years later by Princess Louise, whose artistic temperament was unfortunately aligned with a gift for passing caustic comments, causing the Queen to regard her as 'the most difficult' of her daughters. The independent streak in her nature propelled her into an unhappy marriage with a Liberal Member of Parliament, Lord Lorne, heir to the dukedom of Argyll, whose interest in women was not very noticeable and not many people were surprised that the marriage was childless, perhaps not even consummated.

When Prince Arthur, undoubtedly his mother's favourite child, was born, on 1 May 1850, he, too, 'was rather blue' but soon became 'nicely pink'. As he grew up the Queen waxed lyrical; she told his governor she had 'adored little Arthur from the day of his birth', and to Prince Albert she confided that Arthur was 'dearer than all the others put together'. She would not hear a word in his disfavour; it gave her a pang 'if any fault is found in his looks and character'. The idea that her third son should have been born on the birthday of Arthur Wellesley, Duke of Wellington, the most famous and universally revered man in her kingdom (always, of course, excepting Prince Albert), so appealed to the Queen that it was the reason she had him christened Arthur, and she invited the Duke to be a godfather. The health of Victoria's fourth son, the unfortunate Leopold, was a constant worry. When he was ten an epidemic of measles rampaged through the family. 'We were very anxious about Leopold,' Albert told his brother, 'but God protected him.'

Bertie's childhood was blighted by three factors over which he had no control: the existence of an exceptionally clever and lively elder sister, parents who lived in dread that he might follow the Hanoverian example of princes who went off the rails, and his constantly being compared by his mother with his father, whose

'First May 1851'. The Duke of Wellington presenting a birthday gift to his
godson, Prince Arthur. Painting by F.X. Winterhalter.

superhuman abilities and virtues no son could ever hope to emulate.
It was surprising that the future Edward VII did not have a nervous
breakdown or turn into a thoroughly unpleasant man. As it transpired, his own children, and in particular George V, worshipped
him. Victoria and Albert's high-flown ideals were not in themselves misconceived, but along with an overcrowded educational
programme they placed the three eldest boys, in particular Bertie,
in a straitjacket from which there was little chance of escaping into
normal boyhood and adolescence. When Alfred, for example, was
thirteen and was sent – an exciting adventure for any lad – on a
visit to his uncle, Prince Ernest, Albert wrote: 'In the small Palace,
I suppose it was not possible to lodge Alfred with his tutor. But
as a rule, I do not like it if he is not under his control.'

Bertie was constantly under the control of a tutor (his first was appointed when he was not yet eight) and an equerry, both in attendance during an informal visit to Germany in 1860. He was to pay a visit to Weimar, 'but only for lunch'. On his way to Coburg 'he might see the Meiningen family for a moment'. He was to be involved in 'no ceremonies whatever'. On the other hand, Prince Ernest was told, 'He likes to ride. He would also be very happy if he could shoot a mountain-cock, if one is to be had.' His parents had nothing against him going to the theatre on a Sunday '*but he must go to church in the morning*'. Shooting birds was to remain a major pleasure; his visits to churches, as Supreme Governor of the Church of England, were strictly on condition that the sermon lasted no longer than ten minutes.

Alfred, the most enquiring and gifted of the boys, learned to play the violin in secret in order to surprise his parents, and he presented another obstacle to Bertie; he was much more persistent in his aims, which appealed to their parents, whereas Bertie spent much of his time in a trance. It was quite obvious that it was Alfred of whom they approved, and as Prince Albert observed to his brother, there were 'only two eyes between him and the throne', the two eyes of the lackadaisical Bertie. It cannot have been much fun having parents who would cheerfully have swapped you for a younger brother, or who thought it prudent, in eighteenth-century fashion, to separate their children, Alfred being shunted off to the Royal Lodge in Windsor Great Park in 1855 while Bertie was condemned to stay at Osborne on his own (with a tutor in attendance, of course) while his parents sauntered off to Balmoral. Many of Albert's expressions regarding the children were whimsical and slightly off beam; Bertie was not to be permitted entry to the London season 'as long as he is neither fish nor flesh, as the old saying is'. Although Albert's favourite child was almost certainly

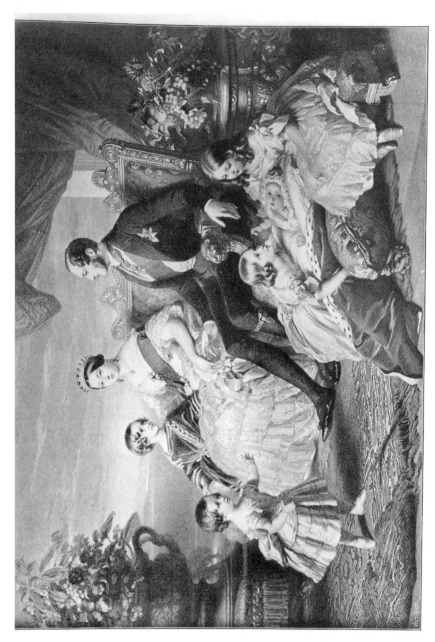

Royal Group, 1848, engraving from a painting by F.X. Winterhalter.

his eldest, there is no doubt he believed, as did the Queen, that they all inhabited a man's world, in which a woman's accomplishments should more or less be contained to child-bearing. Vicky 'really possesses extraordinary qualities for her age and sex' he let slip in a letter to his brother when the Princess Royal was seventeen.

Victoria's appreciation of her well-brought-up, well-groomed children was most apparent when they behaved with decorum at grand assemblies, got up theatrical performances or made a fuss of her on her birthday. 'We spent yesterday very happily,' the Queen wrote from Osborne to Princess Augusta of Prussia on 25 May 1852. 'My beloved husband was extremely affectionate to me and gave me the most beautiful presents . . . There was dancing in the evening and Helen [Helena, aged six] was allowed to join for the first time. You may well imagine how dignified she was! The dear children took the greatest pains to give me pleasure, Vicky in particular! I enclose this letter which she wrote to me, for you to read, as I think it is truly pretty, and she wrote it all by herself. Please return it to me!' It would have been rather astonishing had the Princess Royal not written a letter by herself; she was twelve.

While planning a visit to Coburg, Prince Albert reminded his brother that 'Victoria likes to dance, especially at small *thés dansant*. You might arrange some.' But Prince Ernest was warned that on a Sunday 'we would not go to a ball nor to the theatre'. There was also no need for him to 'arrange a chase', that is to say, a hunt, 'as Victoria does not like such pleasures and *I* prefer to stay with her'.

Music and paintings gave the Queen most pleasure, but the theatre ran a close third. From Windsor Castle she wrote to the King of Prussia to say she was attempting to 'revive and elevate the English drama' which had 'greatly deteriorated through lack of support by Society. We are having a number of classical plays in a small, specially constructed room which you occupied, the Rubens room,' she told the King, 'and I never enter it without the most vivid recollections of your dear visit, already seven years ago. May it soon be repeated!' The Queen often referred to the King's Drawing Room in the magnificent suite of state rooms built overlooking the North Terrace as the Rubens Room, for the good reason it was hung with fine examples of that painter's work. In 1853 she had the children 'acting Racine's *Athalie* (naturally abridged)', Victoria informed one of her royal correspondents, 'and I really must say that it was a great success . . . Vicky and Alice really acted excellently.'

Victoria was not in the least prudish about putting on plays during Lent. And in addition to the classics she enjoyed light-hearted entertainments organized by the household. A piece called *Caught at Last* included comic songs rendered by 'the Hon. A. Yorke.' Alick Yorke was something of a court jester, a fey dandy who overdid the use of the scent bottle and sported enormous buttonholes and rings. It was Alick Yorke, who ended up with a knighthood, who once, at Osborne, recounted a risqué joke which caused a good deal of laughter but which the Queen failed to catch. Unfortunately for Yorke, she asked him to repeat it; when he did so it was he who received the famous retort, 'We are not amused', but it is most unlikely, as many people imagine, that the Queen laid emphasis on the word 'we', using it rather as people say 'one' when they mean 'I'. 'We are *not* amused!' would have been her way of administering an only half-hearted rebuke. She was probably very amused indeed but did not care to admit it.

And yet there was a deadly serious side to the Queen's character, never more evident than in the training of her children in royal duty and obedience to God. Alice, for example, was confirmed at Windsor at the age of fifteen. 'The Archbishop [of Canterbury,

John Bird] will examine Alice privately,' Albert intoned to his brother, 'together with the Dean of Windsor (her teacher), before Victoria and me, in her room on Wednesday. On Thursday afternoon, when the other children have looked for their Easter eggs, the Confirmation will take place in the private chapel, and on Good Friday, in the morning, we shall all take Communion, before the church service, which will be in the afternoon.'

The children were not so much organized as regimented. They began in the nursery in Class I, moving up into Class II when they were six. French, German and religious instruction were regarded as essential, Victoria undertaking the Princess Royal's initiation into the mysteries of faith, the Prince of Wales for some reason being instructed by one of three governesses hired, one coming from Germany, another from Switzerland. Bertie's first tutor was the unfortunately named Henry Birch; he had previously taught at Eton and now undertook to brief the young heir to the throne in geography. The children were kept at work six days a week, without school holidays as such, but family birthdays, which came round with increasing frequency, were treated as days off. Birch believed the curriculum devised by Victoria and Albert too much of a strain for a young boy, especially a child like Bertie who had no pretence to intellectual gifts, and endeared himself to Bertie by rewarding as well as punishing him. His sister Vicky endured a far less punishing regime; she was a precocious learner anyway, and by the age of ten she was fluent in German, which was just as well as she was destined to become Empress of Germany. It was on the occasion of her pending marriage to Prince Frederick William of Prussia in 1858 that Queen Victoria delivered herself of a broadside, addressed to Lord Clarendon, worthy of her great predecessor, Elizabeth I:

It would be well if Lord Clarendon would tell Lord Bloomfield [the minister at Berlin] not to entertain the possibility of such a question as the Princess Royal's marriage taking place in Berlin. The Queen never could consent to it, both for public and private reasons, and the assumption of its being too much for a Prince Royal of Prussia to marry the Princess Royal of Great Britain in England is too absurd, to say the least . . . Whatever may be the usual custom of Prussian Princes it is not every day that one marries the eldest daughter of the Queen of England. The question therefore must be considered as settled and closed.

Outright in her opinions at the best of times, Queen Victoria never hesitated to pass derogatory remarks about her children in letters. When Leopold was six, the Queen told Vicky that his manners were 'despairing' and his French 'more like Chinese than anything else'. In 1856 she had written to Princess Augusta of Prussia to say that Leopold was 'rather ugly'. In the same year the Princess was told bluntly: 'I find no special pleasure or compensation in the company of the elder children. You will remember that I told you this at Osborne. Usually they go out with me in the afternoon (Vicky mostly, and the others also sometimes), or occasionally in the mornings when I drive or walk or ride, accompanied by my lady-in-waiting. And only very exceptionally do I find the rather intimate intercourse with them either agreeable or easy.' Her husband's company was all she needed, as she admitted to Vicky on 2 March 1858, some five weeks after her marriage at the Chapel Royal in St James's Palace. 'You said in your long letter that the happiest time for you was when you were alone with Fritz; you will now understand why I often grudged you children being always there, when I longed to be alone with dearest Papa! Those are always my happiest moments!'

It was hardly a subtle justification for avoiding intimacy with her children as they were growing up; at this stage Vicky, who eventually bore eight children, had no one to keep her company but her husband. And for some time after she had left home, and was a married woman, the Queen treated Vicky as though she was still a schoolgirl. She wanted Lady Churchill, who had accompanied Vicky to Berlin, to let her know 'exactly how your hours are – what you do – when you dress and undress and breakfast etc'.

'I am in a constant fidget and impatience to know everything about everything,' Victoria told King Leopold, meaning the details of Vicky's new life on the Continent, but she could not resist adding: 'To-morrow is the eighteenth anniversary of my blessed marriage, which has brought such universal blessings on this country and Europe! For what has not my beloved and perfect Albert done? Raised monarchy to the highest pinnacle of respect, and rendered it popular beyond what it ever was in this country!'

She ticked Vicky off for writing 'on that enormous paper – for it will go into no box or book'. And she was not best pleased to be told by Lady Churchill that 'the rooms at night are so awfully hot'. She could hardly bear to know that Vicky was happy anywhere but in England, for she was frankly jealous of her new son-in-law, much though she and Albert had welcomed the alliance. 'That you are so happy is a great happiness and comfort to us,' she told Vicky on 15 February 1858, 'and yet it gives me a pang, as I said once before, to see and feel my own child so much happier than she ever was before, with another . . . You see, my dearest, that I never admit any other wife can be as happy as I am – so I can admit no comparison for I maintain Papa is unlike anyone who lives or ever lived and will live.' Queen Victoria was not the easiest mother in the world.

'Now I must tell you that you numbered the pages of your letter wrong,' the Queen was admonishing her daughter on 22 February 1858, 'and then I must scold you a little bit for not answering some questions; but above all for not telling me what you do.' Vicky had failed to answer a single question, all on separate sheets of paper, about her 'health, cold sponging-temperature of your rooms etc'. Her 'good dear child' was still 'a little unmethodical and unpunctual'. Vicky's letter 'received today [2 May 1859] of the 30th ought to be numbered 84 instead of 78!! So that the next would be 85 – or – if you have written since – the one you write after this would be 86. If you numbered them down in your remembrancer as I do,' she was sternly rebuked, 'and looked before you wrote, you would not make mistakes.' On 22 June 1858 Vicky had been asked: 'Do you know that you've got into a habit of writing so many words with a capital letter at the beginning?' Victoria might have had greater cause for complaint had her daughter started to plonk a capital letter in the middle of a word.

Even while scolding Vicky the Queen was complaining to her about her brother the Prince of Wales. Referring to Prince Alfred's efforts to join the Royal Navy, she wrote to Vicky on 9 March 1858: 'Affie is going on admirably; he comes to luncheon to-day (which is a real, brilliant Osborne day) and oh! when I see him and Arthur and look at . . . ! (You know what I mean!) I am in utter despair! The systematic idleness – disregard of everything is enough to break one's heart, and fills me with indignation.' Bertie was 'so idle and so weak', the Queen reminded Vicky three weeks later, and she told her: 'We must look out for princesses for Bertie . . . Oh! if you could find us one!' Not that she approved of marriage as a general rule. On 3 May she wrote: 'I think people marry far too much; it is such a lottery after all, and for a poor woman a very doubtful happiness.' She sent Vicky just the kind of encouragement a young bride must long for when she wrote on 16 May: 'The poor woman is bodily and morally the husband's slave. That always sticks in my throat.' On hearing that Vicky was pregnant (Prince Frederick William had written to Albert to tell him), the Queen told Vicky that she had received 'the horrid news' and immediately brushed aside any pleasure at the prospect of becoming a grandmother with a further swipe at her heir: 'The only one of all the children, who neither drew, wrote, played [she meant a musical instrument] or did anything whatever to show his affection – beyond buying for me a table in Ireland – was Bertie. Oh! Bertie alas! alas! That is too sad a subject to enter on.'

'Poor Bertie', as the Queen so often called him, had more or less sunk beneath the burden of his parents' expectations. When he became seventeen he was given an annual allowance of £500, mainly to spend on clothes, but he was instructed never to wear

Albert Edward, Prince of Wales 1859, after F.X. Winterhalter.

anything extravagant. He was also told to try and emancipate himself 'as much as possible from the thraldom of abject dependence on servants'. Life was composed of duties, he was informed, 'and in the due, punctual and cheerful performance of them the true Christian, true soldier and true gentleman' was recognized. 'Bertie continues such an anxiety,' the Queen told Vicky on 9 April 1859, 'I tremble at the thought of only three years and a half before us – when he will be of age and we can't hold him except by moral power! . . . Oh! dear, what would happen if I were to die next winter!' Victoria was only forty. 'Dear Affie is our great delight,' the Queen told Vicky on 7 March 1860, 'so full of fun and conversation and so full of anxiety to learn – always at something, never an instant idle – such steam power, such energy it is such a great pleasure to see this – but the contrast with someone else is sad.'

But Vicky was not to be drawn. 'You don't once enter into any of my observations upon Bertie,' the Queen complained. 'It is such a proof of my confidence in you when I speak to you so openly about your brothers – that your silence seems strange to me. Poor Bertie, I pity him.' Vicky herself was never free of her mother's intolerant strictures. When the poor girl muddled up the Queen's accession and coronation days (she was expected to write with congratulations), she received 'a grand scold!' She was also told in no uncertain terms not to 'stoop when you sit and write . . . remember how straight I always sit, which enables me to write without fatigue at all times'. Stooping was 'a mere bad habit. Now pray don't do it.'

Terrified of her children's sexuality, Victoria found it impossible to tell Princess Helena, aged twelve, the exciting news that her sister was expecting a baby. 'Those things are not proper to be told to children,' the Queen explained to Vicky, 'as it initiates them into things which they ought not to know of, till they are older.

Affie [fourteen and about to enter the navy] knows nothing either.'

The Queen thought Leopold 'a very common looking child'. Louise was very naughty and backward, while Alfred's letters were 'too shockingly and disgracefully written'. As for Helena when she grew up, she did not improve in looks and had great difficulty 'with her figure and her want of calm, quiet, graceful manners'. But it was Bertie, as ever, who 'vexes us much. There is not a particle of reflection, or even attention to anything but dress!' the Queen told Vicky. 'Not the slightest desire to learn, on the contrary, il se bouche les oreilles [his hearing is muzzled] the moment anything of interest is being talked of!' To some extent she blamed his current tutor, Frederick Gibbs, who 'certainly failed during the last 2 years entirely, incredibly – and did Bertie no good'.

The Queen could be just as outspoken about her grandchildren. In 1871 Princess Helena was under doctor's orders to winter in the south of France, leaving her four children in the care of the Queen. The youngest, not quite two, was Princess Marie Louise. 'Children very well but poor little Louise very ugly', was the uncompromising telegram Victoria sent to her daughter. When she was older, and learned about the telegram, Princess Marie Louise asked an unrepentant Queen Victoria: 'Grandmama, how could you send such an unkind telegram?' To which the Queen replied: 'My dear child, it was only the truth!' As Princess Marie Louise remarked in her memoirs: 'All the same, I did not think it very nice to inform the whole of the French telegraph authorities that the Queen of England had an ugly granddaughter!' Marie Louise, who died only in 1957, developed into a very handsome woman but endured a most unhappy marriage to Prince Aribert of Anhalt.

Three days before Christmas 1858, Vicky was informed: 'Dear Papa is still not quite well – he went yesterday evening with Bertie (who understood not a word of it) to see the Westminster boys act one of their (very improper) Latin plays.' As for Bertie's appearance: 'Handsome I cannot think him, with that painfully small and narrow head, those immense features and total want of chin.' She may have forgotten that he was a Hanoverian, and no doubt had inherited his 'want of chin' from herself.

As with the birth of Leopold, the Queen's final confinement in 1857, when she gave birth to Princess Beatrice, was eased by the administration of chloroform. Another indication that Beatrice was intended to be the last addition to the family was her nickname, Baby, with which she was saddled well into adult life. She was also fated to fulfil the Queen's demand that she 'MUST' have a married daughter living with her. In a perfectly organized world, that is to say, one organized exclusively for the convenience of the Queen, at least one of her five daughters would have had the decency to remain unmarried, but every one of Victoria's children, even the sickly Leopold, found a spouse. So when eventually Beatrice plucked up courage to seek permission to marry Prince Henry of Battenberg, permission was granted on condition that she and Prince Henry made their home under the Queen's roof. Beatrice became a glorified lady's companion, always available to read the newspapers to her mother after breakfast, to run errands, to help entertain guests, to sympathise when family or domestic misfortunes befell, to help supervise mammoth holiday migrations to the south of France and to write and answer letters.

Baby seems to have been a very pert little girl, as is often the case with the youngest of a large family. She was only four when her father died, and on her young shoulders fell much of the great weight of her mother's prolonged bereavement. She needed somehow to create a more normal, affectionate relationship with the Queen than perhaps any of the other children, and in this she was assisted by Victoria's apparent willingness to indulge her. Told, not too strictly, that Baby must not have a certain delicacy, Beatrice replied, 'But she likes it, my dear', mimicking her mother's voice while helping herself. She was a sturdy little girl, too, being hoisted on to a pony at Buckingham Palace for the first time on her second birthday.

Queen Victoria ended up with forty grandchildren and thirty-seven great-grandchildren and like so many grandmothers she found it easier to show affection to her grandchildren than to her own offspring, for they made no demands on her; they were somebody else's responsibility. She was extremely generous with gifts, and made it a habit, for example, always to present her grandchildren with a gold watch on their tenth birthday. When Princess Marie Louise, Princess Helena's younger daughter, attained her tenth birthday in 1882, the Queen wrote to her from Osborne:

Dear Little Louise,
On this your tenth birthday I write to express my best wishes, praying that God may bless and protect you for many years and help to make you a good, truthful, affectionate little girl, dutiful and loving to Papa [Prince Christian of Schleswig-Holstein], Mama and Grandmama, and kind and good to all around you. I hope you will like your watch and spend a happy birthday . . .
Ever your loving Grandmama, V.R.I.[3]

And with non-royal children – she liked to ask them if they knew who she was – the Queen was perfectly at ease, and easily amused by them. In 1887 one of Lord Kilmarnock's little boys was unwell, and having read a story in which the hero wrote to his monarch he took it into his head to write to Victoria. The letter had been posted before his horrified father discovered his son's indiscretion, and Lord Kilmarnock hastened to apologize – by which time, however, the Queen had written and posted a reply. She had been delighted 'with the little letter of this little boy', she instructed her private secretary to inform Lord Kilmarnock, 'as nothing pleases her more than the artless kindness of innocent children'. She often invited the children of members of her household to visit. One such was Victor Mallet, one of her numerous godchildren, whose mother, Marie Mallet, had been appointed a maid of honour in 1886, and after her marriage became a woman of the bedchamber. In 1896, when Victor, later in life a distinguished diplomat, ambassador to Madrid and later Rome, was staying at Windsor, he produced a toy and said to the Queen: 'Look at this pig. I have brought it all the way from London to see you.' The Queen roared with laughter.

10

Albert's Treadmill

Leaks to the press about the activities of the royal family are no novelty. Viscount Torrington, a lord-in-waiting, sent to J. T. Delane, editor of *The Times*, a detailed description of Christmas at Windsor Castle in 1860, the last Christmas, as it happened, ever to be shared by Queen Victoria and the Prince Consort:

> The Queen's private sitting-rooms, three in number, were lighted up with Christmas trees hung from the ceiling, the chandeliers being taken down. These trees, of immense size, beside others on the tables, were covered with bonbons and coloured wax lights. Some of the trees were made to appear as if partially covered with snow. These rooms contain all the presents for the royal family the one to the other. Each member gave a present to one another, so that, including the Prince of Hesse [Prince Louis, newly engaged to Princess Alice] and the Duchess of Kent, every person had to receive thirteen presents.
>
> Even as in a public bazaar, where people jostle one another, so lords, grooms, Queen and princes laughed and talked, forgot to bow, and freely turned their backs on one another. Little princesses, who on ordinary occasions dare hardly look at a

gentleman in waiting, in the happiest manner showed each person they could lay hands on the treasures they had received.

In another room the Queen and Prince Albert distributed gifts to the household, Lord Torrington receiving a set of gold dress studs and a pocketbook. For others there were salt cellars, a sugar bowl and a claret jug. Those who normally remembered to bow had long ago adopted what became known as the Coburg bow, a swift nod from the neck, and definitely not from the waist.[1]

The farm and manor houses that stood on the Osborne and Balmoral estates meant little to Queen Victoria, but there was an early-nineteenth-century house in the Home Park at Windsor, just to the south of the castle, Frogmore, which had strong family associations and grounds which served as a private garden for the castle. At least two previous buildings had stood on the site of the Frogmore House Queen Victoria knew and which today is open to the public, the land having become royal property in the reign of Henry VIII and certainly known as Frogmore by the time of Elizabeth I. When George III came to the throne Frogmore was leased by the Crown to a Mrs Egerton, but Victoria's grandmother, Queen Charlotte, managed to reacquire the lease, and she turned Frogmore into one of her favourite homes. She commissioned James Wyatt to design the present house, and it was her vice-chamberlain, Major James Price, who applied a gift for landscape gardening by digging out a canal where a mere stream had trickled through the grounds; the soil thus excavated was thrown up to form artificial banks for planting trees and spring bulbs, and an improvized island was contrived together with the lake on which Prince Albert delighted to skate.

Frogmore was assigned by Victoria to her mother, and it was at Frogmore that the Duchess of Kent died. After Princess Helena's marriage to Prince Christian of Schleswig-Holstein, Frogmore House became her first married home, where she gave birth to two of her four children, Albert and Helena Victoria. Later on it was the home of Queen Victoria's cousin, the popular, jolly and somewhat overweight Duchess of Teck, mother of the future Queen Mary. Queen Victoria had a teahouse erected in the grounds, where she would sometimes take breakfast before attending to her state papers.

'I am sitting in this dear lovely garden – where all is peace and quiet, and you only have the hum of the bees, the singing of the birds, the occasional crowing and crackling from the poultry-yard,' she reported from Frogmore to Vicky on 10 July 1867. 'It does my

Duchess of Kent's Mausoleum, Frogmore.

poor excited and worried nerves good.'² Three days later: 'I have breakfasted here with Louise and Beatrice in order to be quiet before this tremendous affair of the Sultan's visit.' By this time the gardens had become the sacred resting place of both her mother and Prince Albert, having gradually been built up as a sort of Victorian memento mori. On a bank by the lake Baron Stockmar was commemorated by a Celtic cross. Another cross was raised for Lady Augusta Stanley, a lady-in-waiting who thoroughly annoyed the Queen by marrying the Dean of Westminster when she was forty-one. King Leopold was told that Lady Augusta had 'most unnecessarily decided to marry', but the Queen melted when Lady Augusta died. Her inscription reads: 'In gratitude and affectionate remembrance of her faithful labours for thirty years.' Two dogs are buried at Frogmore, a pug called Basko, owned by Prince Henry of Battenberg, the husband of Princess Beatrice, and a pet 'For years the attached and faithful follower of HRH the Duchess of Kent'.

Did Victoria believe that her mother had been Sir John Conroy's lover? She so hated Conroy that as a girl she could have been capable of believing almost anything to his detriment. But although Conroy was a plausible, manipulative man, and the Duchess of Kent a young, twice-widowed, lonely and vulnerable woman, there is no concrete evidence that theirs had been a sexual relationship. And certainly by the end of the Duchess's life the Queen had transmogrified her mother into some sort of saint. Her death, on 16 March 1861, was the most dreadful day of her life, she told King Leopold. The Duchess had been 'that precious, dearly beloved tender Mother' without whom she could not imagine life. 'I held her dear, dear hand in mine to the very last, which I am truly thankful for!' Too overcome with woe to attend the funeral ten days later, Victoria recalled that she had 'never been near a coffin before', which, bearing in mind her age – forty-one – would indicate a fairly charmed life, or one in which the Queen had deliberately avoided attending funerals.[3] She had, however, managed to kneel by her mother's coffin, 'overwhelmed with grief.'

'It is dreadful, dreadful to think we shall never see that dear kind loving face again,' Victoria wrote in her journal on 9 April, 'never hear that dear voice again!' One of her great comforts was 'to go to Frogmore, to sit in her dear room', and she repeated the fact that 'she had never been near a coffin before'.

Rather than follow the advice of Prince Albert by removing to Buckingham Palace for a spell, she resolved to hang on to her unhappiness, much of it caused by guilt and remorse when she recalled her cool conduct towards her mother in the early days of her reign. Albert's father had been the brother of Victoria's mother, and on his death he had been buried in Coburg in a new mausoleum built by Albert and his brother. On a visit to Germany in 1860, Victoria and Albert had inspected and admired the mausoleum and decided in principle on a mausoleum for themselves. The Duchess of Kent had conceived a whim to join her brother, but when Albert pointed out to his aunt the inconvenience of dying in England and being buried in Germany the Duchess asked him to build a mausoleum for her in the grounds of Frogmore. And work on the mausoleum, situated on one of Major Price's home-made hillocks, had actually commenced before the Duchess died. It was here that she was eventually laid to rest.

Meanwhile, the hunt was on to find a suitable bride for the Prince of Wales. Apparently when Bertie met the Princess of Meiningen in Berlin she 'did not please him', and anyway, she was not strong. Marie of the Netherlands was admitted to be 'clever and ladylike' but too plain – according to the Queen; too ugly in the opinion of Prince Albert. And she, too, was 'not strong'. 'Poor

King Edward and Queen Alexandra at the time of their marriage.

Addy', Princess Alexandrine, a niece of the King of Prussia, turned out to be neither 'clever or pretty'. The field had been narrowed down to Princess Alexandra of Denmark, and Vicky was instructed to 'find out everything about her education and general character'. Was she 'clever, quiet, not frivolous or vain, fond of occupation etc. The looks and manners we know are excellent,' the Queen wrote, but did she seem 'very *outrée* Danish?' The subject was so important, the choice so circumscribed, that the Queen was sure her daughter would 'set about at once finding out all these things'. It was so very important, Vicky was reminded, 'with the peculiar character we have to deal with'.

By 19 June Victoria was writing to Berlin to tell Vicky: 'Dear Papa and I are both so grateful to you about all the trouble you have taken about Princess Alix. May [Bertie] only be worthy of such a jewel! There is the rub! When I look at Louis and at the charming, sweet, bright, lively expression of the one and at the sallow, dull, blasé and heavy look of the other I own I feel very sad.'

Vicky and her husband, with their children William and Charlotte, soon afterwards paid a visit to Windsor, and on 17 August, armed with wreaths, they all trooped off to the Duchess of Kent's mausoleum, 'and into the vault which is *à plain-pied*, and so pretty − so airy − so grand and simple, that, affecting as it is, there was no anguish or bitterness of grief, but calm repose!'

Having spent some nominal time at Christ Church, Oxford, hemmed in by courtiers, Bertie had become attached on a very temporary basis to the Grenadier Guards, and his parents attended a field day at the Curragh Camp near Dublin, when 'Bertie marched past with his company, and did not look at all so very small . . . At the Review they played one of [her mother's] marches, which entirely upset me.' With Bertie's future now settled, the Queen wrote on 1 October to Vicky to say that she and Prince Albert could not sufficiently thank her and her husband for all their 'love, affection and kindness in this important matter. Bertie is certainly much pleased with her but as for being in love I don't think he can be, or that he is capable of enthusiasm about anything in the world . . . he is so different to darling Affie!'

In this letter Victoria allowed herself a rare criticism of Albert. 'You say no one is perfect but Papa,' she wrote. 'But he has his faults too. He is very often very trying – in his hastiness and over-love of business – and I think you would find it very trying if Fritz was as hasty and harsh (momentarily and unintentionally as it is) as he is!'

The truth is, with Victoria's willing connivance, Albert was acting as King in all but name, Victoria being only too ready to hand over the political side of her duties to his care. And until a type-writer made its appearance at Windsor Castle at the very end of the century, forty years after Albert's death, and then only to be used 'sparingly', every letter, often of inordinate length, was of necessity handwritten. Britain had acquired an enormous empire over which the Queen reigned, and the cabals and letters that flowed from the Court of St James's by the middle of the nine-teenth century to the furthest corners of the world were far in excess of those of any previous reign. Yet still the Queen had failed to appoint an officially recognized private secretary; everything of importance passed through the hands of the Prince Consort or was initiated by him. Albert had become very tired and run down, plagued by toothache, rheumatism and acute insomnia. And his life had not been made any easier by continual worry about the unstable emotional condition of the Queen, by having such a neurotic 'fidget' to pacify who most of the time burdened him with excessive adulation.

With the arrival of a typewriter at Windsor Castle in 1900 it is interesting to track Victoria's entry into the twentieth century. In 1895 she had a lift installed at Windsor. The following year an internal telephone had appeared with outside lines connecting the castle with the post office, the railway station, Buckingham Palace and Marlborough House. It was also in 1896, on 23 November, that the Queen noted: 'After tea went to the Red Drawingroom, where so-called "animated pictures" were shown off, including the group taken in September at Balmoral. It is a very wonderful process, representing people, their movements and actions, as if they were alive.' On 8 August 1898, at Osborne, the Queen spoke into a phonograph to send a message to the Emperor of Ethiopia. By 1899 electric lights had been installed at Balmoral.

Thanking Prince Ernest from Holyhead on 6 August 1861 for his good wishes for his birthday, Albert wrote: 'I go on working at my treadmill, as life seems to me.' These were the words of a deeply depressed, disillusioned and world-weary man of forty-two. During the last summer of his life Prince Albert had even found himself in acrimonious correspondence with his brother, who had warned Bertie against marriage with Princess Alexandra. Albert reiterated the Queen's list of complaints about the various princesses on offer, adding the additional information that the daughter of Prince Frederick of the Netherlands was 'too ugly' and that a sister of Prince Louis had been considered but rejected on the grounds that 'it would connect us for a second time with Darmstadt'. It was Bertie's wish to marry soon, he added, and indeed it was 'in his interest morally, socially and politically' to do so. Albert remained terrified, especially now that Bertie was in the army, that he would soon succumb to sexual desire, and ironically he had reported to Prince Ernest from Osborne on 12 July that Bertie was 'busy with his military studies'. No doubt he was, but it was during his ten-week attachment to the Grenadier Guards that Bertie fell for the charms of a local camp follower. He was, after all, twenty and no more cut out than most young men of his age for a life of celibacy. His parents had a fit, fearing that any woman with whom Bertie slept might become pregnant and demand to be married to him, or perhaps produce someone else's child and pretend it was the Prince's.

Desperate for a scapegoat, for years the Queen was to blame the shock of Bertie's youthful indiscretion for his father's death, due to follow so closely on the heels of that of her mother. In fact, on 22 November 1861 Prince Albert drove to Sandhurst to inspect new buildings in progress. It never stopped raining, and the Prince caught a severe chill. A few days later he wrote in his diary: 'Am full of rheumatic pains and feel thoroughly unwell. Have scarcely closed my eyes at night for the last fortnight.' By this time Bertie was briefly entered as an undergraduate at Cambridge. Anxious to pry into his son's affairs, Albert now took the road to the Fens, which entailed another strictly unnecessary journey in atrocious weather. On 5 December the Queen noted: 'He did not smile or take much notice of me.' The Prince had a 'strange, wild look'. When at last Prince Albert was persuaded to go to bed it was to the Blue Room that he retired, the room in which both George IV and his brother William IV had died. The doctors prescribed beef tea. They never grasped that the Prince was dangerously ill, a victim, it is now generally believed, of typhoid fever, the drains at Windsor still being in need of attention. Whatever the precise cause of his death it was undoubtedly assisted by a fatalistic attitude of mind. 'I do not cling to life,' he once told the Queen. 'You do, but I set no store by it.' He had even gone so far as to predict, 'I am sure if I had a serious illness I should give up at once. I should not struggle for life.'

The Queen told King Leopold that her 'poor dear Albert's rheumatism' had turned out to be 'a regular influenza, which has pulled and lowered him very much'. But she was optimistic that in two or three days he would be 'quite himself again'. Her bulletins to her uncle may in part have been to reassure King Leopold but in part to boost her own morale. 'Every day . . . is bringing us nearer the end of this tiresome illness.' By 12 December the Queen was writing of gastric fever, but, she assured King Leopold, 'there is nothing to cause alarm'. She said she could not sufficiently praise the skill, attention and devotion of her physician-extraordinary, Dr William Jenner, 'who is the *first fever* Doctor in Europe'. No fewer than five medical practitioners of one sort or another had been hovering around. The Prince had two days to live.

At seven o'clock on the morning of the fatal day, 14 December, the Queen began her vigil. 'It was a bright morning,' she remembered, when she came to record the events in her journal, 'the sun just rising and shining brightly.' The doctors told her they were still very hopeful, and that she might go out for a breath of fresh air, 'Just close by, for half an hour'. So Victoria attempted to walk on the terrace with Princess Alice, but burst into tears and went indoors again. 'Sir James [Reid] was very hopeful; he had seen much worse cases. But the breathing was the alarming thing.' The doctors may have been very hopeful, but it was hopefulness based on ignorance; they had no idea what to do. The Queen bent over the Prince and said, in German, 'It is your little wife.' She asked, again in German, for a kiss. 'He seemed half dozing, quite quiet.' Victoria left the room for a few minutes, 'and sat down on the floor in utter despair. Attempts at consolation from others only made me worse.'

The eighteen-year-old Princess Alice understood the situation only too well, and had no doubt that her father was about to die.

Last photograph of the Prince Consort.

She told her mother to return. Victoria held the Prince's left hand, already cold. His breathing was now quite gentle. 'Two or three long but perfectly gentle breaths were drawn, the hand clasping mine.' And he died. 'I stood up, kissed the dear heavenly forehead and called out in a bitter and agonizing cry, "Oh! My dear Darling!"'

Victoria, in time-honoured tradition, exonerated the doctors, and then, rather surprisingly, flung herself into the arms of the Prince of Wales, telling him to devote the rest of his life to her comfort.[4]

II

'The Queen is an Odd Woman'

The day following the Prince Consort's death, four doctors signed the briefest of bulletins: 'The Queen, although overwhelmed with grief, bears her bereavement with calmness and has not suffered in health.' Even so, and taking a longer-term view, in his short but vivid life of Queen Victoria, Arthur Ponsonby, a page of honour to the Queen when he was a boy, wrote: 'There can be no question that the Queen's sense of proportion was dislocated by her loss. She nursed her grief until woe became a luxury almost amounting to self-indulgence.'[1] A large part of the problem was the Queen's lack of intimacy with her children and her former overreliance on her husband. Having just lost her mother as well she felt peculiarly isolated by the eminence of her position. Other than King Leopold there was no one any longer to call her Victoria; even her cousins addressed her as Madam. It was only as an older and more balanced woman that she learned to share her bereavements, of which she suffered a great many, with her ladies-in-waiting.

Initially, however, statues and monuments arose. In 1862 Buckingham Palace remained closed, as did the State Apartments at Windsor. The Queen had herself photographed with selected children gazing with adoration at a bust of Albert, whose rooms remained eerily undisturbed.[2] The pattern of remorseless mourning was set on the first anniversary of the Prince's death, when a bust was placed on his bed and three services were conducted in the Blue Room. For the first year following his death Prince Albert's coffin had lain in a vault in what is now the Albert Memorial Chapel, adjoining St George's, while the mausoleum he and Victoria had promised themselves was being built in the garden at Frogmore, not fifty yards from the much smaller mausoleum Victoria had so recently had erected for her mother.

The exterior, clearly visible through the trees from the Long Walk, looks like nothing so much as a north London synagogue. The interior, in the Romanesque style, was the work of a Dresden professor, Ludwig Grüner. The Queen had chosen the spot forty days after the Prince's death, and three months after his death she laid the foundation stone. 'The mausoleum is making rapid progress,' Queen Victoria reported to Vicky on 11 June 1862, 'and the interior, as proposed, promises to be very fine. Alice went to see the statue at [Baron Carlo] Marochetti's which is finished and which she says is most beautiful and so like now.' She meant the Prince Consort's effigy. 'It overcame all who saw it. How I long for it to be in its place! It will be such an object and such a comfort to go to and sit by!'

The imposing tomb of Queen Victoria and the Prince Consort is the centrepiece of the mausoleum, the Queen having taken the precaution of having her own white marble effigy sculpted at the same time as Albert's, so that although she was eighty-one when she died she is captured in the mausoleum for all time aged forty-two. She discarded the welter of rings that normally adorned her chubby fingers and wears only her wedding ring, while on her left wrist is carved the diamond bracelet that contained a miniature of Prince Albert and a lock of his hair.

The Albert Memorial Chapel, Windsor.

On 17 December 1862, although the interior of the mausoleum was still not finished, and only a temporary sarcophagus was in position, the building was consecrated by Samuel Wilberforce, Bishop of Oxford since 1845, who said that 'the sight of our Queen and the file of fatherless children' was one of the most touching scenes he ever saw. 'Woke very often during the night, thinking of the sacred work to be carried out at 7 o'clock,' Queen Victoria wrote in her journal the next day. 'At that hour the precious earthly Remains were to be carried with all love and peace to their final resting-place by our three sons (for little Leopold had earnestly begged to go too).' The missing son was Alfred, at sea with the Mediterranean Fleet. The Queen did not attend the removal of Albert's coffin to the mausoleum, but she received a report from Princess Alice that 'all had been peacefully and lovingly accomplished'. In the afternoon she drove to Frogmore House, and from there she walked across to the mausoleum, where the Dean of Windsor, Gerald Wellesley, 'with a faltering voice read some most appropriate Prayers. We were all much overcome when we knelt round the beloved tomb. When everybody had gone out we returned again and gazed on the great beauty and peace of the beautiful statue. What a comfort it will be to have that near me!'

An immediate consequence of the Prince Consort's death was the long-overdue appointment of a private secretary to the Queen. The choice of the man to hold the post of confidential adviser and discreet liaison officer between the monarch and her ministers was Lieutenant General Charles Grey, already well known to the Queen for his work as private secretary to Albert. He held the appointment until his death, following a stroke, in 1870. 'Good, excellent General Grey,' the Queen wrote of him, 'his discretion, sense and courage made him invaluable.' By dint of historical precedence the Lord Chamberlain may be the most senior member of the royal household, but a succession of influential and respected private secretaries, starting with General Grey, ensured that the choice of private secretary was the more crucial. Victoria's private secretaries – Sir Henry Ponsonby, who succeeded his wife's uncle, General Grey, in 1871 and held the post for a quarter of a century, and Sir Arthur Bigge, private secretary for the last five years of her reign and before that assistant private secretary – would never have presumed to take over Prince Albert's role as policy-maker; what they did instead was accelerate the development of constitutional monarchy. They tendered to the Queen impartial advice (and she sometimes asked for theirs) while keeping the Prime Minister, the Foreign Secretary or the Home Secretary, as appropriate, aware of the Queen's desires and opinions.

There are today only three people with direct access to the

sovereign – the Lord Chamberlain, the private secretary and the Dean of Windsor, and it was Queen Victoria who made it perfectly plain to Gladstone in 1882 that she alone would appoint the Dean of Windsor. The Queen's Free Chapel of St George Within Her Castle at Windsor is, like Westminster Abbey, a Royal Peculiar, but whereas the Dean and Chapter of Westminster are appointed on the advice of the Prime Minister, Queen Victoria set a precedent whereby the monarch to this day interviews and appoints the Dean of Windsor and the canons as well. When Gerald Wellesley, with whom Queen Victoria had formed a very close relationship, died in 1882, she wrote to Sir Henry Ponsonby to thank him 'for his letter of sympathy on a *universal & irreparable* loss, which is crushing to her! *Irreparable!* The last of her valued *old* friends & the *most* intimate of all.' Windsor without him, she added, 'will be strange & dreadful'. She went on to say that 'the bare thought of replacing or rather filling up the beloved Dean of Windsor's place (for he cannot be replaced)' was very painful to her, but she feared it must be faced. 'The Queen,' she said, 'is glad that Mr Gladstone sees that the appointment of Dean of Windsor is a personal & not a political appointment; she will therefore not expect Mr Gladstone to suggest names to her.'

What the Queen wanted, she explained to Ponsonby, was 'a tolerant, liberal minded, broad church clergyman who at the same time is pleasant socially & is popular with all Members & classes of her household – who understands her feelings not only in ecclesiastical but also in social matters – a good kind man without pride'. The person she had in mind was one of her chaplains, the Vicar of Newport on the Isle of Wight, Canon George Connor. She only regretted he was not of 'higher social rank', but he came 'of a good family' and was 'a thorough gentleman'. He was, in fact, father-in-law of the Bishop of Newcastle. She had not 'the slightest idea' whether Canon Connor would accept; he did, and promptly died the next year. His successor as Dean of Windsor was Randall Davidson, later Archbishop of Canterbury, with whom both the Queen and Ponsonby formed a warm friendship. Davidson's biographer, Bishop George Bell of Chichester, wrote in 1935 that Ponsonby 'came to rely more and more on the younger man's shrewd judgement for help in all manner of political and general problems'. Their relationship was a good example of two members of the Queen's household working in tandem for the benefit of Victoria, Davidson himself commenting that Ponsonby 'showed great capacity in all political matters, advising the Queen admirably and communicating with her Ministers in exactly the right sort of way'.

The Queen was powerless, however, to prevent the sort of squabbles that all too often break out in what should be the cloistered calm of any collegiate establishment. The cantankerous John Dalton, tutor to two of Victoria's grandsons, Prince Albert Victor and Prince George, and father of a future Labour Chancellor of the Exchequer, Hugh Dalton, became a canon of Windsor in 1884. He found it 'an almost unbearable irritation' to think that there were 'other people who had an equal right with him to a voice in the Chapter. He approached every meeting,' it was said, 'determined to fight over the smallest detail, only to prevent his colleagues, whom he despised, from having their way.'

He remained at Windsor for more than forty years. 'Those damn minor canons – all fools!' he would expostulate in the cloisters. When he failed to acquire the deanery in 1917 (it went to a godson of Queen Victoria's, Albert Baillie), he gave his former pupil, King George V, 'one of the worst hours he had ever spent'.

Within a year of Canon Dalton's installation the Queen was minuting, for the benefit of her private secretary: 'As Tutor Mr Dalton never said "Grace" but as Canon he does & [the Queen] hears has done so in Latin. Pray tell him it must be in English and only *one*.' The Queen took the keenest interest in the choice of preachers, not only at Windsor but on the Isle of Wight. A list of possible preachers at Osborne in 1879, submitted by the Dean of Windsor, did not meet with her approval: the Dean of Westminster '*Too long*'; The Dean of Christ Church, Oxford 'Sermons are like lectures'; Dr Bradley 'Excellent man but tiresome preacher'. Four other names, those of Mr Roberts, Mr Birch, Mr Tarver and Mr Rowsell, received equally curt dismissals. 'The Queen likes none of these for the House. The last of all is the *only good* Preacher excepting Dean Stanley [of Westminster] & he is too long. Mr Rowsell unfortunately reads very disagreeably but those crossed [Roberts, Birch and Tarver] are most disagreeable Preachers and the Queen *wonders* the Dean mention them.'

When, in 1893, ill health, it was said, prevented the chaplain at Hampton Court (like Windsor, a Royal Peculiar) from continuing in office, and it was urged that for some years he had given satisfaction, the Queen returned the following minute: 'This is a mistake. He *never* gave satisfaction & was most interfering and disagreeable.' Writing from Balmoral to her husband on 31 May 1897, Marie Mallet said: 'We had a dismal preacher yesterday, Dr Mitchell. He discoursed on death and worms and judgement for thirty minutes and we all felt inclined to howl.'

Henry Ponsonby's appointment as private secretary on the death of General Grey displayed the radical and independent nature of the Queen. Ponsonby was the eldest son of a severely wounded survivor of the Battle of Waterloo, and when it became known that the Queen intended offering Ponsonby the post the Duke and Duchess of Cambridge and Prince Christian, the husband of Princess Helena, all voiced their disapproval, for if Ponsonby himself was a radical his wife's views, as he admitted himself, 'were

General Grey.

very extreme'. Both Henry and Mary Ponsonby, of whom the Queen grew very fond, had been contributors to the *Pall Mall Gazette*. But the Queen had known Ponsonby as an equerry and realized he had picked up useful experience by assisting General Grey. He certainly knew what might be expected of him – the passing of unpalatable messages. On one occasion the Queen considered a young lady-in-waiting too heavily made up, but instead of having a word herself, or sending a message through the Mistress of the Robes, she said: 'Dear General Grey will tell her.' 'Dear General Grey' declined to do anything of the sort.

Victoria was a great one for sending messages and memos, many of which took ages to decipher, for her handwriting was pretty appalling, and the older and more blind she became the longer it took to comprehend her wishes. It was through the Dean of

Windsor that the Queen sent a hint to Ponsonby not to permit his wife to compromise him in her conversation. Ponsonby had received promotion just at a point when the Queen was becoming increasingly isolated. During a protracted visit to Balmoral, Ponsonby and Sir Thomas Biddulph, Keeper of the Privy Purse, were bemoaning 'the present state of affairs' because they thought the Queen was 'getting to like to be still more alone and to see no one at all, governing the country by means of messages through footmen to us'. Sir Thomas Biddulph was one of those servants whose true worth the Queen only felt able to acknowledge after their death. 'Dear excellent Sir Thomas Biddulph,' she wrote when he died, 'was one of the best & kindest of men, & so straight-forward, sensible & true. The Queen is greatly upset by it.'

Queen Victoria was quite incapable of putting her head round the door and speaking to a courtier face to face. One of her ladies-in-waiting, Horatia Stopford, became known as the Queen's Messenger, and was even entrusted to convey a reprimand to Ponsonby. Such was the circulatory nature of communications at court that when, in 1888, the Duchess of Teck, always hard up, wanted to borrow a carriage to convey her from Windsor Station to see the Fourth of June celebrations at Eton (she could quite easily have walked), she got her daughter to submit the request, a reply from the Queen being returned by Miss Stopford to Henry Ponsonby for transmission to the Duchess: 'The Duchess of Teck may have a carriage tomorrow but Sir Henry must make it very clear that it is not to be asked for again.'

Jane, Marchioness of Ely was another lady-in-waiting entrusted with messages, but as she had a speech defect and tended to whisper, the verbal ones often lost a good deal of their import; Sir Henry Ponsonby declined to 'strain his ears to hear her'. Three weeks in waiting at a stretch is the normal rota today, but in 1876

Sir Thomas Biddulph was reporting from London to Ponsonby: 'I saw Lady Ely today. She . . . was principally taken up with her own health and waiting. She says she cannot go on as it is, that it is killing her, and asked what to do. I said write plainly to the Queen what you can do, and make it clear that if HM cannot agree to your terms, you must resign. I think this would bring the Queen to reason, if firmly done. She says six weeks at a time is the utmost possible, and that all the Doctors urge her to do less.'

Victoria had even begun to bypass her private secretary, sending letters and telegrams to the Prime Minister through Lady Ely. Ponsonby had a 'very serious talk with Princess Alice who takes the gloomiest possible view of all the talk, even abroad, of retirement and not even seeing much of or talking to her children'. By 1892 things had got so bad that Ponsonby found himself writing to his cousin, Sir Spencer Ponsonby-Fane, Comptroller to the Lord Chamberlain, to say: 'Princess B seems to think it possible that HM wd go to one Drawing Room. But HM in sad and mournful tones said to me she was damned if she would.'

Queen Victoria's Drawing Rooms were held in the Throne Room at Buckingham Palace at three o'clock in the afternoon, 'with full evening dress, feathers and veils', according to her granddaughter, Princess Marie Louise. Apparently, 'The ladies who were to be presented always kissed Her Majesty's hands; daughters of peers, in addition to kissing hands, were also kissed by Her Majesty on the cheek . . . Her dear Majesty wore on top of her lace veil the little diamond imperial crown.' The Princess adds in her memoirs that the Queen usually remained for an hour 'and then either the Princess of Wales or my mother [Princess Helena] used to carry on in her place. But it was Her Majesty's Drawing Room.'[3]

Little over a year after the Prince Consort's death a woman of the bedchamber, the Hon. Mrs Bruce, was writing to the Lord

Drawing Room at St James's Palace, 1861 – the last attended by the Prince Consort.

Chamberlain to say: 'The Queen desires me to let you know that Her Majesty wishes the Ladies of the Corps Diplomatique, the wives of the Cabinet Ministers and the Ladies of Her Household to be in black, with black feathers and gloves at the first Drawing Room. All other ladies may be in colours.' Notwithstanding the bulletin issued on 15 December 1861 by the doctors, to the effect that bereavement had not affected the Queen's health, in February 1864 it was clear that the Queen was ducking out of royal duties on the pretext of ill health. It was announced that 'Levées would be held by the Prince of Wales, for the Queen, before Easter, and probably a Drawing Room by the Princess of Wales on behalf of Her Majesty. Levées and Drawing Rooms will likewise be held by the Prince and Princess of Wales after Easter. The Queen's health is still unequal to the performance of State ceremonials and Her Majesty's physicians have decided that any such exertion would be prejudicial to Her Majesty's health.'

It was the thought of being the centre of attention in a room virtually full of strangers without Albert at her side that the Queen could not tolerate – not that Albert had cared greatly for ceremonial court occasions. 'To-day there is to be a Drawing-Room, not one of the most agreeable things,' he had written to his brother from Buckingham Palace on 18 April 1844. Many of the ladies who attended the Queen's Drawing Rooms found the occasion disagreeable, too. 'It seems impossible that Her Most Gracious Majesty can be aware of the suffering ladies go through at a Drawing Room,' 'A Loyal Subject' wrote to *The Times* on 7 May 1874. 'At the last, many left their homes at 12 o'clock, and were not home again till after 7 o'clock.

'During the whole of this time they could get no refreshments, and during three hours of it they were fighting their way through an anxious crowd, in addition to which the greater part had not the honour of passing by Her Majesty, as fatigue naturally obliged her to leave.

'The same fatigue which affects Her Majesty also affects her subjects, while they suffer, besides, from being without refreshment for so long a period.'

'A Mother' followed up this letter two days later with one saying that she had two daughters who had set out at one o'clock with lovely Paris dresses 'looking as fresh as two pretty women can look' only to return home at six-thirty 'pale and exhausted, with their dresses torn and spoilt', and one of them had been laid up with a severe headache ever since. She was quite sure that if the Queen had the least idea of the sufferings of ladies 'in that fearful crowd', she, 'whose kindness is proverbial', would be horrified.

In 1884 the Queen had a perfect excuse to cancel all Drawing Rooms – the death of Prince Leopold. Even when he was grown up Prince Leopold's life had been ruled and regulated by royal decree. In 1878, when the Prince was twenty-five, Henry Ponsonby was writing: '[The Queen] has laid down absolute rules for what he is to do, coming such a day and going such a day – never to dine out or go to a club – to come to Osborne in July and leave it the day the Regatta begins and all in that strain. I cannot support such a system and for one thing know it is useless to try it on. Will the Queen never find out that she will have ten times more influence over her children by treating them with kindness and not trying to rule them like a despot?'

It was Ponsonby who intercepted a telegram sent to Windsor Castle announcing the sudden death of Prince Leopold in Cannes. 'Another awful blow has fallen upon me and all of us today,' the Queen wrote in her journal, again sanitizing someone safely dead. 'My beloved Leopold that bright, clever son, who had so many times recovered from such fearful illnesses, and from various small accidents, has been taken from us! To lose another dear child, far from me, and one who was so gifted, and such a help to me, is too dreadful!' With haemophilia, Prince Leopold, Duke of Albany, was lucky to live to be thirty and to have married and fathered two children – a son, Charles, Duke of Saxe-Coburg, born after his father's death, who unfortunately became a Nazi, and Princess Alice, Countess of Athlone, who lived until 1981 and became a great repository of stories about Queen Victoria. The Prince of Wales went to France to collect the body of his brother, the Queen venturing as far as Windsor Station to receive the coffin and follow it to the Albert Memorial Chapel, where Leopold, for some unknown reason, now lies buried. He shares this Victorian Gothic Revival resting place with an irredeemable half-wit, his nephew Prince Albert Victor, Duke of Clarence and Avondale, elder son of Edward VII, who performed one useful act by dying in 1892.

Of Princess Helen of Waldeck and Pyrmont, married to Prince Leopold in 1882, Henry Ponsonby's son Arthur has written: 'She is the single instance quoted in the letters [the correspondence of Henry Ponsonby] of a member of the family who refused to write to the Queen when there was any trouble, refused to send messages through an intermediary and insisted on confronting her "face to face". In one quoted instance the interview must have been lively, as after it the Duchess of Albany did not appear at the Queen's table but dined alone with her husband.' In the year of Leopold's death, Bertie suggested that the Queen might take just one Drawing Room. Her reaction was conveyed to Ponsonby by Miss Stopford:

Balmoral Castle, June 7, 1884: The Queen has just received your note concerning the Drawingrooms, and I am desired to tell you that HM will not *hear* of any being held this year – that even

if there was ONE the Queen would not allow either Princess
Christian [Helena] or Princess Beatrice to attend, and that the
Princess of Wales could not be *alone* – that a Drawingroom held
this Season would have to be in very deep mourning, which
would be undesirable, in short the Queen will not hear of it,
and begs that nothing more may be said to her about it.

Even Prince Alfred felt obliged to approach his mother through
an intermediary, usually Ponsonby. At a time when Ponsonby was
still an equerry, and was in waiting at Osborne, the seventeen-
year-old Prince turned up after a long absence. 'The Queen is an
odd woman,' Ponsonby recorded. 'I believe she is as fond of her
children as anyone. Yet she was going out driving and started at
3.25 p.m. Just as she was getting [to her carriage] up comes the
advance Groom to say Arthur had arrived and was following, yet
she wouldn't wait for one minute to receive him, and drove off.'

The Queen regimented and upbraided her household just as she
did her adult children. Instead of having a quiet word with
Ponsonby at Balmoral one Sunday in July 1885 she sent him a four-
page letter of complaint and instructions because both he and his
assistant were absent from the castle at the same time. When a
letter from the chargé d'affaires in Coburg was opened by the
wrong person 'as a common letter', the Queen was '*much* annoyed'
and Ponsonby was informed: 'It must *not* happen again.' He was
told, too, that he could 'send the Queen questions about anything
thro' Miss Phipps [Harriet Phipps, a woman of the bedchamber]
who is very clever, quick & discreet & is quite able to do what
Lady Ely & Miss Stopford do' – that is to say, to act as an intermediary between the Queen and her private secretary. The only
explanation that comes to mind for Victoria's refusal to do business with Ponsonby direct is that she declined to have any man

take the place physically of Prince Albert. She also shied away from personal confrontation because she dreaded the possibility of being contradicted. If life at Balmoral was anything to go by, she might just as well have dispensed with a Master of the Household – and a Mistress of the Robes while she was about it – for she had her finger on every single pulse. She decided the day on which every member of the household should arrive and depart. She even supervised meals for the servants. The equerry-in-waiting was not permitted to give orders to the stables or the Highlanders, maids of honour had to be chaperoned, the Queen decided who was to ride which pony and attendance at church was obligatory.

If a maid of honour was without a title or prefix she was granted the rank and precedence of the daughter of a baron, so that at least, for instance, she would be known as the Hon. Susan Baring. Often the young ladies were appointed sight unseen. Marie Adeane went straight into waiting at Windsor in 1886 without ever having previously met the Queen. With her mother, she stood before dinner in the corridor. When the Queen arrived from her private apartments, she beckoned to Lady Ely, indicating that she was to present the new maid of honour. Marie curtsied. The Queen gave her her hand to kiss, then kissed her on the cheek, pinned on to her left shoulder a maid of honour badge – a miniature of herself surrounded by diamonds and mounted on a ribbon bow – and proceeded into dinner.

Hence the household remained a fairly closed shop. Alick Yorke, known to the family as Nunks, was Marie's uncle, and it was he who had been told by Victoria to sound out Marie's mother, Lady Elizabeth Biddulph (for a short time before her second marriage a woman of the bedchamber), to see if Marie would care to be a maid of honour. Marie's grandfather, the Earl of Hardwicke, had been a lord-in-waiting. Writing from Balmoral to Lady Elizabeth on 30 September 1887, Victoria said it would be a pleasure to have a granddaughter and niece 'of those whom I have known so long', and added: 'We are pleased to have your brother Alick, who is always pleasant and very useful here.' His main duty was to make people laugh.

Marie's own duties were carefully enumerated. Could she speak, read and write French and German? Could she play the piano and read easily at sight in order to play duets with Princess Beatrice? Could she ride? And was she 'engaged, or likely to be engaged to be married?' Like Queen Elizabeth, Victoria had a strong aversion to her household, even the men, getting married. During her second waiting, at Osborne, Prince Henry was instructed by the Queen to command Marie to sing. 'I really can't, sir,' she stammered, and was let off. 'However,' she told her mother, 'I had to read a horrid duet with Princess Beatrice, the Queen sitting close by; I believe I got through it pretty well but I could hardly see the notes and simply prayed for the end.'

Marie Adeane had been appointed only because another maid of honour, Louisa Brownlow, had no sooner been appointed than she announced her engagement. The Queen was apparently 'much put out'. When her doctor, Sir James Reid, had the temerity to become engaged to another maid of honour, Susan Baring, Lady Lytton told Princess Christian that the household was 'full of jokes and chaff' but the Queen was very upset. She refused to see Sir James for three days, and he got back into her good books only by promising that he would never do it again. Someone else who disgraced himself, at the age of seventy-two, was the Duke of Argyll, father-in-law of Princess Louise; a year after the death of his second wife he married a maid of honour, Ina McNeil. The first intimation of this intended desertion from her court reached the Queen when she received a 'rather startling letter' from the Duke.

Victoria was particularly fond of Marie Adeane, and when she married Bernard Mallet in 1891 she gave her a cheque for £1,000, an Indian shawl and a diamond brooch. Writing from Windsor Castle on 26 June that year, Marie told Bernard: 'I have just had an interview with the Queen, almost the farewell one, and it is far worse having to say "Goodbye" than even I had expected. I did my best not to break down but all "in vain", and the kinder the Queen was the more I cried. It is really dreadful to think I shall never see her in the same way again.'

Marie had already done rather well by way of perks. She told her step-sister Violet Biddulph in 1888: 'The Queen has just given me a Balmoral Tartan Shawl and a very superior Cairn-gorm to fasten it with. I think I shall sport it at Ledbury and astonish the neighbours.' On 19 November 1889 she wrote: 'The Queen gave me some beautiful lace yesterday. I think it is Irish hand-made and a good pattern, there are several yards of it, plenty to garnish an elegant evening dress.' On 26 May 1890: 'I have had no duty of any sort to do except the answering of sundry epistles congratulating the Queen on her birthday. Her Majesty gave me a new photo of herself taken at Aix and a pair of little German glasses in remembrance of the day.' Seven years later: 'The Queen has given me a dear little brooch in pink and grey enamel with small diamonds as a memento of the Jubilee.' Three days after Christmas 1897 she was reporting from Osborne to her mother: 'I have some charming presents, large gold spoons from the Queen, a stand for miniatures from Princess Beatrice, a lovely old silver spoon from Princess Louise and a lovely little silver tray from the Duchess of Albany.'

A duty shared by ladies-in-waiting and the maids of honour was the sometimes chilly experience of driving out with the Queen. On 5 October 1895 at Balmoral, Lady Lytton was told that she would be required to drive with the Queen and Princess Christian at 4 p.m., 'so I went at once to dress warm', she recorded in her diary, 'as the order included (from the Scotch Piper who sings his words and is very difficult to understand) tea at some lodge, and I knew we should be home late . . .' She continued:

> The process of getting her Majesty into the carriage is intricate, with a green baize plank slanting up from the door-step. Then the Indian servant supports the Queen the most, and so gently, and without any fear or nervousness, then there were cloaks, shawls and frills offered by different hands. Princess Christian seemed terribly afraid of taking too much room, and sat right forward and I opposite. Then the many rugs were brought in turn, and finally a lovely new green rug, reversible cloth with white plaid the other side. 'This was a present given to me the other day, and a beautiful one,' the Queen said . . . We stopped at a cottage and the Queen gave a woman a dress so kindly and the small talk never stopped and when the Queen dozed at times the Princess and I went on talking.

At tea they 'all ate much more than we ought'. Some of the letters to which the ladies-in-waiting were called on to send suitable replies called for ingenuity, to put it mildly. 'The Queen, Windsor Castle: Dear Queen, I want a pair of twins. They must be a boy and a girl, and the girl must be one minute older than the boy. Please send them quick. Your affectionate subject . . . '

Cold drives were not confined to Balmoral. 'I have just come in quite frozen from a one and a half hour drive with the Queen,' Marie Mallet reported from Osborne on 16 January 1888, 'the wind north-east and freezing hard.' That month there was 'dense fog for four days', and letters were delayed 'as the steamers won't run in such dangerous weather. We have to go out just as usual but it is odious and even the Queen complains of the damp.'

Outings for the Queen's ladies were sometimes on foot. 'I went for a long walk with the Queen this morning,' Marie Mallet wrote from Balmoral on 11 November 1889, 'and felt very tired after it. It is no joke trotting up these mountains after a chair drawn by the most stalwart of ponies at the rate of at least 4 miles per hour! We were out from 11.20 to 1.10.'

There is no doubt that the Queen's ladies felt a deep and sincere affection for her, but they were sometimes drawn to the tedium of life at court by the prospect of a salary, albeit not a very large one. Although Lady Lytton's husband had served as Viceroy of India and ambassador to Paris (where he died in harness), bad management of his assets had reduced the family's income to £1,900 a year and she still had a son at Eton. As her daughter Emily declared she was a republican and would never contemplate becoming a maid of honour, Lady Lytton accepted the Queen's invitation to fill a vacancy that had occurred among her ladies-in-waiting 'caused by an event which has grieved me deeply, viz the death of my dear & valued friend the Dowagr Duchess of Roxburgh', largely because £300 a year beckoned, the sum her daughter had turned down. Marie Mallet was offered only £200 a year on her appointment as an extra woman of the bedchamber in 1895, but it was enough to tempt her back.

'Dear Marie,' the Queen wrote from Osborne on 8 August, 'Your kind letter gives me much pleasure and I need not say how truly I rejoice at the prospect of having you again about me.

'I trust you will not find the duties of your new office too onerous. Harriet Phipps will be able to tell you all about them. Ever, Yours affly, V.R.I.'

Unfortunately, Miss Phipps left instructions in her will for all her papers to be destroyed (why did she not destroy them herself, one wonders?), just one instance of invaluable social history going up in flames, but Marie Mallet's letters are among the most interesting records of the last years of Victoria's reign that happily have been preserved. 'The Queen sent for me directly after lunch yesterday,' she wrote to her husband from Balmoral on 17 October 1895, 'and greeted me so warmly and in such an affectionate manner that I had the tears in my eyes. She said, "I am so very glad to have you back, dear Marie, you will remember how very angry I was when you married!"' As far as work was concerned, Marie told Bernard: 'I really believe there is less to do than I have always imagined and that my principal business is to listen attentively and then hold my tongue.

'Last night while dressing to dine with the Queen Princess Beatrice knocked at my door and invested me there and then in petticoat and dressing jacket with the Order of Victoria and Albert, Third Class!4 It is quite lovely, just like Mama's, so I need not describe it further. It made me look very smart and I swelled visibly with pride when I appeared in the Drawing Room.'

Three days later she was writing to say: 'I began my new duties last night by reading to the Queen till past 12, but the interest and excitement kept me wide awake and mercifully I had no inclination to yawn. Harriet gave me a message from the Queen to the effect that she intends increasing my salary . . . £50 per year, from her own Privy Purse.' It was an extraordinary example of the Queen sending a message to one lady via another instead of speaking direct.

At Balmoral Marie considered herself 'very well lodged on the sunny side of the house' with a 'cosy little sitting-room' next to her bedroom; it contained 'a sofa, writing table with drawers, two other tables and a fairly comfortable armchair'. She was 'also entitled to one dwarf palm in a pot, and "The Times", "Morning Post" and

Queen Victoria and Beatrice, Princess Henry of Battenberg, in the Queen's
sitting room, Windsor Castle, 1895.

the "Scotsman" daily'. These she studied 'with a view to reading tit-bits to the Queen in the evening but as she has all the telegrams at once and does not care for controversy it is not always easy to pick out what may interest her'. On 25 October Marie had driven with the Queen, who had been so 'talkative and amusing' that she and a fellow lady 'had much ado to keep from immoderate laughter'. On coming upon a company of gypsies 'the Queen insisted on speaking to several of them and gave them money'.

On 4 November Marie told her husband:

You asked me to describe my day, so here it is. Breakfast at a quarter to ten, then general conversation till about eleven, when we repair to our respective dens and do what writing we have for the Messenger (this morning I have only two letters to answer and two telegrams to send). When the Queen goes out about twelve we all emerge and walk for an hour weather permitting which it has *not* done lately; at one we write again or read. I sometimes play duets with Princess Beatrice or read aloud to her and occasionally I see the Queen and take messages to Sir A Bigge [Sir Arthur Bigge, assistant private secretary] or 'Nunks' [her uncle, the groom-in-waiting]. At two we have a sociable meal and have coffee afterwards in the Billiard Room where we gossip and wait for driving orders. By 3.30 to a quarter to four we all drive out or on our own; tea at 5.30, more talk, then to our rooms again and we pay each other friendly visits, finally dinner at nine (if with the Queen), quarter to nine if with the household.

At eleven the Queen leaves the Drawing Room and I wait in my bedroom till I am summoned at twenty or a quarter to twelve to go to the Queen in her Sitting-room where I talk or read and take orders till about 12.30, then 'Good-night' and I fly to my bed and hot-water bottle! I do not keep up my maid. This routine never varies by a hair's breadth, as soon a revolution as to drive in the morning and walk after lunch, and boiled beef on Thursday and 'mehlspeise mit ananas' on Friday recur with unfailing regularity.

The courts of George II, George III and to a large extent those of George IV and William IV, although they may have differed from Victoria's in particularities, were equally renowned for following the sun on its invariable course. At least for the household – and the servants – the setting in which Victoria's routine was played out varied with moves between Windsor, Balmoral and Osborne and, for those fortunate enough to be chosen, with journeys to Italy and the south of France.

In her isolation and essential loneliness the Queen was, of course, far more dependent on her ladies than they were on her. The death of Prince Henry of Battenburg in 1896 provides a telling example of the relationship between the Queen and her ladies. Marie Mallet wrote to her husband, now private secretary to A. J. Balfour, to say, 'The gloom is very great . . . The Queen sent for me before dinner and talked a long time holding my hand and crying most bitterly . . . then I went to Princess Beatrice and we both sat and sobbed for half an hour.'

On returning to Balmoral for the first time as a woman of the bedchamber, Marie told her mother: 'My welcome here was even warmer than I had expected and the extraordinary thing is that everything is so exactly the same as when I left five years ago that I feel as if I had not even been away at all! The same chairs in the same places, the same plum cake, even the number of biscuits on the plate and their variety, absolutely identical, the same things said, the same done, only some of the old faces gone and a selection of new dogs follow the pony chair.'

It was small wonder that at the commencement of her third waiting, at Balmoral in October 1896, Marie was writing:

Our life here is intensely monotonous and I always feel when I return to it, even after months of absence, as if I had but left the week before. If I were a Queen how differently I should act but there seems a curious charm to our beloved Sovereign in doing the same thing on the same day year after year. Our drive on Saturday to the Bridge of Dee a good 35 miles on a chilly afternoon returning home in the dark after six could hardly be called pleasure, but the Queen enjoyed the sense of continuity as she had always done, talked the whole time and when getting out of the carriage after being wedged firmly for three and a half hours wondered why her knees were so stiff.

In addition to the Queen's affectionate if somewhat eccentric subjects, Marie Mallet now found herself instructed to write letters to numerous dignitaries, including the Bishop of Ripon, Sir Walter Parratt (Master of the Music) and the Dean of Windsor. When it came to delving into a War Office box, having, of course, been instructed by the Queen to do so, and to reading various communications to her, Sir Arthur Bigge became 'rather cross'. He thought it 'absurd that military messages should go through the Ladies! But this', Marie commented, 'is the natural result of having a Sovereign of 80. I am sure I wish she *would* see her Gentlemen oftener. I frequently am invited to put my nose into other people's affairs and dislike it.' The Queen even asked Lady Lytton to write to Lord Salisbury on the matter of a peerage.

Depending on the mood of the Queen – and that often depended on whether someone had died or not, but she could certainly sparkle if she felt like it – dinners at Windsor and Balmoral were as often as not a major ordeal. 'For the last two days the Queen's dinners have been appallingly dull,' Sir Henry Ponsonby noted in 1878. 'I really have nothing to say nor has anyone else.' Three years later: 'We had a dinner with the Dukes of Edinburgh, Connaught and Albany and their two Duchesses [Leopold was not yet married] which with Princess Beatrice makes a large element of Royalty. But the Queen keeps the conversation entirely under her control and does not allow any of them to talk too much.' He often referred, however, to the liveliness of Princess Louise's conversation at dinner and the relief this gave to the atmosphere of dullness, even gloom.[5] At one Balmoral dinner Ponsonby reported: 'We had a fierce discussion headed on each side by the Queen and Princess Beatrice as to whether if you were condemned to one or other you would rather live at the Equator or the North Pole. Princess Beatrice was for the Equator but the Queen fierce for the North Pole. "All doctors say that heat is unwholesome but cold wholesome."' For all her flinging open of windows, the Queen was not immune from colds. An early dinner attended by Ponsonby he found 'painfully flat partly I think because [the Queen] had a cold, partly because she sat between Leopold who never uttered and [Lord] Gainsborough who is deaf'.[6]

For somebody as averse as Queen Victoria to contradiction it must have been a welcome release of tension even to argue with her daughter. At Balmoral in 1898 the Queen and Empress Eugénie, widow of Napoleon III, 'discussed the state of the Italian army with much heat, contradicting each other so vigorously that we all shook with internal laughter', so Marie Mallet told her husband. 'It was most amusing to see two people who are never contradicted playing the game with each other. Neither gave way.'

The Gentlemen of the Household were spared invitations to lunch, often taken by the Queen, when she was at Windsor, in the

Oak Dining Room in the private apartments, seated in a small gilt armchair upholstered in crimson brocade. On a table nearby she would first lay out her handkerchief, fan, gloves and vinaigrette. She drank wine at formal meals but the Highlanders had given her a taste for whisky. She enjoyed, too, a glass of mulled port, and at Balmoral, in 1888, she was introduced, by Marie Mallet, to perry. At dinner on 2 November that year she ate, 'with evident relish and many expressions of admiration as to size, beauty and flavour', one of a consignment of Herefordshire apples sent to Scotland by Marie's step-father. 'I have never tasted perry and only cider once or twice in my life,' the Queen told Marie. 'Do you think your mama will send me some?' Both cider and perry duly arrived, and on 10 November 'the Queen partook of both for lunch and thought them quite delicious but she preferred the perry'.

The Queen's appetite was prodigious. In 1897 Reginald Brett, later second Viscount Esher, and his wife dined at Windsor. 'The Queen ate of everything,' he wrote in his diary, 'even cheese and a pear after dinner. No "courses". Dinner is served straight on, and when you finish one dish you get the next, without a pause for breath.' This uncivilized method of serving dinner, which might have appealed to Henry VIII's courtiers, was also recorded by Marie Mallet, who once said: 'The service was so rapid that a slow eater such as myself or Mr Gladstone never had time to finish even a most moderate helping.' What Marie described as a 'simple meal' could consist of soup, fish, cold sirloin of beef, a sweet and dessert, and always it was rushed through in half an hour. Claret or sherry was poured by a piper, champagne was served by butlers and the sweets were handed round by Indian servants.

One of the Queen's many godchildren, Alberta Ponsonby, who lived at Windsor until 1945 and in fairness, it must be said, did not like the Queen, told the diarist James Lees-Milne that dinners at the castle were 'interminable and dreadful'. No one, she claimed, was allowed to speak (or not above a whisper), and the Queen used to address her family in German. But she may have struck a bad night or been a biased witness. At mealtimes, as on many other occasions, Victoria was capable of great shafts of kindness. 'Edith, here is a bracelet for you,' she suddenly said to Lady Lytton at dinner one evening. One certainly gets the impression that dinner parties to which only ladies were invited were far more relaxed and enjoyable than those to which the gentlemen came.

'We had a most cheerful Ladies' Dinner last night,' Marie Mallet recalled at Balmoral in 1898, 'the Queen in excellent spirits, making jokes about her age and saying she *felt* quite young and that had it not been for an unfortunate accident she would have been *running* about still!' The accident to which the Queen would have been referring occurred at Windsor on 17 March 1883 when she was about to go out in the afternoon, 'missed the last step', as she recorded herself, 'and came down violently on one leg, without actually falling, which caused violent pain in my knee'. John Brown helped her 'with great difficulty' into the carriage, and on returning to the castle it required both Brown and a footman called Lockwood to get her to her room. Instead of resting, she 'struggled into dinner' on the arm of Princess Helena. The Queen was sixty-four at the time of this mishap from which she never really recovered. It eventually necessitated the use of a wheelchair, which makes a claim by Arthur Ponsonby that the Queen was still dancing at the age of seventy-two rather hard to believe.

In the summer of 1890 the Queen knew that Lady Ely was dying, 'Yet the final telegram was a shock and she cried bitterly', Marie Mallet told her husband. 'We had a Ladies' Night last night and the Queen wore jet and hardly uttered.' Two days later Marie reported that 'most meals have been funereal. Of course, this is quite natural for the Queen was devoted to poor Lady Ely. Her Majesty says that if she had been at Windsor she would have gone to the funeral.' That would have been an honour indeed, for it was almost unheard of for Victoria to attend even family funerals, although she told her doctor, Sir James Reid, that she was never depressed at a funeral! The court had remained in mourning, however, since the death of Prince Albert, the Queen and her ladies-in-waiting invariably dressed in black. The maids of honour were permitted white, grey, mauve or purple, unless, of course, court mourning for a specified period was ordered for some English or foreign royal, when even the maids wore black with jet jewellery.

Oddly enough, the Queen's refusal to wear anything but black does not seem to have had any noticeable economic effects. In 1861, while still a married woman, Victoria spent £3,890 on clothes and five years later £4,052. In 1872 the bills came to £4,242. She was by nature extravagant and had no conception about the sort of economies ordinary people had to make. In 1897 government ministers were so concerned about the maintenance costs at Buckingham Palace and Windsor Castle that the Queen cut down on the numbers of different kinds of bread she had for breakfast and gave orders that her bed, which invariably accompanied her to the Continent on holidays, was not to be repaired. (In 1890, on a visit to Aix-les-Bains and Darmstadt, the Queen travelled incognito as Madame la Comtesse de Balmoral.)

Victoria invited Bernard Mallet to Windsor on one occasion as a surprise for his wife. 'Very little conversation at dinner,' he noted in his diary, 'except in a low voice. It lasted little over half an hour. The Queen as she rose said of the wind, which was howling outside, "What a melancholy sound!"' When he was summoned to talk with her in the corridor 'she immediately put me quite at ease with her great amiability of manner and evident interest in what was said. She laughed more than ever, and I had a stronger impression than ever of her charm, which consists of extreme womanliness, and great commonsense, together with sincere and evident interest in what she is saying. No mere making of conversation but real sympathy and interest.' This was a verdict echoed by his wife: 'Her interest is real and not the least put on.'

As Minister in Attendance, Lord James of Hereford, who had described Balmoral as 'cold as death', one night at Osborne recalled: 'We talked, as usual, in a very subdued tone, but the Queen often leant her head towards us and listened to our conversation.' Just before leaving the dining room, Lord James told Princess Helena an extraordinary anecdote about a dog belonging to Sir Henry Wolff, ambassador at Madrid. It appeared that the dog's dinner had been overlooked while Lady Wolff was entertaining, so the dog went into the garden, bit off a forget-me-not and placed it on Lady Wolff's lap. The Princess implored Lord James to repeat the story for the benefit of the Queen, who 'looked responsively round'. She 'laughed heartily and said, "But can it be true?" "Your minister at Madrid, Ma'am, is always remarkably accurate in his statements of facts," said Lord James. "Ah, so I understand," said the Queen, with a very sly look.'

There is no doubt whatever that wealthy Victorians ate far more than was good for them; a substantial breakfast, at least a three-course lunch and a bounteous dinner, not forgetting a solid tea of bread and scones and cakes between lunch and dinner. In Scotland the Queen often called on tenants for tea, or arranged for a picnic tea to be sent on ahead to be eaten in a lodge. After one such excursion Lady Lytton recorded: 'The Queen had a good appetite and after two scones, two bits of toast and several biscuits she said, "I am afraid I must not have any more."' And the household were expected to keep up with their royal mistress. Marie Mallet's description sent to her step-sister of the gastronomic excesses of a train journey from Balmoral to Windsor is not fit reading for a Puritan. 'My dear,' she wrote, 'I can't tell you how much food we were provided with.' There were hampers stuffed 'with every kind of cold meat' and 'enough cake and biscuits to set up a baker's shop' accompanied by tea, claret, sherry and champagne. 'But this was evidently not deemed sufficient to support life, so we had a hearty tea at Aberdeen, where royal footmen rushed about wildly with tea kettles gazed at by a large crowd, and a huge dinner at Perth, with six courses . . . and at 11.30 p.m. on our arrival at Carlisle we partook of tea and juicy muffins.'

There were members of the Queen's household in a strangely anomalous position: her doctors. Until late in her reign Victoria declined to acknowledge her physicians, her German secretary or the Windsor librarian as members of the household, with whom they did not even eat. On one memorable occasion, when the Queen wished her doctor to attend after dinner, she sent a note to the Master of the Household to say, 'The gentlemen and Sir James Reid are to come this evening to a Drawing-room'. Dr Reid had joined the Queen's retinue on 8 July 1881, as resident medical attendant, at the age of thirty-one. He spoke fluent German, which would have been recommendation enough, and in the peculiar way the Queen had, she eventually promoted him unofficially to confidential adviser. In 1894, on the welcome resignation of Gladstone, she told him to write to the Earl of Rosebery to urge him to accept the premiership in order to protect her health; she wanted a holiday in Florence.

Reid began his stint at court on £400 a year. Victoria eventually raised his salary to £1,500, and he went on to serve both Edward VII and George V. His Windsor lodgings, which he thought 'very comfortable', had a 'splendid view', he told his mother, 'right down what they call "the Long Walk"'. On his first visit to Osborne he wrote home to say: 'I think I am getting on pretty well, though altogether I have not done *one day's* work since I left you!' That situation was soon to change. Other specialists had appointments: Dr William Hoffmeister was surgeon apothecary at Osborne, Sir James Paget was sergeant surgeon to the Queen, Dr James Ellison was surgeon apothecary at Windsor, Sir John Williams was called in as *accoucheur* to Princess Beatrice. But it was Reid who lived, while in waiting, at the Queen's beck and call. A summons to see her four or five times a day was nothing unusual. She tended to fuss over her health, but when she was not falling about (in 1892 she tripped over a carpet and fell heavily) she had little to complain about except sometimes insomnia and often flatulence, usually brought on by eating too many heavy puddings too quickly. More soothing than any medication were the highly indiscreet chats she had with Reid before retiring for the night. And Reid frequently found himself in attendance on the Queen's grandchildren and visitors. Like his uncle and namesake, Prince Leopold, Duke of Albany, Prince Leopold of Battenberg suffered from haemophilia and had to be watched like a hawk, and his sister Princess Ena, when six, nearly died after falling off her pony. From the royal family and distinguished foreigners there were the usual perks – a gold cigarette case, for example, from the Emperor of Russia.

Like so many strong-willed women who hate to be thwarted, Queen Victoria could induce insomnia or other imaginary symptoms of ill health, which in turn resulted in sympathetic attention. Some of the recipes or prescriptions at Dr Reid's disposal have a positively medieval ring about them: 'Dover's Powder', 'Tincture of Henbane'. In July 1889 he recorded: 'I was obliged to give [the Queen] 5 grains of Dover and one of Calomel as she insisted on having something of the sort. She had an excellent night, but Mrs MacDonald [Annie MacDonald, wardrobe maid, who served the

Queen for forty-one years] says she is dreadfully cross today, and that they can hardly get on with her at all. I believe it is entirely owing to the Royal Grants Commission not getting on as she wishes, for she has been in a vile humour since Wednesday evening when she got a box on the subject from Lord Salisbury.' Reid went on to explain:

Ponsonby told me yesterday that the Royal Grants Committee do not quite see their way to recommending grants to any of Her Majesty's children except the Wales family, and that this has made the Queen angry. I am afraid to give her more Dover's Powders for fear of establishing a habit. The Queen said again that she could not sleep. Nevertheless she declined to go to bed till the usual time, 1.30; and as her undressing etc takes an hour, it was about 2.30 when she got to bed. She could have quite enough if she would sleep when she can, but she *won't* and *refuses* to sleep either earlier at night or later in the morning than her usual hours.

Reid, who reported in the early years of his appointment to the Queen's physician-in-ordinary, Sir William Jenner, told Jenner in 1889 that the Queen had suffered 'a very severe attack of acute indigestion with gastric pain and nausea. I was up with her till 5.30 a.m. It was caused, I believe, by her eating among other things a very heavy indigestible sweet at dinner; and I trust she will be more careful in future.' Even on holiday Reid was pursued by running commentaries on his patient's symptoms. 'Since you left,' the Queen wrote, dispensing with her usual mode of reference to herself as 'the Queen', 'my indigestion seems not very good. I had no pain but rather an oppression after meals, and a rising after all I ate and acidity, as well as a slight headache most mornings which goes off later. The bowels are right, upon the whole, but there is an inclination to griping and the day before yesterday there was a good deal of bile. I think that perhaps tomorrow evening that powder with a little salt in the next morning will be a good thing.'

In common with most of her subjects, the Queen endured dental problems, and as old age crept up so her eyesight began to fade. With the amount of reading and writing with which she had filled her days, she found this the hardest disability of all to bear. As did her household, who now spent hours trying to make out the meaning of illegible letters. 'My eyes are troublesome,' the Queen wrote to Reid in the winter of 1892. 'I can get none of the spectacles to suit; they are wrongly focused, and at night reading is very trying and difficult, though I still at times find dark print not too unreadable. I can see much better without glasses. I am sure some can be got to suit.'

Reid was not even the Queen's optician. But so dependent did she become on him that she was selfish enough to summon him back from his honeymoon because – she said – her shoulder was aching. Reid had been foolish enough only to go as far as Taplow Court with his bride – just around the corner from Windsor. When the Queen discovered how many family and household were planning to attend Reid's wedding at St Paul's, Knightsbridge she complained there would be no one left to pour her tea (a page would not suffice, it seems) and Princess Beatrice had to cut the reception and return to her mother's side.

Having been appointed a Companion of the Order of the Bath, Reid, entirely for snobbish reasons, declined a knight bachelorhood, and in the Queen's Birthday Honours List for 1895 he was made a Knight Commander of the Bath. Two years later he became a baronet. He has left an interesting account of his private investiture at Balmoral:

I was 'introduced' to the Queen's presence by Edwards [Sir Fleetwood Edwards, an assistant private secretary], and went down on one knee, when Her Majesty touched me on each shoulder with a sword and said 'Sir James'. (She insisted on doing it with a Claymore, instead of an ordinary sword, as this place is in the Highlands!) I then kissed her hand and remained kneeling, when she put round my neck the red ribbon and badge of the Bath, and handed me the star which is worn on the coat. I then kissed hands again and got up, and it was all over. She had never seen the top of my head before, and was surprised, she said, to see my hair was so nearly gone! I dined last night with the Queen, and should not wonder if I do so again tonight in my new warpaint!

It is an interesting account because it contains a number of differences in procedure compared with modern practice. Today the Queen does not name her subject. There is no kissing of the sovereign's hand at an investiture, and a newly dubbed knight stands to receive the insignia.

Sir Henry Ponsonby referred to one of the Windsor doctors as 'a very good man, a very great bore and a very bad doctor, who is a great gossip and wearies my life out with grievances and quarrels'. Although medicine made giant strides during Victoria's reign, the track record of doctors, denied as they were any twentieth-century aids to medicine, was as often as not one of failure. Yet they were thought to be infallible. Sir Douglas Powell was sometimes invited to dine. During the interminable standing after dinner Sir Douglas surprised the assembled company by fainting. As he was carried out, the Queen asked what had happened. On being informed all she said was: 'And a doctor, too!'

12

The Loss of a Real Friend

Only Queen Victoria could have employed both a chief dresser and a head dresser, the latter the appropriately named Mrs Tuck. After the death of Prince Albert, what they and the other dressers did all day it is hard to imagine. It was not as if the Queen was for ever sitting for a portrait or slipping out to fulfil some royal engagement. The great swaths of black satin in which the Queen festooned herself when she got up served just as well for breakfast, lunch, a drive in a carriage, tea in a cottage, dinner and the reception of Cabinet ministers. In the early years of Victoria's reign there was a principal dresser, Marianne Skerrett. Her first German dresser, 'a most valued and excellent servant', the Queen told her uncle, Leopold of the Belgians, died after nearly seven years in service. She had been '*perfection* in every sense of the word'; news of her death had 'quite overset' her. But her aunt, the Duchess of Gloucester, was only moderately sympathetic; *her* dresser had been with her for fifty-two years, and she told Victoria: 'If anything was to happen to Miss Gold I should not know what to do without her.'

It was not just that ladies like Queen Victoria could not iron a handkerchief or button up a dress; they made real friends with their personal maid or dresser. She was the first person they saw in the morning and the last at night, an eager ear for gossip from the dining room, for amusing anecdotes from the drawing room. It is easy to envisage the sort of rapport that existed between Victoria and her personal servants by recalling a famous occasion when, after the Queen had made one of her assistant private secretaries, Frederick Ponsonby, wait three years before allowing him to marry, her dresser ventured to suggest a tea service alone was not much of a present; she thought the Queen's largesse should stretch to a silver coffee service as well. 'Am I giving this present,' the Queen demanded to know, 'or are you?'

Length of service had been a hallmark of royal servants since long before Victoria came to the throne, and her own staff were generally slow to desert her, partly because she tried to make their lives as interesting and varied as possible. Marianne Skerrett, in her role as personal secretary rather than dresser, was a forerunner of Harriet Phipps, answering begging letters and dealing with tradesmen, and with artists as eminent as Sir Edwin Landseer. She spoke both German and French and was no mere maid, but took a hand in engaging the other dressers and wardrobe maids. She was with the Queen for a quarter of a century, 'a person of immense literary knowledge' and 'of the greatest discretion' in the opinion of the Queen, although others of more lowly rank thought her 'a sharp clever old maid as ever lived, and very plain spoken', which may have been precisely what appealed about her to Victoria.

The wardrobe maids received £50 a year, Skerrett £200, which put her on a financial footing with a woman of the bedchamber. There was, of course, far more to a dresser's duties than laying out the Queen's wardrobe and helping her get in and out of her garments. Any lady's maid would have been expected to possess the rudiments of millinery and dressmaking, and to be able to dress her mistress's hair. If a riding habit was spattered with mud, it was a maid's task to get it clean, and throughout her career she would seldom stray far from a copy of *Mrs Beeton*.

Life for a wardrobe maid or a dresser before Victoria went into permanent mourning in 1861 was much more glamorous than it was following the death of the Prince Consort. For a levée at Buckingham Palace the Queen might wear 'a train of white and gold moiré antique silk . . . trimmed with gold blonde lace and red velvet bows', and a gown of white satin. Or perhaps a train 'of pink satin, covered with English lace and trimmed with bows of white satin'. For her birthday Drawing Room in 1856 the Queen wore 'a train of light blue silk, embroidered all over with a palm pattern in gold, silver and red'. For a state ball the same year she wore a dress of 'Indian muslin embroidered with gold sprigs, and a broad gold border in bouquets, trimmed with bunches of red cactus, and green leaves ornamented with diamonds'. In July she appeared at a ball given by the Duchess of Gloucester in 'a magnificent dress of cerise-coloured tulle'. Shortly after his marriage, Prince Albert was writing from Windsor to tell his brother that Victoria 'was lovely to look at yesterday at dinner. She had a very low-necked dress, with a bunch of roses at her breast which was swelling up from her dress.'

In the manner of any well-brought-up upper-middle-class lady, the Queen took good care of her servants. When her dresser Frieda Arnold had a 'fearful headache' and a heavy cold, 'The Queen sent a friendly little man in a black truck coat and kid gloves' to see her twice a day; he was Dr Henry Brown, apothecary to the household at Windsor from 1837 to 1866. On New Year's Day 1855 the dressers were given tickets for an evening concert in St George's Hall at Windsor, a very elaborate affair with an orchestra of 140 and a chorus of 75. The Queen could never be described as a snob;

she stood as godmother to the daughter of one of her dressers.

The dressers took their meals in the steward's room, along with the housekeeper, pages, visiting ladies' maids and valets. There was also a servants' hall, and the numbers of meals prepared for the different dining rooms required catering and culinary skills of a high order. In 1855 the daily average of beef, lamb and pork consumed when the Queen was in residence either at Buckingham Palace, Windsor or Osborne came to 629 pounds. Transport logistics were equally daunting. A state visit to France entailed getting fifteen ladies and gentlemen of the Household, their maids, valets and footmen, two royal pages, a hairdresser, two valets for Prince Albert, a messenger, two dressers, a wardrobe maid and two police inspectors among others on to the royal yacht, a new ship capable of a speed four times faster than any available escort.

Even before crossing from Southampton to the Isle of Wight, wardrobe maids and dressers were treated with amazing consideration. On the train journey to Southampton they were provided, so that they had something to eat before the sea crossing, with 'ham, capon, bread and butter and port-wine'. And the Queen was just as devoted to Prince Albert's servants as to her own. One of his valets, Isaac Cart, had been with the Prince since Albert was eleven. When Cart died in 1858, the Queen wrote of him: 'He was invaluable; well-educated, thoroughly trustworthy, devoted to the Prince, the best of nurses, superior in every sense of the word, a proud independent Swiss, who was quite *un homme de confidence*, peculiar but extremely careful, and who might be trusted in anything . . . He was the only link my loved one had about him which connected him with his childhood, the only one with whom he could talk over old times. I cannot think of my dear husband without Cart! He seemed part of himself! We were so thankful and proud of this faithful old servant, he was such a comfort to us.' Albert had, in fact, also brought with him to England a riding master, Wilhelm Meyer. When Meyer retired in 1867 the Queen gave him a carriage and horses.

Anyone of humble origin took her fancy. When in 1887 a sergeant was convicted of embezzlement it was suggested that he should be deprived of his Victoria Cross, instituted for all ranks for 'conspicuous bravery' by Queen Victoria in 1856. 'The Queen cannot bring herself to sign this,' she minuted. 'It seems too cruel. She pleads for mercy for the brave man.' To drunkenness below stairs she turned a Nelsonian eye, unlike Lady Lytton, who managed to find 'sad cases of drink amongst the servants'. It always 'distresses one to see so much of it' she told Lord Edward Pelham-Clinton, Master of the Household.

A visit to Baden-Baden in 1872 enabled the Queen to meet up again with two of her former maids, Frieda Arnold and Sophie Weiss, and to Frieda's daughter she presented a set of jewellery. When in 1890 Frieda's husband died the Queen wrote to say: 'These lines accompany an enamelled photograph of your dear husband which I have made for you. Please accept also the expression of my deep sympathy on the irreplaceable loss which you have suffered. May God console and protect you!' It was precisely this sincere personal touch the Queen exercised where her servants were concerned that endeared her to them so much. And their numbers were truly enormous. At least two dozen grooms were stationed at Buckingham Palace alone. At Windsor there were at least fourteen beaters. John Whiting, a Page of the Back Stairs, was photographed in 1858 resplendent with gold watch chain; he was then in the fifty-second year of his service, his memories of the court stretching back to the reign of George III. John Meakin, born in 1816, had by 1898 woven the Queen's hose for sixty years; for sixty years, too, Ann Birkin sat embroidering the Queen's hose.

Such continuity of service gave the Queen herself a sense of security, and anyone who had served three previous monarchs could be relied on for fascinating anecdotes.

The Queen's consideration for her servants was legendary.[1] On 14 November 1865 the Keeper of the Privy Purse was writing to the Lord Chamberlain to say: 'Mrs Blake, the widow of old Blake, who was a page of King William's, and for 60 years in the Royal Service, died upon the 11th. She lived in a small cottage at Bushey, called Hawthorne Lodge, and she has left a daughter, Amelia, who is afflicted with a spinal complaint, and, in consideration of the services of the family, for I believe they have all been Royal Servants, the Queen is anxious that this poor woman should be permitted to continue to occupy this cottage.'

On 25 May 1866 the Queen gave a tea party for the servants' families. 'They will dance a little afterwards,' she wrote in her journal. When John Turnball, clerk of the works at Windsor, died that year, the Queen hastened to view him in his coffin. Two years later, when a messenger who had been in service forty-seven years suddenly died in a cab, the Queen went to see his body 'in his last bed, looking peaceful with a smile on his face'. She refused to sack an old lamplighter at Windsor just because he was drunk, and when her servants were ill she never hesitated to visit them; she felt they were part of her family. On 16 July 1886 she went to see her 'poor excellent footman Lockwood, who has been ill since the winter and is gradually wasting away. His emaciation is fearful to see.' She recalled that after her fall at Windsor he had carried her for more than three months. He 'was a devoted faithful servant. It made me very sad to see him like this.'

At Balmoral in 1895 the Queen attended the funeral of a young nephew of John Brown, and afterwards she sat for half an hour with his mother, 'weeping with, and helping her', so Lady Lytton recorded. As the lad's father had 'kept himself up with whiskey and had to be supported by two at the ceremony', it was deemed better that the Queen should see him another day. Despite the emotional ordeal, the Queen called at three other cottages, 'had the women out and gave them stuff for dresses so kindly. She had a nap at the end but Miss Phipps roused her before we got home.' Later that year the Queen stopped at a cottage 'to see a stout "Maggie".

'"Have you got any money?" said the Queen to the Scotch servant, a stout man who can't move without being so blown he can't speak.

'"Aboot twelve shillings."

'"Ah, that won't do *at all*, I always give her five poond," answered the Queen with the Scotch accent.'

At Balmoral the Queen was very much the lady of the manor, for ever distributing alms and popping into the local shop, which, in fact, the Queen and Prince Albert had built for Mr and Mrs Symon when they first found them in the village in 1848. In September 1896 the Queen had taken the Tsar of Russia to meet Mrs Symon, and between them the Queen and the Tsar practically emptied the shop. On 27 January 1897, while at Osborne, the Queen wrote in her journal: 'Heard when we were at breakfast . . . that dear old Mrs Symon at the shop in the village at Balmoral had passed away . . . She was quite an institution; and everyone high and low used to go and see her.'

Even the servants of her household were fussed up by the Queen. On the last day of August 1899, very near the end of her life, 'The Queen received all the servants and gave Checketts [Lady Lytton's maid] a nice fitted box with her own hand. Checketts could not sleep for thinking of the honour,' Lady Lytton told her daughter, 'and was inclined to cry.'

The Queen at Osborne House, 1866. On the seat are the Princesses Helena and Louise. Her Majesty is attended by John Brown.

The servant more indulged and ultimately mourned than any other was the notorious John Brown. He was notorious not because of his relations with the Queen, although they were looked on with disdain by family and courtiers alike, but because he was so stunningly rude and offhand with those very members of the royal family and household who despised, indeed loathed, him. John Brown was a rough-hewn, hard-drinking, down-to-earth, out-spoken Highlander, an egalitarian who believed himself to be the equal of any man or woman born, with the one exception of the Queen. The Queen he revered as his sovereign, but as a woman he knew perfectly well how isolated and lonely she was, and how she yearned to be treated like an equal. Her household would never have dreamed of doing so, her children were either in awe of her or they were frankly afraid of her. With the Queen, Brown formed precisely that relationship of familiarity unique to the English upper middle class and their personal servants. If he went further than many in his position might have done, it was because he was a Scot; one minute he was addressing the Queen as Your Majesty, the next as Woman. And the Queen responded with a silent inner thankfulness; somebody had actually noticed that she was a woman as well as a queen. Within the limits of their relationship John Brown never overstepped the mark. After his death, Victoria may have exaggerated her sorrows or rubbed her family's nose in her loss by erecting so many statues and busts, but it was in her nature to grieve so openly; far more to the point is that she wrote in her journal: 'It is the loss not only of a servant but of a real friend.'

John Brown was born in 1826 at Crathie on the Balmoral estate, and had it not been for Queen Victoria, who assigned to him the role of personal attendant and gave him accommodation at Windsor Castle, where he died, it is unlikely he would ever have left the Highlands. His father was a crofter, his maternal grandfather a blacksmith. Brown began his unique career as a stable lad, and as soon as the Queen and Prince Albert came upon Balmoral he was appointed gillie to the Prince. Hence, on fishing and shooting expeditions he got to know his royal employers well, and they him. He was immensely efficient and quite fearless. He treated the Queen and Prince Albert with abrupt courtesy; he was never insolent but he never fawned. For Victoria and Albert he was the ideal travelling companion, with his broad Scottish common sense and intimate knowledge of the terrain.

Had the Queen merely retained Brown's services out of doors after Prince Albert's death trouble would never have brewed, but she gave him carte blanche to take over the organization of many indoor events. The household came to detest the high jinks that epitomized the gillies' balls, with John Brown bellowing instructions and dancing with the Queen.[2] It is interesting that in editing his father's letters Arthur Ponsonby thought it safe to write: 'Nothing . . . that John Brown said or did was of the smallest consequence except perhaps his seizure of the mad youth who pointed an unloaded revolver at the Queen when she was passing in her carriage in London in 1872.' So anxious was he to airbrush Brown out of history that he chose to ignore the occasion in Windsor on 2 March 1882 when a man called Roderick Maclean fired into the Queen's carriage as she was leaving the railway station for the castle. Brown, as usual, was on the box. Maclean must have been a lousy shot, for he missed not only the Queen but Princess Beatrice and the Duchess of Roxburghe. An Eton boy belaboured Maclean with his umbrella. The Duchess at this stage still thought the shot had been some sort of joke, but 'Brown, however, when he opened the carriage, said, with a greatly perturbed face, though quite calm, "That man fired at Your Majesty's carriage" '. In her own account of the drama the Queen added, 'Nothing can exceed dearest Beatrice's courage and calmness, for she saw the whole thing, the man take aim, and fire straight into the carriage.'

Ponsonby's judgement depends on your point of view. As far as the Queen was concerned, it was sufficient just to have John Brown about her; that he may not have sat in the Cabinet or become Archbishop of Canterbury was hardly the issue. The household would have been exasperated, for instance, because Brown was in attendance during a state visit from the Sultan of Turkey in full Highland dress; and because his name was mentioned in a sarcastic, almost republican, article in *Vanity Fair*, in which the Queen was criticized for using Windsor Castle for hurried calls '*en route* between Osborne and Balmoral'; and because he was frequently drunk on duty without once being reprimanded by the Queen, whereas Victoria could send stinging rebukes over trivial misdemeanours to her household.

It is true that Henry Ponsonby had to expend valuable time and energy preventing rows between Brown and the Queen's children; and that on one extraordinary occasion Ponsonby actually found himself undertaking Brown's duties. Ponsonby discovered the Queen seated in her carriage waiting to go for a drive. He hovered in order to bow her off. The carriage failed to move, however, as there was no John Brown in sight. Without a word to the Queen, Ponsonby made his way to Brown's room, found him flat out on the bed, locked the door, and again without a word mounted the box and drove off. There was not much the Queen could say. Sir John Cowell, at one time Master of the Household, had more than one occasion to remonstrate with Brown over the amount of alcohol consumed in the servants' hall, but instead of supporting the head of her household the Queen invariably sided with her drunken gillie.

Brown suffered from a skin complaint called erysipelas, which it is thought exacerbated his irritable nature. It also reduced his resistance to infection, as must his chronic intake of whisky, and he caught a chill on some madcap expedition at Windsor to enquire after Lady Florence Dixie, who had allegedly been attacked by two men dressed as women and stabbed with a knife. Her St Bernard was said to have put the men to flight. Dr James Reid thought Lady Florence 'rather a queer customer' and believed she had invented the whole story. Whatever the truth, the outing cost Brown his life. By the evening following Brown's visit to Lady Florence, Reid noted that he was suffering from delirium tremens, and not surprisingly no one had the courage to tell the Queen how ill her faithful attendant was. She knew, however, that Reid's father had suddenly died, yet she insisted that Reid should remain at Windsor to nurse Brown. On the morning of 29 March 1883 Prince Leopold broke the news to his mother that Brown was dead. 'Am terribly upset by this loss,' the Queen recorded in her journal, 'which removes one who was so devoted and attached to my service and who did so much for my personal comfort.'

At the instigation of the Queen, *The Times* carried an obituary. Before burial at Crathie (Victoria would frequently stop off at his grave to lay flowers), Brown's body remained for a week in his room in the Clarence Tower, overlooking the East Terrace, and just as she had done with Albert the Queen gave orders that his room was to remain undisturbed. She compelled members of the household, whose lives he had made so difficult, to attend a Congregationalist service in the room before his body was removed, and shops in the town closed – or were told to close – out of respect. Had the Queen deliberately intended to foster outlandish rumours about her relationship with John Brown, she could not have gone about it more thoroughly.

To Brown's sister-in-law Victoria wrote: 'Weep with me for we all have lost the best, the truest heart that ever beat. My grief is unbounded, dreadful, and I know not how to bear it, or how to believe it possible.' With scant regard for Ponsonby's feelings, she wrote to him to say she was 'utterly crushed. The loss of the strong arm and wise advice, warm heart and cheery original way of saying things and the sympathy in any large and small circumstances is most cruelly missed.' Prince George of Wales was admonished never to forget his 'poor sorrowing Grandmamma's best and truest friend'. Plaster of Paris busts and gold tiepins were churned out as memorabilia. A life-size bronze statue by a distinguished Viennese sculptor, Edgar Boehm, appeared in the garden at Balmoral – removed to a more secluded spot by Edward VII, to the grounds of a house the Queen had built for Brown. In the holy of holies, the sacred Royal Mausoleum at Frogmore, John Brown's memorial tablet was to be the single tribute to anyone who was not a member of the family. As she frequently did when stricken by grief, the Queen lost the use of her legs.

If the Queen had made a bit of a fool of herself over John Brown, it was a dress rehearsal for the absurdities of her employment of the Munshi. Immensely proud of having been proclaimed Empress of India in 1876, genuinely interested in the subcontinent and without a shred of racial prejudice, in 1887 Victoria hired two Indian servants, the first of many, over whom she fussed like a mother hen. Reams of instructions about their welfare flowed from her pen: when they were to wait, what they were to wear, how to keep them warm. One was a strikingly good-looking Muslim called Abdul Karim, twenty-four years old and married; his wife was invited to join him at Balmoral. Abdul gave the Queen lessons in Hindustani so she gave him the appellation Munshi, meaning teacher. Like Prince Albert so many years before, the Munshi began by blotting the Queen's letters, but it

St George's Hall, Windsor Castle.

was not long before he was reading them, too. Advised by Prince Louis of Battenberg, the son-in-law of Princess Alice, that her Hindu subjects in India might resent this favouritism, the Queen gave way and promptly appointed the Munshi her Indian Secretary, giving orders that all photographs of him serving at table were to be destroyed.

The Queen had already caused offence to her household by issuing instructions that after dinner the Munshi, about whom Dr Reid thought the Queen was 'off her head', was to join them in the billiard room. When she announced that the Munshi was to accompany her on holiday to Cimiez, the household put their collective foot down and issued an ultimatum: if the Munshi went to France they would resign in a body. Even the Queen realized she would be hard pressed to ride out a scandal of this magnitude and relented, but not before, in her rage, she had swept several hundreds of pounds' worth of china off her dressing table. Even the Prime Minister became involved, advising the Queen that the French, not so liberal in racial matters as Her Majesty, might be unkind to her Munshi, so providing her with a let-out.

The Munshi regarded himself as infinitely superior to the other Indian servants employed by the Queen because at home he was considered a gentleman, his father being employed in Agra as a surgeon-general; he was in fact an apothecary in a prison. Rubbish, said the Queen, and made her beloved Munshi, for whose 'sensitive feelings' she felt so sorry, a Companion of the Most Eminent Order of the Indian Empire.[3] But problems with the Indians rumbled on. A brooch given to the Queen by Prince Louise of Hesse went missing and was eventually, rather rashly, sold to a jeweller in Windsor for the equivalent of 35 pence; the household blamed the Indians and the Queen harassed her dressers. From Osborne in 1899 Marie Mallet reported to her mother that the

Royal Group, Osborne House, August 1898.

Left to right: Prince Leopold of Battenberg; Princess Aribert of Anhalt; Prince Edward of York; Duchess of York with Princess Mary; Prince Alexander of Battenberg (on ground); Princess Mary of Connaught; Duke of York with Prince Albert; Queen Victoria; Prince Arthur of Connaught; Duchess of Connaught; Princess Patricia of Connaught (on ground); Princess Henry of Battenberg; Princess Victoria Eugenie of Battenberg; Princess Victoria of Schleswig-Holstein; Prince Maurice of Battenberg.

Queen gossiped a good deal with the Munshi, who was 'ubiqui-
tous here and I am for ever meeting him in passages or the garden
or face to face on the stairs and each time I shudder more'. The
shuddering ceased only in February 1901, when King Edward VII,
without a moment's hesitation, sent all his mother's Indian servants
packing.

13

'*The Dearest Sweetest Smile*'

During the course of her long reign, so far the longest in British history, Queen Victoria received and entertained an enormous number of visitors. Many were politicians, many more were relatives; some came on state visits; various heads of state – of Holland and Russia, for example – more or less just dropped in; at Windsor, in particular, musicians assembled to entertain her. There were guests who came to dinner, others who were expected to put in an appearance at a levée or a Drawing Room, and there were those who were invited to attend a garden party.

The politicians Queen Victoria least enjoyed having to stay were Viscount Palmerston and William Gladstone, Gladstone serving four times as Prime Minister between 1868 and 1894. The Queen complained that he addressed her as though she were a public meeting, but the poor man was simply shy, awkward and in awe of her. As well as serving as a headstrong Foreign Secretary, Lord Palmerston was twice Prime Minister, one of seven members of the House of Lords who held that office during Victoria's reign; at Windsor Castle, in 1839, the fifty-five-year-old Palmerston wandered off through badly lit passages to locate the bedroom of one of the Queen's ladies-in-waiting, who threw him out. When

Viscount Palmerston, from a drawing by Geo Richmond RA.

the Queen was at Balmoral or Osborne it was customary for a member of the government to kick his heels in waiting, one of the most ill favoured being Viscount Cross, the Lord Privy Seal. 'Lord Cross was quite drunk on Thursday evening after dinner,' Marie Mallet wrote to her husband from Balmoral on 13 June 1896, 'and talked so loud and paid such fulsome compliments that Brigge and I could hardly keep our countenances or conceal our disgust but this is strictly "entre nous" for he is in high favour and openly says that the Queen cannot do without him! I overhear him telling her all sorts of tales which I do not believe to be true, for I doubt whether Lord Salisbury would tell him more than he is actually obliged to.'

One of the Queen's elderly ladies, the Countess of Errol, preached abstention from alcohol with all the fervour of a tub-thumping Methodist. At Balmoral that October Marie Mallet recalled, 'Dear Lady Errol's evangelistic efforts culminated in the presentation to Lord Cross of a tract on temperance! He related this last night to the Queen at dinner amid shouts of laughter. I never saw the Queen so amused; but the dear old lady is rather in disgrace especially since she begged the Queen to prevent people visiting Kew Gardens on Sunday.' It seems as though Lady Errol's good works were in vain. 'Lord Cross made an ass of himself as usual last night,' Mrs Mallet wrote from Osborne on 13 February 1900, 'very squiffy after dinner, he began to pay his usual fulsome compliments. I am supposed to have turned from him too haughtily but his ignorance and intemperance disgust me . . . He does not have the same success as he used to in Royal circles, thank goodness.' Arthur Balfour was staying at Balmoral in November 1898. 'A. J. B. was more beloved than ever last night,' Marie Mallet reported, 'and roared so loud at Nunks's imitations of Lord Cross that he could have been heard ten miles off, he simply doubled up with laughter.'

It was small wonder that in the autumn of 1889 the Queen felt considerable anxiety over an intended visit to chilly Balmoral of some envoys from sunny Zanzibar. Viscountess Downe, who had succeeded Lady Ely as a lady of the bedchamber, already had a cold, 'the poor old Duke of Rutland [he was Chancellor of the Duchy of Lancaster] an ordinary chill', according to Marie Mallet, 'and the dear Queen is in rather a fright about the Zanzibar Envoys, one of whom is sixty-three and the other seventy-five, and fears they may catch chills too!' Apparently, they 'were very funny', spoke Arabic 'and presented the Queen with a gigantic letter sealed with a Golden Seal the size one usually sees in a pantomime. They told us they enjoyed the sights of London, especially the Fire Brigade which they say is a sign of good government. They ate their curry very awkwardly. I could see they were dying to fling aside the knives and forks and use their brown fingers. They brought no presents with them which was a disappointment.'

A visitor to Windsor in November 1896 whom Mrs Mallet most decidedly did not like was Horatio Herbert Kitchener – General Kitchener, recently returned from his successful campaigns in the Sudan. Mrs Mallet thought him 'either a woman-hater or a boor, for he would hardly utter to us ladies in spite of many and strenuous efforts at dinner'. He found no difficulty talking to the Queen, however, presenting her with various trophies, including a Crusader's sword. Received in audience at Balmoral two years later, Kitchener was actually invited to sit.

Journeys still took so long and were still relatively so hazardous that early in the Queen's reign visits from overseas royalty were often of a protracted nature. 'The Crown Prince of Württemberg has been here for some time,' Prince Albert wrote to his brother from Buckingham Palace on 10 April 1843. 'He is to stay for some months. It is his first journey and he seems to be rather a stranger to the world.' At a time of poor communications, when heads of state still acted on their own initiative, visits from foreign royalty were also occasions for prolonged discussion of international affairs. On 23 November 1843 Albert was writing from Windsor to say: 'The Hohenlohes left us a week ago and the Nemours are going back to Paris next week.' He thought that the Duchess de Nemours had 'greatly improved' and become 'very reasonable and good-natured'. With the Duke de Nemours Albert had 'fought out many political fights, in great honesty and openness, and understood each other very well'. In 1844 the Queen and Prince Albert received the Emperor of Russia, the King of France and the King of Saxony.

Finding accommodation for overseas guests in 1851, the year of the Great Exhibition, proved a real headache. 'The Prussian suite,'

Albert informed his brother, 'will consist of twenty-nine men. I would therefore beg you to come with a very small suite, if possible only *one* gentleman and *one* lady.' Foreign royalty of a liberal persuasion were always welcome. 'We are very much pleased with our visitors from Portugal,' Albert told his brother when writing on 12 June 1854. He thought his cousin, Prince Pedro, 'well instructed and full of good intentions. He is liberal in politics as well as in religious matters.' Problems of accommodation arose again the following year. 'To-day,' Prince Albert wrote from Buckingham Palace on 21 June 1855, 'Prince Oskar of Sweden is to arrive and Philipp and Charlotte are also coming for ten days. How we are to put them all up, heaven knows.' Terrified that Balmoral, too, might burst at the seams, Albert was writing a month later to say: 'I am pleased to hear that you would like to see Balmoral. We shall go there on 1st September and remain until about the 10th of October. If you come during that time you will be received with open arms. Only one thing I would ask of you, bring as few people with you as possible. In the mountains, far away from all the world, we do not keep a grand Court. Should Alexandrine [Prince Ernest's wife] accompany you, I would ask her to bring only one lady, with her lady's maid, and Alexandrine must also have only one . . . The Prussian family is still here . . . '

Victoria and Albert were immensely hospitable, even if entertaining royalty did provide an excuse to meet people of a similar standing as equals. 'This summer we shall have our house very full,' Albert told Prince Ernest in March 1857. 'We shall not return from Osborne until the end of May. Then Fritz of Prussia, perhaps the Prince and Princess of Prussia, will come too, the young Erzherzog and the Brabants, etc, etc.' In July Prince Albert decided he liked 'the Prince of Hohenzollern better the more I get to know him'. King Leopold and his son and daughter were staying. 'Fritz

The Throne Room, Windsor Castle.

is coming on the 14th or 15th, the Queen of Holland on the 16th. The same day we are going to leave town to go to Osborne. Prince Napoleon will be there and on the 4th of August the Emperor and Empress of the French. We shall be rather crowded in our small house and will not find much quiet time.'

After Albert's death the Queen found the strain of entertaining on her own very great, but in the early years of her marriage she thought it rather fun, and was thrilled when foreign royalty praised the arrangements. After the visit of the Tsar and the King of Saxony, she told King Leopold: 'Both the Emperor and the King are *quite* enchanted with Windsor. The Emperor said very *poliment*: "C'est digne de vous, Madame." I must say the Waterloo Room lit up by that entire service of gold looks splendid; and the Reception Room, beautiful to sit in afterwards.' Not everyone was so appreciative of visits to Windsor, however; in 1851 Lord Macaulay described how a military band 'covered the talk with a succession of sonorous tunes'.

Some idea of the cost and logistics of a state visit can be gained from Victoria's descriptions of the 1855 visit by Napoleon III and his wife, the Empress Eugénie, who saw a good deal of the Queen in her later exile. The Emperor sent fourteen horses ahead of him, and before the royal couple arrived the Queen cast her eye not only over the rooms reserved for them but for their attendants as well. Though rather low, she found them 'nice and clean, with pretty chintz furniture'. She noted that 'a great deal of new furniture has been got, though there was much fine old furniture in store, which has been usefully worked up'. Albert had been dispatched to France to escort the Emperor and Empress, he cutting a comic Ruritanian figure with his absurd waxed moustache, she, on arrival, according to the Queen, 'evidently very nervous'. But as Victoria remarked: 'These great meetings of Sovereigns, surrounded by very exciting accompaniments, are always very agitating.'

'We got on extremely well at dinner,' she recorded later, 'and my great agitation seemed to go off very early.' On the first morning the Queen and the Emperor sat in the White Drawing Room discussing the Crimean War. Then they went for a stroll to inspect the kennels in the Home Park designed by Prince Albert the previous year. On his way back from a call on the Duchess of Kent at Frogmore, the Emperor complimented the Queen on the grass. 'During almost the whole time of the walk, the war and his plans were discussed . . . It was most interesting to hear him and Albert discuss all these matters.' The visit continued with everyone shifting their suites and luggage to Buckingham Palace, for visits to the opera and the Great Exhibition, and when the time came for the

French to depart all the royal children began to cry. The 'dear Empress' pressed the Queen's hand and embraced her three times. Then the Emperor kissed the Queen's hand twice, and she embraced him twice. 'The ladies and gentlemen and our ladies began to be *émues*,' the Queen recalled, 'and I was very near to being set off.'

An interesting man of letters invited to dine at Windsor, in 1859, the year he was appointed a Chaplain in Ordinary to the Queen, was Charles Kingsley, author of *The Water Babies* and at one time a tutor to the Prince of Wales. 'Thank heaven it is all over,' he wrote to his wife Fanny. 'And very like a dream it was, although not an unpleasant one. After dinner I was to be presented and we all stood near the door talking quite freely. Presently she came up and I was taken straight up to her. I had to kneel and kiss hands and I didn't like it . . . Then she began to talk and I to funk. They had had great delight in my books (accent slightly foreign). Then she stopt to think in the shy way she had, between each speech, which makes one in a more awful funk than ever, but she has the dearest sweetest smile woman could have'.[1]

Victoria liked to poke about, and took the keenest interest not only in her visitors' accommodation but in that provided for her household. After his marriage in 1861, Henry Ponsonby rented a house in the cloisters at Windsor. One day when he and his wife were out (it was only a few weeks before the death of the Prince Consort), the Queen, Prince Albert and Princess Alice called at the back door, at the same time as the baker's boy, to look over the house and see if all was well. Gloom and paranoia were soon mostly to prevail, but Lord Stanley, a dinner guest in 1867, found the Queen 'in the best of humours, very large, ruddy, and fat (the tendency increases rapidly) but complaining of her health, saying the work she has to do is too much for her, that she is almost knocked-up and so forth'. And she would put herself out for anyone who pleased her, or she certainly would if they were royal. When in July the same year the Queen of Prussia left the castle, Victoria went to the railway station to see her off, and wrote in her journal: 'Nothing could have been kinder or pleasanter than she was, so discreet, and not interfering in the slightest way with my mode of life.'

But the Queen's mode of life was well and truly interfered with only four days after the departure of the Queen of Prussia when the Sultan of Turkey paid a state visit. He brought with him two nephews, one of them apparently his heir, and his nine-year-old son, a 'dear little boy', who sat next to the Queen at lunch. On her other side sat the Sultan, but as none of the visitors spoke French the conversation must have been rather sticky. Victoria's guests were nothing if not varied; in 1870 she received a Greek Orthodox archbishop. They conversed in German. On 20 June 1873 she wrote: 'Felt nervous and agitated at the great event of the day, the Shah's visit. All great bustle and excitement. The guns were fired and bells ringing for my Accession Day [her thirty-sixth], and the latter also for the Shah . . . I dressed in a smart morning dress, with my large pearls, and the Star and Ribbon of the Garter, the Victoria and Albert Order, etc.'

In 1874 the Duke of Edinburgh's new father-in-law, Tsar Alexander II, arrived at Windsor, but not without mishap. His yacht ran aground on a sandbank and was stuck fast until the tide rose. He was due for lunch at half-past one and did not arrive until 10 p.m. 'We only sat down to dinner, in fact supper, at quarter to 11.' A year later the Sultan of Zanzibar, His Highness Seyyid Barghash, was shown around the castle by the Lord Chamberlain after he had met the Queen, exclaiming later: 'I was indeed wonder-struck with all the sumptuousness that surrounds her.' It seems

Her Majesty the Queen, The Prince of Wales, the Tsar and Tsarina and their infant daughter, photographed at Balmoral, November 1896.

unlikely that an impromptu, indeed chaotic, visit by the Empress of Austria met with Sir Henry Ponsonby's approval. He had been landed with the arrangements, and minuted:

> The Empress of Austria came to England to hunt in March 1876 and sent to say she would call on the Queen at Buckingham Palace or Windsor on her way through. The Queen replied she was busy holding a Court but would see her another day. The Empress sent to say she could come on the following Sunday for luncheon. The Queen did not like receiving her Sunday but could not refuse. All was arranged for her coming to Windsor at 1.30. At 12.15 when we were all in church she telegraphed to say she would come at 1. Service was hurried over and she was received at 1.15 – and left at 1.30. She was blocked up by the snow at Slough and did not get back to London till 4.

In an undated letter from Windsor Castle, probably written in the summer of 1889, Marie Mallet told her husband: 'Today we have been pretty active welcoming and speeding Royal guests. The Princess Clementine [of Saxe-Coburg and Gotha], an old cat with a gigantic ear trumpet, the Duc and Duchess de Montpensier, the Duc and Duchess de Chartres and their daughter. They brought as suite a Spanish lady and gentleman, both bores of the first water. They lunched with us and I had to make French conversation with the man for over two mortal hours. My throat is still quite sore from the effort.'

During a visit to Balmoral from Prince Ferdinand of Bulgaria, Lady Ampthill, who was in waiting, heard 'snorting and snarling' outside her bedroom door, 'and after shaking with terror for some time, visions of burglars, anarchists, etc passing through her brain, she rose, lit the candle, and cautiously opened her door. On the wool mat outside she beheld a gigantic Bulgarian covered with pistols and daggers in full national costume. You can imagine,' Mrs Mallet told her husband, 'how she banged the door and double locked it! This formidable creature turned out to be Prince Ferdinand's body-servant, who finding his master's doormat somewhat hard had moved on to a softer one.'

When King Carlos of Portugal arrived at Balmoral some of the gentlemen had to 'turn out and take up their abode in a tin cottage nearby to make room for the Portuguese suite'. According to Marie Mallet, the King, who was only thirty-two, looked 'fat and pink just like a prize pig'. He ate enormously and took a good deal of exercise 'but the more he takes the more he eats'. After a heavy lunch, 'the "Portugeese", as we call them, were taken for a chilly drive in our wagonette which they insisted on calling a "charabanc", and then scaled a neighbouring hill carrying torches with all of Her Majesty's Highland retainers. A huge bonfire was lighted at the top, whisky dispensed with a generous hand, and then followed Reels.' The King reminded Marie 'of a King in a comic opera'. He was so fat, she said, 'that he bounds rather than walks and his greediness is quite appalling. The gentlemen call him the Champion Liar but as he never addressed a single word to any of us ladies I cannot say we had an opportunity of judging. I however heard him last night describing the capture of a salmon so large that it must have been a whale . . . The Suite kissed and pressed our hands at least four times a day.'

In November of that year – 1895 – the Queen laid on a state lunch at Windsor for some African chiefs, the gentlemen in levée dress. Marie Mallet sat beside Chief Bathoeu, who seemed to her 'the least attractive of the blacks', but she said 'he enjoyed his food thoroughly and ate in a very civilized manner'. They were all teetotal and drank lemonade. After lunch they were received by the Queen in the White Drawing Room, with the Life Guards on duty. They gave the Queen 'three Karosses or rugs of leopard skins of doubtful smell but intrinsic worth', the Queen gave them a copy of the Bible each in their own language, 'and with grateful grunts they retired backwards leaving us much impressed by their quiet dignity and wonderful self-possession. I could see they were immensely impressed but they tried not to show their feelings and succeeded admirably.'

Marie's account of a visit to Balmoral on 25 May 1897 by Leopold II of the Belgians scores full marks for its astute observations. 'Quelle voyage, cher cousin,' the Queen observed, on greeting her uncle's son in 'the chilly front hall'. 'Quelle butte!' was his reply. Marie said he could shake hands with only two fingers 'as his nails are so long that he dares not run the risk of injuring them. He is an unctuous old monster, very wicked I believe. We imagine he thinks a visit to the Queen gives him a fresh coat of whitewash, otherwise why does he travel five hundred miles in order to partake of lunch!' Leopold's exploitation of the Belgian Congo was to become a byword for despotic cruelty.

Victoria's appreciation of music and admiration for those who performed it never faltered, and throughout the thirty-nine years of her widowhood may well have helped to save her reason. Her journal entries are full of references to concerts and solo perform-ances, mainly at Windsor, and to theatrical entertainments, too. 'Had some music in the Red Drawing-room [known today as the Crimson Drawing Room] to which my three children, Lenchen, and the ladies and some of the gentlemen came,' she noted on 4 July 1872. 'Adelina Patti, the famous prima donna . . . sang . . . I was charmed with Patti, who has a very sweet voice and wonderful facility and execution. She sings very quietly and is a very pretty ladylike little thing.'[2]

On 17 May 1877 she wrote: 'After luncheon the great composer Wagner, about whom the people in Germany are really a little mad, was brought into the corridor by Mr Cusins [G. W. Cusins, resident pianist and conductor]. I had seen him with dearest Albert in '55, when he directed at the Philharmonic Concert. He has grown old and stout, and has a clever, but not pleasing countenance.' The Queen had Liszt to play in the Crimson Drawing Room in 1887, and on 17 July 1889 she noted: 'Louise of S-H came to luncheon, and stayed with us to hear Albani and the two de Reszkes sing . . . The two brothers have most glorious voices and sing in the most perfect manner . . . The duet from *Lohengrin*, which is quite a long scene, was beyond anything beautiful, so dramatic, and Albani almost acted it. She was in great force. The music lasted till four, and I could have listened to it much longer. It was indeed a treat.'

Like almost all her contemporaries, Queen Victoria enjoyed the operas of Gilbert and Sullivan, and on 6 March 1891 a performance of *The Gondoliers* was performed in the Waterloo Chamber. The Queen found the Grand Inquisitor 'excellent & most absurd', the dresses 'very gay & smart' and the 'whole ensemble brilliant & well put on the stage, which for an extemporized one was wonderful. I really enjoyed the performance very much. Afterwards I spoke to Mr D'Oyly Carte, & complimented him.' On 2 July the Queen had Pederewski to play, in the Green Drawing Room. 'He does so quite marvellously, such power and such tender feeling. I really think he is quite the equal to Rubinstein. He is young, about 28, very pale, with a sort of aureole of red hair standing out.'

At four o'clock on 26 November, accompanied by an assorted collection of grandchildren, the Queen was back in the Waterloo Chamber 'where the opera of "Cavalleria Rusticana", by a young Italian composer of the name Mascagni, was performed. I had not heard an Italian opera for thirty-one years. The story was most pathetic and touching beyond words. The whole performance was a great success and I loved the music, which is so melodious, and characteristically Italian.'

The very next day: 'A little after six we went down into the drawing-room and had a great treat in hearing Sarasate play on the violin . . . He is very pleasing and modest, and has a very singular melancholy countenance.'

It was at Windsor, in 1894, that the Queen received the young Archduke Franz Ferdinand, heir to the Austro-Hungarian Empire, whose assassination at Sarajevo twenty years later was to trigger the Great War. And on 3 May the following year Victoria, now seventy-six, had the strange experience of receiving at Windsor a fellow sovereign, aged fifteen, Queen Wilhelmina of the Netherlands, who had succeeded her father when she was only ten. The Duchess of Albany, Prince Leopold's widow, was the young Queen's aunt. The Duchess arrived at Windsor with the Dutch Queen Regent, the three of them lunched with Victoria, had coffee in the Grand Corridor and drove to Virginia Water for tea.

Queen Victoria thought Wilhelmina 'very slight and graceful', with fine features and seemingly 'very intelligent', a charming child with 'very pretty manners' and a good command of English. The young girl asked the old woman if she had ever ridden in a hansom, and Victoria admitted with evident regret that she had not. Unintentionally rubbing in her own good fortune, Wilhelmina said: 'I have been in lots, and they are awfully jolly.' Forty-five years later she would be telephoning Victoria's great-grandson, King George VI, appealing for help to repel the Nazi invaders of her country.

14

The Very Last Ceremony

In 1887 Queen Victoria celebrated her Golden Jubilee, twenty-two days being set aside for entertainments of one kind or another. People who for years, perhaps during the whole of their lives, had never set eyes on their sovereign suddenly realized she had reigned for half a century. The only fly in the ointment for Victoria was a shortfall of £6,000 in the public money voted for the occasion, and she found herself dipping into her own Privy Purse to make good the deficit. When ten years later celebrations for her Diamond Jubilee were under discussion, it was heavily hinted that once again the Queen might like to contribute. She declined, saying she was planning to turn out at all only to please her subjects, and in the end the government met the entire bill, which today would be regarded as a sum scarce fussing over, £76,544.

The Queen had grown old remarkably gracefully, undergoing without demur an operation in 1871 for an abscess, but complaining, as old people have every reason to, about aches and pains; but what troubled her most was the gradual loss of her eyesight. And, of course, the longest surviving members of her household had grown old with her. In 1894 Viscount Bridport, a great-nephew of Vice-

The Royal Procession – the ceremony at St Paul's.

Admiral Nelson, was lord in waiting at the age of eighty. General Sir Michael Biddulph, the groom-in-waiting, was seventy. Sir Henry Ponsonby had passed his seventieth birthday, and it must have seemed like an invasion from another planet when his son Frederick arrived on the scene at the age of twenty-seven. He had been personally appointed an equerry by the Queen while still in India, and it was to Ponsonby she had sent a telegram asking him to investigate the background to her beloved Munshi. When in all innocence Frederick Ponsonby reported the true facts, the Queen refused to believe him and declined to invite Ponsonby to dinner for a year. During an entire month on holiday at Cimiez the Queen cut her equerry dead, until on the last day in France she got out of her carriage, turned to Ponsonby and said: 'What a pity it is to leave Nice in such beautiful weather.'

Along with a lengthy memory – at dinner at Windsor Castle in December 1897 the Queen was still talking about the boredom she had endured when taken to hear *Messiah* in York Minster at the age of sixteen – Victoria retained until very near the end of her life a formidable appetite. Dinner on Christmas Day at Osborne in 1897 found a baron of beef and a woodcock pie on the table with a boar's head displayed on the sideboard. To try to alleviate the heat in July 1900 the Queen, while at Osborne, devoured 'a hugh chocolate ice followed by a couple of apricots washed down with iced water' – an ideal recipe for indigestion. In honour of her eightieth birthday the household gave Victoria a dinner at Windsor: consommé, whitebait and trout, a choice of entrées, a soufflé and eggs in aspic. And she never tired of expressing her opinions. At Windsor in 1897 she pronounced football 'very barbarous' but thought cricket 'would not be so bad if the ball were softer'.

Chilly houses she still approved of; at Balmoral in the spring of

1899 Marie Mallet found the house 'colder than I have ever felt it'. But the Queen had only to give Marie 'a dear little brooch with "80" on it in memory of her birthday' for her to 'forget all the inconveniences and worries connected with her service'. Music – Handel excepted – provided pleasure to the end. The Queen had Clara Butt, whom she already knew, to sing at Osborne in January 1899. 'It was nice to see the Queen at a party,' Lady Lytton recalled, 'and she enjoyed it and was so keen.' In May that year Lady Lytton thought the Queen looked 'more marvellously well than ever. Such a good colour and not a bit weary or tired. One can't believe she is eighty. I am now going to my bed,' she told her daughter, 'and hope not to be too cold [the court was at Balmoral]. There are hot pipes in the passages but in the dining and drawing-room it was *bitterly* cold.' Lady Lytton recorded that for her eightieth birthday the Queen's children clubbed together to give her 'three very handsome silver candelabras for the Durbar Room at Osborne', while the old Duke of Cambridge gave her 'a beautiful miniature of George III set in diamonds, which had belonged to one of his aunts'.

Those who knew the Queen well, and apart from her family they were in the main courtiers and those clergy she was fond of, all realized she was two different people: a woman, in the opinion of the Dean of Windsor, Randall Davidson, 'both shy and humble', but a queen who was 'neither shy nor humble [who] asserted her position unhesitatingly'. The Dean thought that what constituted the Queen's 'irresistible charm' was 'a combination of absolute truthfulness and simplicity with the instinctive recognition and quiet assertion of her position as Queen and of what belonged to it'. Arthur Ponsonby, in his brief biography, commented that 'handicapped as she might have been by her small stature and lack of beauty' she had 'acquired a bearing, a carriage and freedom of movement which made a noticeable and positive impression on all who came into her presence'. He thought her dignity did not depend on costume. 'Neither dress, age, figure nor features could deprive her of the astonishing genius of her carriage with which she could with calm assurance assert her presence and command immediate attention in any assembly.'

The Queen was not a witty woman so much as sharp. Told by an earnest clergyman of a house in the East End in which seven people slept in one bed, 'The Queen dryly remarked: "Had I been one of them I would have slept on the floor."'

She seems to have depended for verbal effect on emphasis. Arthur Ponsonby says: 'When in conversation she pronounced somebody or something to be "*most extraordinary*" she was able by the tone of her pleasant and rather flute-like voice to convert the simple words into an expression of the deepest disapproval. So arresting was her personality that inattention in her presence was impossible. So keen was her interest that monarchs, Ministers, courtiers and servants were put on their mettle.' Yet she was so human that her superstition forbade a crossing of the Channel on a Friday.

She could weep with the best of them and rock with laughter: 'She was immensely amused and roared with laughter, her whole face changing and lighting up in a wonderful way.' ' . . . and some-times even the beautiful smile broke across her face in the wonderful way it does.' And as she grew older so her occasions of grief became more genuine. 'All fall around me and I become more and more lonely,' she lamented late in life. One of the most pertinent comments on Victoria's character was made by Arthur Ponsonby: 'She was far from being intellectual; she may often have been igno-rant but she was never stupid.' Considering the inconvenience, discomfort and boredom to which she subjected her politicians and household, Queen Victoria engendered loyalty and love to a remarkable degree. No one who is merely royal can do that.

It was a tragedy that the end of Queen Victoria's life was clouded by the Boer War. It grieved and worried her. She was not surprised that public opinion censured the government but vented her anger against the press by banning delivery of the *Morning Post*. Nevertheless, a surreptitious copy was 'eagerly devoured' every morning 'in the recesses of the Equerries' Room'. The Queen had taken to dropping off to sleep during her carriage rides and while sitting up after dinner. Anniversaries, particularly of deaths and funerals, were still carefully observed, and it was noticed that she was 'anxious and care-worn' and that it 'became harder for her ladies to make her laugh'. The Queen was said to be 'secretly distressed at the bad news' but 'outwardly as cheerful as ever'. 'We are all,' Marie Mallet reported from Osborne on 11 February 1900, 'from the Queen downwards, making things for the troops . . . the Queen turns out khaki comforters as if her bread depended on it.' She told Marie Mallet that she had made many things for the troops during the Crimean War 'but they would give them to the officers, not at all what I intended'.

Spirits soared on 16 February when news reached Osborne of the relief of Kimberley. 'The Queen already looks better.' In the afternoon she went to a children's ward in the County Hospital to give the patients toys. Secret information fed to the Queen that Ladysmith was on the point of being abandoned by the Boers further served to repair her cheerfulness, and she decided to receive Communion, standing at the altar rail leaning on a stick, with her granddaughter Princess Thora helping to support her; she was now beyond kneeling through lameness. The congregation consisted of three of the gentlemen, an old page called Waite and three of the housemaids.

At Windsor on 18 July 1900 the Queen invested a handsome young captain of thirty with the Victoria Cross. He had lost both eyes. Six days later Marie Mallet noted: 'The Queen is certainly less vigorous and her digestion is becoming defective after so many years of hard labour! If she would follow a diet and live on Benger's Food and chicken all would be well but she clings to roast beef and ices!' Provisional arrangements for the Queen to go abroad were put into effect, but in a fairly half-hearted manner; it was thought best to let the Queen imagine she was fit to travel, but no one really believed she was. At Osborne on 31 July a telegram arrived announcing the death of Affie, the Duke of Edinburgh, and the Queen telegraphed to Lord Roberts to say: 'I know the Army will sympathize with my great grief.' Affie's end was a sad one indeed, largely induced by drink, but he had cancer, too. 'I have been interrupted by a summons to the Queen,' Mrs Mallet wrote. 'She gave me her hand to kiss and I knelt down to take it in mine and so we remained for a full five minutes, trying to be calm enough to speak. The Queen cried so gently and seemed so patient and resigned in her great sorrow and finally a calm came over me and I was able to control my voice for I wished to spare her tears if possible.' The next day the Queen was able to manage a smile when a telegram arrived from a sympathetic subject: 'Sincere condolences. Poem follows.'

When news arrived at Balmoral at the end of October of the death in South Africa of Prince Christian Victor, a grandson of the Queen, Marie Mallet wrote: 'Words fail me to describe the pall of sorrow that hangs over this house, the Queen is quite exhausted by her grief . . . as she was not at her best before this shock you may imagine how anxious we feel about her health . . . When she breaks down and draws me close to her and lets me stroke her dear hand I quite forget she is far above me and only realize she is a sorrowing woman who clings to human sympathy and hungers for all that can be given on such occasions.'

Mrs Mallet reported on 2 November: 'The Queen is quite angelic and does her best to keep up, but the effort is very great and cannot be good for her. The curious thing is that she said to me, "After the Prince Consort's death I wished to die, but *now* I wish to live and do what I can for my country and those I love." Do not repeat this but it is a very remarkable utterance for a woman of eighty-two [Mrs Mallet had miscalculated by a year; the Queen was eighty-one] and this is not the first time she has made the same remark. I wonder if she dreads the influence of the Prince of Wales?'

Three days later she wrote: 'The Queen is still far from well but I hope the change to Windsor will do her good. She has so little appetite and yesterday we had a thick fog worthy of London, which made her perfectly miserable.'

On 6 November: 'I actually made the Queen laugh at dinner last night by conjuring up a vision of "Nunks" as a Bishop in full canonicals . . . I could kill the cooks who take no pains whatever to prepare tempting little dishes and would be a disgrace to any kitchen. How I would like to work a sweeping reform, we are abominably served just now. The footmen smell of whisky and are never prompt to answer the bell, and although they do not speak rudely, they stare in such a supercilious way. As for the Queen's dinner it is more like a badly arranged picnic.'

Victoria was about to take a last look at her beloved Balmoral. By 7 November she was in Windsor, where staffing arrangements were no better than they had been in Scotland. 'The servants here are too irritating,' Mrs Mallet wrote on 8 November. 'The Queen only ordered one small dish – nouilles – for her dinner last night and it was entirely forgotten, so she had nothing. The cooks should be drawn and quartered and the

Clerks of the Kitchen strung from the Curfew Tower; their indifference makes me boil with rage.'[1] She added later: 'The "Munshi" has . . . returned after a year's absence in India. Why the plague did not carry him off I cannot think, it might have done one good deed!'

On 9 November the Queen herself noted in her journal: 'Had felt better through the day and free from pain, but I still have a disgust for all food.'

Next day: 'Had an excellent night, but my appetite is still very bad.'

On 11 November: 'Had a shocking night, and no draught could make me sleep as pain kept me awake. Felt very tired and unwell when I got up, and was not able to go to church to my great disappointment.'

On 12 November: 'Had again not a good night and slept on rather late. My lack of appetite worse than ever. It is very trying.' Nevertheless, the Queen managed to hold a Council and then had a half-hour's drive. And she did seem to be on the mend; on 13 November 'she enjoyed her coffee and egg for breakfast', according to Marie Mallet, who told her husband that Sir James Reid was 'devoting all his energies to getting her better and I have the utmost confidence in him. He is very nice to me and tells me everything, which is a comfort.'

The following day Mrs Mallet decided that the Queen was better after a good night 'but a large luncheon party and shouting to the Princess of Wales [who was very deaf] exhausted her and she was in pain and very feeble after it. Of course we must be anxious for the next few days but there is no reason why she should not pick up again and regain her appetite, but she resents being treated as an invalid and as soon as she feels a tiny bit better she overtires herself and collapses.' But she was still capable of springing

Queen Victoria in 1899.

surprises, if in a somewhat roundabout manner. One afternoon she sent for Marie Mallet and told her to ask Sir Fleetwood Edwards for the insignia of a Knight Grand Cross of the Order of the Bath with which she wanted to invest the late Prince Christian Victor's younger brother, Prince Albert, at tea time. Alas, there was no G. C. B. insignia to be laid hands on in the castle at such short notice, so the ceremony had to be postponed. 'Rather like a fairy tale,' was Bernard Mallet's comment.

Marie Mallet did not accompany the Queen to Osborne, from where Sir James Reid wrote to her on 4 January 1901: 'The Queen is now much better. She has continued to improve ever since she consented to be treated as an invalid; and she now causes me no present anxiety.' But in the medical report Reid wrote the day after the Queen died, he mentioned that she had manifested 'unusual fatigue' as a result of her journey from Windsor to Osborne on 18 December, 'with symptoms of nervous agitation and restlessness which lasted for two days'. She seems to have celebrated Christmas and seen in the New Year in the normal way, but by 16 January 1901 she 'showed for the first time unequivocal symptoms of mental confusion'. The following day she suffered a slight stroke, but she struggled to recognize visitors despite increasing drowsiness, and until the very end her heart continued to beat quite steadily. She lingered peacefully until 22 January, seemingly aware, until within only a few minutes of her death, of the presence of those members of her family gathered in her bedroom. However, whether she was really aware that it was the Kaiser, the least trusted or favoured of her grandchildren, who had elbowed his way to the top of the couch where she lay, ostentatiously supporting the eighty-one-year-old Queen and Empress, whose world, and many of whose family connections, he would within a few years blow to pieces, no one knows.

The funeral procession of Queen Victoria at Windsor.

The Queen's body lay in state in the dining room, watched over by Grenadier Guards. On 1 February the funeral cortège passed through East Cowes bound for the royal yacht *Alberta* and eventually the Royal Mausoleum at Frogmore, the coffin draped with a white and gold pall. On 2 February, at the station at Windsor, Frederick Ponsonby gave orders for the carriage to move. When it did so, two of the horses began to kick and plunge, and away went the traces. Unaware that the coffin was still stationary, the front of the procession began to make its way to the castle. Ponsonby dashed out to stop them, and then ran back to the new King, Edward VII, to tell him what had happened. Prince Louis of Battenberg suggested getting the naval guard of honour to drag the gun-carriage, and this, to the chagrin of the artillery, they did. Thus are traditions established, dead sovereigns having been dragged by the navy ever since.[2]

The Master of the Household, Lord Edward Pelham-Clinton, had earlier returned to Windsor to supervise the funeral. He recorded in his diary on 1 February: 'Very busy all day, constant telegrams altering arrangements for rooms by sending more Royalties – I begin almost to despair of succeeding, but think all is settled. I get out for a few minutes to go to St George's and ask Lady Bigge if she can take in any of the suite. To my great relief she takes in three.'

The next day there were '70 Royalties', as Lord Edward called them, to lunch. 'Guests about 600 or 700 in St George's Hall. A Royal dinner of 25. Household do – 24.' There was a service in St George's Chapel the next morning, but probably not attended by the cooks, whose recent incompetence would not be countenanced by 'poor Bertie' much longer. 'Royal dinner 27. Household do – 35.'

Victoria was taken to lie beside Albert in the Royal Mausoleum on the afternoon of 4 February. 'A most beautiful and impressive ceremony altogether,' Lord Edward remembered. 'The King most kindly allows me to throw the earth on the coffin . . . the last, the very last, ceremony that can be performed.'

The Royal Mausoleum.

Notes and References

Chapter 1: The Corporal Marries

1   When Thomas Creevey called on the Duke of Wellington at his hotel in Brussels to learn at first hand what had occurred at Waterloo, the Duke told him the battle had been 'a damned nice thing', meaning a close-run thing, 'the nicest-run thing you ever saw in your life'.

2   On 5 July 1820 a Bill of Pains and Penalties was introduced in the House of Lords. Its aim was to prove Queen Caroline's adultery and to deprive her of her title. When on the Bill's third reading on 10 November the government's majority was reduced to nine, the Prime Minister, Lord Liverpool, thought it unlikely to pass in the Commons and it was dropped. On 19 July the following year the Queen failed to gain admittance to Westminster Abbey for the coronation of George IV, and she conveniently died six weeks later.

3   *The Creevey Papers*, ed. John Gore (Batsford, 1963).

Chapter 2: The Kensington System

1   In recent years, those who have had apartments at Kensington Palace include the Prince and late Princess of Wales, the late Princess Margaret and her former husband, the Earl of Snowdon, Princess

Alice, Duchess of Gloucester, the Duke and Duchess of Gloucester, the late Princess Alice, Countess of Athlone, and Prince and Princess Michael of Kent.

2   The earldom of Nottingham became amalgamated with an earlier seventeenth-century earldom of Winchelsea, the family adopting the surname Finch Hatton.

3   No maids of honour have been appointed since the death in 1936 of George V.

4   In the 1993 Missing Persons volume of the *Dictionary of National Biography*, Elizabeth Longford plumps for typhoid. In *Queen Victoria in her Letters and Journals* an equally distinguished historian, Christopher Hibbert, writes that Victoria had been very ill, 'possibly with tonsillitis'.

5   When Sir David Wilkie came to paint the scene of Victoria's first Council, as meetings of the Privy Council are always called, he annoyed her intensely by depicting her in white, to emphasize her innocence, when she was in fact wearing mourning for William IV.

Chapter 3: 'Very Pleasant Large Dinners'

1   The Queen's Lodge was very properly demolished by George IV, in 1823.

2   *Court and Private Life in the Time of Queen Charlotte*, ed. Mrs Kernon Delves Broughton (Richard Bentley & Son, 1887).

3   During Victoria's reign Clarence House became a London home for her mother and later her second son, Alfred, Duke of Edinburgh.

4   *The Country Life Book of Royal Palaces, Castles & Homes*, Patrick Montague-Smith and Hugh Montgomery-Massingberd (1981).

5   Letter of 3 July 2001 to the author from Mr Alex Galloway, Clerk of the Council.

6   Charles Greville's sister Harriet had married Lord Francis Egerton Leveson-Gower, changing his name in 1833 to Egerton, his father

being the first Duke of Sutherland. In 1846 Lord Francis was created Earl of Ellesmere.

Chapter 4: Lady Flora and Others

1 Grand Duke Alexander was the son of Nicholas I. He succeeded to the Russian throne in 1855 as Alexander II, and was assassinated in 1881.

Chapter 5: 'Windsor is Beautiful and Comfortable'

1 Since Queen Victoria's reign one other monarch to date has never lived at Windsor Castle: Edward VIII.
2 Probably the two most accessible are *Windsor Castle* by Sir Owen Morshead (Phaidon Press, 1951) and *Windsor Castle: Past and Present* by Michael De-la-Noy (Headline, 1990).
3 *Windsor Castle*, ibid.

Chapter 6: A Strange Chinese-Looking Thing

1 In 1772 the Royal Marriages Act stipulated that no member of the royal family might marry beneath the age of twenty-five without the consent of the sovereign, and if, after the age of twenty-five, consent was still withheld, twelve months' notice was to be given to the Privy Council. The Act remains in force today.
2 In 1811 George IV, at that time Prince of Wales, was appointed Regent of the United Kingdom of Great Britain and Ireland. He succeeded to the throne in 1820.
3 *My Mistress the Queen* (Weidenfeld & Nicolson, 1994).
4 Over the years a substantial quantity of furniture has been returned to the Royal Pavilion, initially by Queen Mary and later by Queen Elizabeth the Queen Mother. Restoration work had proceeded in various stages over a period of a hundred years when in 1975 an

arson attack caused severe damage to the music room. In recent years the gardens have been re-landscaped; the stables were long ago transformed into a concert hall, library and museum; and today, thanks to meticulous scholarship and workmanship, the Royal Pavilion is fully restored and can be viewed in all its redecorated and refurnished Regency splendour.

Chapter 7: 'A Perfect Little Paradise'

1   By 1862 Queen Victoria was so wealthy that she could afford to pay £220,000 for the Sandringham estate in Norfolk, which she gave to her eldest son.

Chapter 8: 'No Pudding and no Fun'

1   In contrast to Balmoral Castle, Birkhall, which dates from 1715, is in the style of a sturdy and very attractive manor house. *The Country Life Book of Royal Palaces, Castles and Homes* (ibid.) states incorrectly that the estate was given to the Duke of York, later George VI, after his marriage. It belongs in fact to the sovereign, and was loaned to the Duke and Duchess of York before they came to the throne, first by George V and later by Edward VIII. As Queen Elizabeth the Queen Mother, the former duchess occupied Birkhall as a guest of Queen Elizabeth II from 1952 until her death 50 years later.

2   Montague-Smith and Montgomery-Massingberd, ibid.

Chapter 9: Poor Bertie

1   Queen Victoria's eldest daughter was styled the Princess Royal from birth, only the fourth English princess so known, the previous holders of the title being the eldest daughters of Charles I and George II and the daughter of George IV. Likewise, Bertie was known as the Prince of Wales from birth, the eighteenth since the

future Edward II was proclaimed Prince of Wales in 1301.

2   David Duff cites 'private information' for this story in his book *Albert and Victoria* (London, 1972).

3   Queen Victoria had been declared Empress of India on 12 May 1876, and from that date no longer signed herself Victoria Regina but Victoria Regina et Imperatrix.

Chapter 10: *Albert's Treadmill*

1   Since the time of Prince Albert the Coburg bow has been adopted as correct etiquette at all the courts of Europe.

2   Queen Victoria was spared the building of London Airport, which placed Windsor Castle on its direct flight path, and all is no longer 'peace and quiet' by a long way.

3   When Princess Augusta, a daughter of George III, died in September 1840, and Queen Victoria was seven months pregnant, Prince Albert wrote to his brother to say: 'To get out of the way of the funeral ceremony, which will take place, according to the old fashion, at Windsor, we are going to Claremont for five days. As far as possible, all sad impressions must be kept from Victoria.' Claremont in Surrey had been the country home of George IV's daughter, Princess Charlotte, and Prince Leopold. After Charlotte's death and Leopold's eventual election to the throne of Belgium, King Leopold retained the impressive property with its beautifully landscaped park as his English home. Late in the twentieth century it became a girls' boarding school.

4   Also present at the death of the Prince Consort were Princess Helena and the Queen's half-brother, Prince Charles of Leiningen, and his wife.

Chapter 11: *'The Queen is an Odd Woman'*

1   *Queen Victoria* (Duckworth, 1933).

2   On 25 March 1862 an official memorandum from the Lord

Chamberlain read: 'It is Her Majesty's command that the Blue Room at Windsor Castle in which His Royal Highness the Prince Consort died should remain in its present state and shall not be made use of in the future.' Such an edict could hardly be binding on Victoria's successors, and her grandson George V used the Blue Room as a sitting room, but he left it furnished as it had been in his grandfather's day, even having the room photographed so that housemaids, when they dusted, would know exactly where each object was to be replaced. But later in his reign he began to tire of living in a museum, and he complained to the dean that 'with one room in which my father slept kept with a dressing gown over the chair, and my brother's room with his toothpaste undisturbed', if it went on like that 'you'd never have any rooms left to live in'.

3   In Edward VII's reign the Drawing Room became a presentation for debutantes, the debutantes being presented to the King and Queen by their mothers providing they themselves had been presented at court; if they had not, some other lady who had been presented had to deputize. Formal presentations exclusively for debutantes were abolished in favour of garden parties early in the reign of Elizabeth II.

4   An order now defunct, not to be confused with the Royal Victorian Order, instituted the following year.

5   But with her acerbic tongue and tendency to quick judgement, Princess Louise was not universally popular. 'Princess Louise has just arrived [at Osborne],' Marie Adeane reported to her future husband on 24 January 1891. 'She is fascinating but oh, so ill-natured I positively dread talking to her, not a soul escapes.'

6   Queen Victoria's refusal to have rooms in any house properly heated was so notorious it is a wonder she retained a household at all. Marie Mallet described the drawing room at Osborne as Siberian, and from Balmoral, on 4 November 1896, Mrs Mallet reported: 'The Queen quite apologised yesterday for enjoying the cold weather so intensely. "I always feel so brisk" said she! It is more than her daughters or Ladies do!'

Chapter 12: The Loss of a Real Friend

1 Prince Arthur received a severe rebuke from the Queen when he started throwing his weight around and was told he must 'not treat servants etc like many do, as soldiers, which does great harm and which especially in the *Queen's home* is totally out of place and she will not tolerate it'.

2 The custom of occasionally dancing with one's servants was a consequence of the Age of Enlightenment. In Salzburg, in the eighteenth century, 'Lorenz Hübner, a priest and writer devoted to the history of the city, could be seen dancing with his cook at the gathering in the city hall'. *Mozart: A Cultural Biography*, Robert G. Gutman (Pimlico, 2001).

3 The Order of the Indian Empire was instituted in 1868. No conferments have been made since India was granted independence in 1947.

Chapter 13: 'The Dearest Sweetest Smile'

1 In Victorian times no drinks would have been served before dinner, and, for the ladies, none afterwards; they probably drank tea or coffee, and the gentlemen could perhaps look forward to a whisky in the smoking room. The strangest custom by far at court was for guests to sit down to dinner without first having been presented to the Queen. Guests invited to stay the night at Windsor Castle nowadays are received by the Queen shortly after their arrival, when generous drinks are served, the guests again assembling in one of the drawing rooms for more drinks before dinner. After the meal, the gentlemen drink port at the table, and following a tour of the State Apartments and the library more drinks are provided before the Queen and the Duke of Edinburgh retire.

Another interesting comparison between Victoria's household and the present establishment are the numbers of ladies-in-waiting appointed. In addition to the Mistress of the Robes the Queen makes do with only a couple of permanent ladies of the bedchamber and four permanent women of the bedchamber.

2   The Queen's reference to three unnamed children and Lenchen – her daughter Princess Helena – is ambiguous and is impossible to comprehend clearly.

Chapter 14: The Very Last Ceremony

1   The Curfew Tower stands in the Lower Ward of Windsor Castle, overlooking Thames Street. Built in 1227 by Henry III, it has a wooden top added in the nineteenth century in imitation of the medieval fortifications at Carcassonne in south-west France.

2   So far, Edward VII, George V and George VI. The former Edward VIII was not accorded a state funeral, and his coffin was transferred from Windsor Castle to the Frogmore cemetery by car.

Index

Page numbers in italics refer to illustrations

275

Marie
947-
723-
4842